Blount Springs

Alabama's Fountain of Youth

Greg Burden

Blount Springs, Alabama's Fountain of Youth

Copyright 2014
All rights reserved.
by Greg Burden

Printed in the United States of America.

No part of this book may be used or reproduced in any manner whatsoever without written permission except in the case of brief quotations embodied in critical articles and reviews.

Fifth Estate
2795 County Hwy 57
Blountsville, AL 35031

First Edition

Cover Designed by An Quigley

Printed on acid-free paper

Library of Congress Control No: 2014933630

ISBN: 9781936533404

Fifth Estate, 2014

Table of Contents

Chapter 1	The Beginning of a Dream	1
Chapter 2	A Highly Renowned Watering Place	12
Chapter 3	George Mason Goff	17
Chapter 4	An Irishman Comes to Town	31
Chapter 5	Up From the Black Belt	37
Chapter 6	The South & North Alabama Railroad	42
Chapter 7	The War of Northern Aggression	50
Chapter 8	Devastation and Rebuilding	60
Chapter 9	Col. Frank Jackson	66
Chapter 10	A New Hotel, Cholera, and the Press	79
Chapter 11	L'Orient, a Ghost Town Within a Ghost Town	88
Chapter 12	Press, Picnics, and Politics	96
Chapter 13	A New Partner and a New Hotel	107
Chapter 14	The Great Southern Cave	116
Chapter 15	The Golden Age	123
Chapter 16	The Blount Springs Hotel	140
Chapter 17	The Gay Nineties	152
Chapter 18	Crime, Fire, and Politics	163
Chapter 19	Dawn of a New Century	173
Chapter 20	Life After the Fire	189
	Photographs	199
	References	209

Preface

It was serendipity that started the research resulting in this book. Looking at Facebook one day, I ran across a new page called Blount Springs Alabama History. It was created by Mike Tumlin and now it is my pleasure to call him a friend. He inspired me to dig deeper and share information I found with a growing audience of interested new friends. The page ended with over 5,000 likes.

I had a passing interest in the area before due to traveling through there most of my life, but I had no idea of the amazing history those little hills and valleys held, just waiting for discovery. As a child I first learned of Blount Springs and that it was a historic site as I rode on numerous excursions to Birmingham with my parents in the 1960s. Sometimes we would stop and smell the sulphur at the springs and I had read the historic marker several times. Later as teenagers my friends and I roamed around exploring. It served as just another spot to visit as we broadened our scope of places to visit, but I still had no idea of the wonder and history of the myriad events that occurred at Blount Springs.

Looking for information and pictures of Blount Springs to publish on Facebook also led me to Amy Rhudy and the Blount County Museum. What a wonderful repository of history and interesting items it is. She has provided a wonderful atmosphere for research and been a great help in amassing information and inspiration to pull this together for others to enjoy. She pushed me to in writing this book and I will forever be indebted to her for getting me to take that step and attempt something I always thought I would enjoy.

My family has had to contend with my obsession with Blount Springs for over a year now. Besides hearing all the details, ad nauseam, they've read drafts, edited, and re-edited for me. I also dragged my mother all over the state to various archives and museums looking for information.

I know I've left something important out of this writing, or there is one other scrap of information I could have found if I just had a few more days to work on it. Please forgive me for anything I have forgotten and my hope is this will spur others to dig into their family records and old photographs. This could produce more information about one of the most fascinating eras and places of Alabama history. This subject needs to be further explored and my sincere hope is this book will entertain and inform people. I hope it does in such a way that more will become interested in the past and learn from it, and even more, to explore it further, and produce better works about this intriguing area known as Blount Springs.

1

The Beginning of a Dream

Deep in the piney woods of what would become Central Alabama was a beautiful land of hills, rocks and bubbling springs that evolved into a place of healing and enjoyment for many of the state's elite. This area started out as hunting grounds for various natives of the land since it really wasn't suitable for crops due to its hilly and rocky nature. It was the perfect environment for deer and other denizens of the forest.

There is a legend that a silver mine was operated by Spaniards and Native Americans together for several years before the area was settled by men from Georgia, South Carolina and Tennessee. In a handwritten document, dated August 2, 1876, John Swann of Tuscaloosa told the story of the lost mine. According to his account the story was related to him by Abner Y. Densmore. Densmore lived for many years near Red Hill, about twenty miles from Blount Springs. There was an old shop on Densmore's place that older residents told him had been built by Spanish explorers to process the silver they mined at the Springs.

The Spaniards were driven out of the country at some point and the natives began mining and processing the silver by wagon loads by themselves. After a while they moved on and filled in the mine so the white men could never find it.

The Mississippi Territory
The History of Alabama For Use in Schools by William Garrot Brown

A generation or so later, another generation returned looking for the mine their fathers had told them about. They were to look for a certain beech tree with strange markings on it. The mine was never found again but the shop was partially standing in 1876. Many older locals attested to the fact of the mine's existence. This is the only evidence supporting the legend of the silver mine.

The Mississippi Territory was created by the United States just before 1800. The Georgia Cession was added in 1802 and became what we now know as Mississippi and Alabama. The Territory was split in half when Mississippi became a state in 1817.

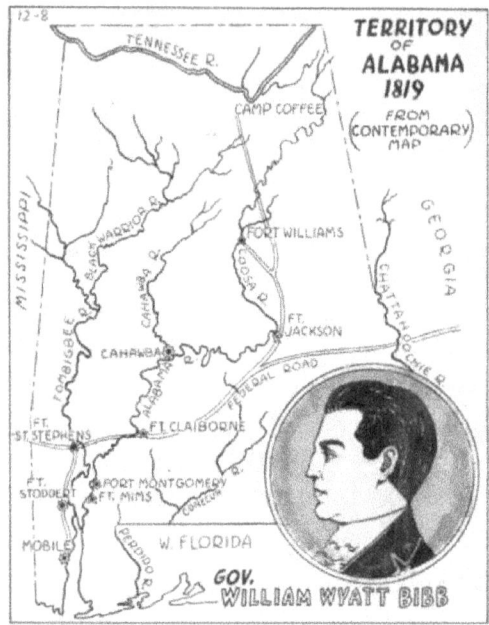

Territory of Alabama 1819
Alabama Dept. of Archives & History,
Montgomery, Alabama

An almost mirror image of the new state would become the Alabama Territory. It was thriving in the north at Huntsville and the south at Mobile. In between were enough settlers to bring a vote in Congress to create the Alabama Territory but the majority population was still Cherokee, Choctaw, Chickasaw, and a multitude of tribes lumped together and called Creeks. This new territory was established by an Act of Congress on March 3, 1817. St. Stephens in South Alabama was selected as the capital but Huntsville remained a great influence on the state.

Huntsville was first settled by white men around 1805 and became an important city in the Mississippi Territory. Cotton was selling for 30¢ per pound in the East and people were willing to move from Virginia down the Great Valley Road into Tennessee and then beyond for cheap, fertile, government owned land. Many of those new settlers came

Luther Morgan
Ancestry.com

further south to Twickenham, a new town that would later be renamed Huntsville, built near Hunt's Spring. LeRoy Walker bought much of the land here and was behind naming the new town.

As more people moved into the area and anti-British sentiment grew, Twickenham became much less desirable as a name and it was changed. The Tennessee River Valley proved to be one of the best places to grow cotton and the town of Huntsville flourished with 25 cotton gins, two banks, two newspapers and a courthouse.

After the Creek War of 1812-1814, many of the Tennessee Volunteers who served with Andrew Jackson remembered the beautiful lands they'd seen during their march to defend the settlers. Some were granted land in the newly claimed territory for their service in avenging the Indians for the Fort Mims Massacre and other events, while others were just ready to buy better farmland. The land office in Huntsville stayed busy with all the new settlers moving in.

During this time Luther Morgan, a former soldier and adventurer, established himself as a trader and merchant in Huntsville. He began exploring south of the Tennessee River Valley looking for land to claim in this raw wilderness. Around 1800 hunters had stumbled across some springs and there was talk about them in Madison County. No one knew exactly where they were and perhaps this fired the imagination of Luther Morgan.

Around 1817, Morgan's old acquaintance from his service with the Tennessee Volunteers, Davy Crockett, came through the Alabama hinterland looking for a new place to settle. Tennessee was getting too crowded for him. Crockett came to Alabama and traveled with a group of old friends from Tennessee that had fought in the Creek War a few years before. They included Jim Lanier, Tom Brandon, Luther Morgan, and three others named Robinson, Frazier and Rich.

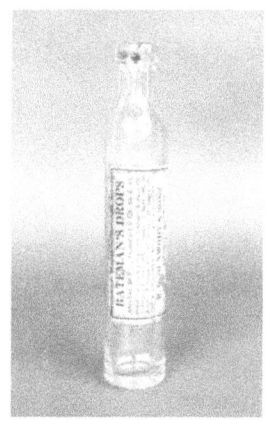

Bateman's Drops
Museum of American History

The last three continued with Davy all the way to present day Tuscaloosa where they camped. Their horses wandered off and he chased them back across the route they'd come. He almost died when he was struck by a mysterious sickness. Two friendly Indians carried him to a cabin in Jones Valley. It was the cabin of Jesse Jones who had settled there on Village Creek in 1815. Mrs. Jones nursed him back to health with good food and a full bottle of Bateman's Drops. He said in his autobiography that this threw him into a sweat and for good reason. The Drops were tinctured opium.

After Crockett left the care of Mrs. Jones, he went back up the trail and spent a couple of weeks with his old friend Luther Morgan at his camp at the sulphur springs of Blount County. Morgan had discovered those sulphur springs he had been looking for and built a wigwam there. Crockett tells of staying with him in his wigwam and about Morgan's pet bear chained to a nearby beech tree. Unfortunately the bear is only given mention in Crockett's account.

In Huntsville Morgan was a trader in whiskey, bacon, cotton bags and the hemp rope used to wrap cotton bales, turning a tidy profit of $4,000 as early as 1812. He increased his earnings to $15,000 in 1815 and used his profits to invest in town lots and the area of the springs he'd found during his wanderings. By 1819 Morgan also built a home in Huntsville and started developing and advertising his Blount Springs resort. His home and store were next to each other , just a block away from the most important building in the newly founded town, the courthouse. Morgan had everything lined up to be a very successful and rich man.

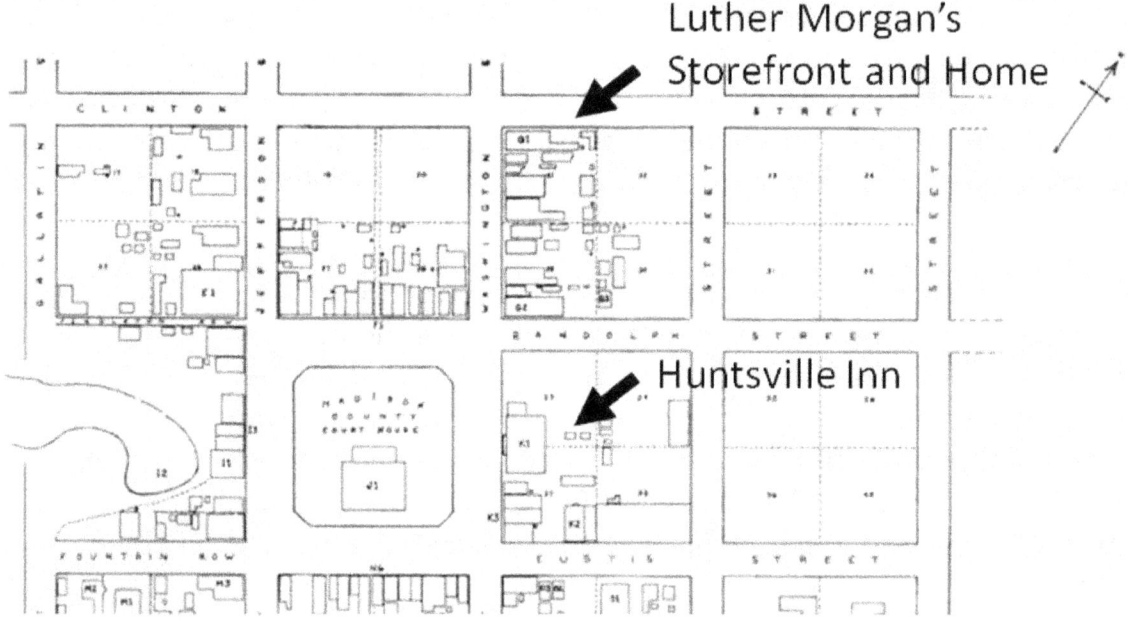

Huntsville Street Map in 1819
huntsvillehistorycollection.org

Sometime after 1818 he bought the land that contained the now famous springs in Blount County. The legal description of the spot where the springs are located is the Southwest quarter of Township 13, Range 2 West, Section 6

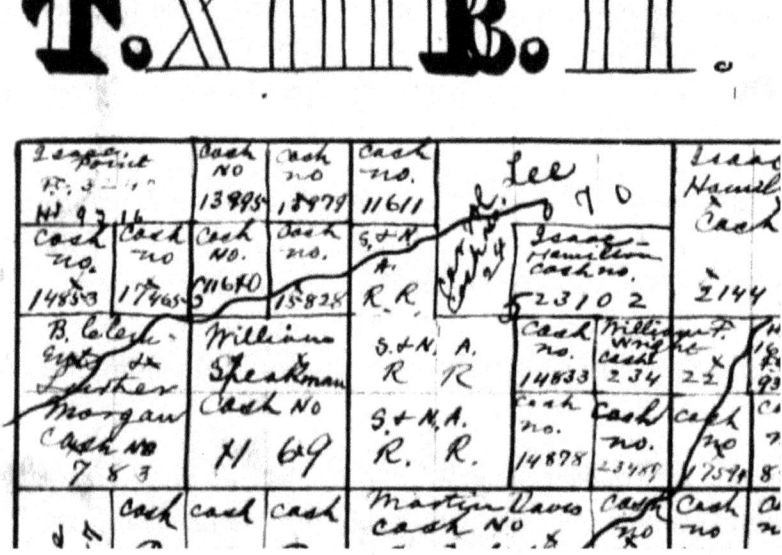

Plat Map Showing the Original Purchasers in Township 13 Range 2 West
Blount County Records

Morgan wasn't alone in thinking the little valley would be a great place to live. In 1818 Jonas Byars moved from North Carolina and settled in a cave about a mile and a half from the springs. By 1820 he built the first log cabin in what is now Blount Springs and started farming. Hunting was good in the area and it supplemented the food that could be grown in the rocky soil. He would raise his family here and have a great impact on Blount County.

Jonas came from the Spartanburg district of South Carolina and his wife, Sarah Davis Byars was from the Greenville district. Byars served as county commissioner, tax collector and justice of the peace in Blount and was one of the trustees for the building of the courthouse in Blountsville. The town of Elizabeth, New Jersey was named after his grandmother.

The very first improvement Luther Morgan made in Blount County was building his wigwam, his bear always chained to the beech tree. This he used as a trading post for the natives and scattered settlers that had moved nearby. As he ran the trading post he also constructed several small cabins around the sulphur springs.

Morgan had grandiose plans of making the springs into the largest and most luxurious bathing resort in the Southeast. Cotton prices were still up, his business in Huntsville was growing and all his investments were paying off. He felt like everything he touched did well so this would be another in a long line of successes. Little did he know that all his enterprises would come crashing down only too soon.

Huntsville, Alabama 1819 Constitution Hall is on the left
legislature.state.al.us

Huntsville continued to grow and prosper so it was only fitting that they needed somewhere to go to relieve their complaints and rest from their hard labors. Luther Morgan provided just such a place and advertised heavily in the two local papers of the time.

Chapter 1 – The Beginning of a Dream

In 1819 the elite of the Alabama Territory gathered in Huntsville to create a Constitution for the new State of Alabama. William Wyatt Bibb, governor of the Territory and other leaders came and stayed at the Huntsville Inn. In that building was written the first Constitution of Alabama. The admission of Alabama as the 22nd state was finally official December 14, 1819.

Overproduction and the Panic of 1819 caused the price of cotton to go down drastically. It was assumed this was a temporary drop, but by 1823 prices were down to around 11¢ a pound.

Huntsville still grew and by 1830 Madison County had a population of 27,990, about half white and half slaves. During all this time Morgan continued to try to grow his businesses. He built a warehouse and a meat house on Franklin Street, plus a new brick storefront on Commercial Row. He brought his sons into the business and they speculated on bringing more products into Huntsville. They formed a new company called Luther Morgan and Sons. All their property was heavily mortgaged to pay for these expansions, including their homes.

```
RATES
AT
BLOUNT SPRINGS
Boarding, Lodging, use of Baths,
    &c. &c. per week,   -   -   - $6
Keeping horse per Do.   -   -   3 50
Children under 12 years and ser-
    vants per Do.   -   -   -   3 00
Stage Fare each way,   -   -   5 50
  The above for the present season will be
the charges by the proprietors.
  N. B. The stage for the above place
leaves the Huntsville Inn every Wednesday
morning at half past 8 o'clock.
```

The Southern Advocate of 1825
Alabama Department of Archives and History, Montgomery, Alabama

The Huntsville Inn was very well established and became the starting point of a stagecoach route that went weekly to Blount Springs. The stage left the Inn each Wednesday at 8:30 and fare was $11.00 for the roundtrip. Things were going well for the resort at the time and he increased his holdings by building 30 cabins to rent to his clientele.

Early in 1824 cotton fell to 10¢ a pound and many fortunes were lost. Merchants were closing their doors and business fell off at Blount Springs too because the majority of it came from Madison County. Luther Morgan and Sons fell on hard times, mostly due to their overinvestment in Blount Springs. These investments had diverted valuable resources they needed to keep their Huntsville operation going.

In a desperate effort to keep things solvent with their wholesalers from Baltimore and New York, a deed of trust was established mortgaging the Blount Springs property, the stores and homes in Huntsville and five slaves. This happened January 17, 1825. The money was borrowed from William Patton, Benjamin Patterson and George J. Rodgers and the parcel described as "The Southwest quarter of section six in Township thirteen of Range two west." This tract was 160 and 45/100 acres. There was also a second tract of 160 acres in the Southeast quarter.

The Southern Advocate of 1826
Alabama Department of Archives and History, Montgomery, Alabama

When this deed of trust was signed it ended the company of Luther Morgan & Sons, but another company started as Samuel D. Morgan & Company. Samuel Dold Morgan was Luther's eldest son. Continuing their Huntsville businesses, they also used some of the money to add fifteen cabins and a twenty- room lodge.

Rates were cut for children and servants and more advertising proclaimed that music and dancing were to be provided for the pleasure of the patrons. Also announced were the availability of billiards, hunting, fishing, ninepins and other entertainments, quality liquors among them.

Samuel Morgan
Ancestry.com

They managed to keep their various enterprises going for a few years but they couldn't make the payments on their large debt. All this effort and the improvements to their properties were in vain as cotton prices continued to fall. Finally the property had to be sold at public auction to satisfy their debts. Since everything had been put up for mortgage to keep things afloat, the Morgans lost everything. These Morgans included Luther and Ann, Samuel and Matilda, Calvin and Henrietta, Alexander and America. The year was 1833.

Samuel and Matilda moved to Nashville in 1833 and started the house of Morgan, Allison & Company. Samuel concentrated on improving his credit for a few years and must have succeeded because during the panic of 1837, the Legislature of Tennessee, with full faith in the stability of his firm, authorized his house to issue scrip. This priviledge was a great endorsement of the government's faith in him.

Samuel worked hard to do well in Nashville and tried to make a mark across the South. He founded industries and constantly urged the development of the mineral resources of the South. He didn't forget his years in Huntsville and built a cotton mill there, along with another one in Lebanon, Tennessee.

In 1875 he founded the Tennessee Manufacturing Company in Nashville, which became the Warioto Cotton Mills in 1908. The Nashville-Chattanooga Railroad became the first launched in Tennessee and he was the biggest factor in its founding. Morgan & Company was his dry goods store in downtown Nashville. Everything he touched seemed to be successful after his early failures in Huntsville and Blount Springs.

Years earlier twins Calvin and Alexander made trips to faraway Lexington to buy hemp rope to resale in Huntsville and the Mississippi Territory. During these trips Calvin also managed to win the heart of Henrietta Hunt, daughter of one of the wealthiest men of Kentucky, John Wesley Hunt. Calvin was not your ordinary adventurous frontiersman, so he was also able to convince her father he was worthy. He loved to read and had attended Cumberland College in Nashville before becoming one of the partners in his father's businesses. One of the businesses in which Calvin took particular interest was a pharmacy. He ran this business from the front of his home. Because of all the other endeavors of the family the pharmacy was closed in 1831. He decided to pack up Henrietta and their son, John Hunt Morgan, and take up his father-in-law's offer of managing one of his farms near Lexington. Calvin became very successful in his new occupation.

Calvin Morgan's Home and Pharmacy on Clinton Street
The Morgan House

John Hunt Morgan grew up to become, arguably, the most famous and successful Confederate Raider of the War. He was known for leading a raid that ranged the farthest north of any Southern excursion. Morgan was ordered to move behind the Union lines and divert troops and resources from Vicksburg and Gettysburg.

He crossed the Ohio River and hit Southern Indiana and Ohio. Several small towns were invaded without much loss on either side. When he learned that his men had taken Masonic jewels he found the men and the jewels were returned to their rightful place in the lodge. He was a Freemason himself. During July he captured and paroled several thousand Union soldiers.

Gen. John Hunt Morgan
Wikimedia Commons

After a few more skirmishes in small Indiana and Ohio towns, 700 of his men were captured while they were trying to cross back over the Ohio River into West Virginia. Only 200 escaped, along with Morgan and most of his staff. The captured troops were sent to Camp Douglas in Chicago. Morgan and the remainder of his men continued making their way back into the Confederate lines, but were captured two weeks later.

Five of Morgan's officers in captivity
Wikimedia Commons

The entire raid was a media sensation in the Northern papers, notably Harper's Illustrated Gazette. The public waited breathlessly for word of their move and then were thrilled with the details of Morgan's capture and later escape.

They escaped into Kentucky by hiring a small boat to take them across the Ohio River. Through the assistance of sympathizers, they eventually made it to safety in the Southern lines. Coincidentally, the same day Morgan escaped, his wife gave birth to a daughter, who died shortly afterwards, before Morgan could return home.

Even though he made good his escape after a phenomenal raid, Bragg never truly trusted him again. Morgan was placed in command of the Trans-Allegheny Department of Eastern Tennessee and Southwestern Virginia. He lost his good and trusted men when he couldn't take that group with him. Bragg ordered them to stay with his command,

Chapter 1 – The Beginning of a Dream

perhaps hoping to diminish the fame and admiration of Morgan.

Harper's Illustrated Drawing of the Ohio Raid

Some of the methods of his new troops were called into question and a Board of Inquiry had been called to determine whether Gen. Morgan should continue to lead these men. He was suspended from duty until the Board met and ruled, but he decided to ignore those orders and move against the enemy as a sort of vindication of his methods.

He moved his troops toward Greenville, Tennessee and felt he should be at the front of the column as it moved across the country. This was a dangerous move in itself but nothing disastrous happened then.

It was decided to make headquarters at the Williams home on the outskirts of Greenville and guards were set accordingly. One major mistake was made when a vital roadway was left unguarded, the very road that a unit of Yankee cavalry charged down, towards the Williams home. It appeared they knew exactly where to go and it was speculated that Morgan was given to the Unionists by friendly parties. As the troops exchanged fire with the guards posted around the house, Morgan and his officers ran into the gardens and vineyard by the house.

Ironically the only man killed was Morgan. The Union Troops said he was shot only because he resisted arrest. The facts did not support this idea as he was shot in the back. Celebrating his death allowed the other raiders time to escape. The citizens of the town asked for the body to give it a proper burial but instead it was thrown over a horse like a prized kill and paraded up and down the street to the cheers of the troopers. Morgan's body was stripped and then thrown into a ditch.

One of his staff officers was soon taken prisoner and asked to make positive identification of the body while it lay in the ditch. After pleading with the commander the body was finally released and sent to his wife in Abingdon, Virginia in early September. A funeral was held for him there and then the body continued to Richmond for a Confederate States funeral to honor him as one of their heroes. Thousands came out of respect for the hero and he

Dedication of Gen. John Hunt Morgan Statue in Lexington, Kentucky
R. Burl McCoy Collection, Lexington History Museum

was buried in Hollywood Cemetery with full military honors. In 1868 his family brought the body back to Lexington, Kentucky for his third and final funeral and second burial. Over 2,000 people attended his homecoming and he is still the center of stories and legends about his exploits during the War. On October 17, 1911 more than 10,000 people came to honor one of their sons for his contribution to their state's history and the "Lost Cause" when a statue of the Rebel Raider was dedicated on the lawn of the courthouse in Fayette County, Kentucky.

2

A Highly Renowned Watering Place

Luther Morgan and his family had worked hard to save their properties but cotton prices continued to fall, their other ventures failed, and the Blount Springs cottages and land were auctioned to satisfy their debts. John H. Harris and James Perine were the purchasers at that auction of March 20, 1828. The two men bought the property for $8,000 and took out a mortgage to satisfy the sale (this mortgage was paid in full August 13, 1833).

The deed explained some of the particulars as it transferred from Morgan to Perine and Harris:

> *...and whereas by said Deed it was stipulated and agreed that if the said Luther Morgan, Samuel D. Morgan, Calvin G. Morgan and Alexander G. Morgan should fail to pay off the amount of money in said deed specified at the time therein specified, then upon the happening of such failure of payment, the said William Patton, Benjamin Patterson and George J. Rodgers can proceed to sell said property in said deed specified to the highest bidder on a credit of twelve months at the court house in the Town of Huntsville, giving two months public notice of the day and place of sale in some paper published in the town of Huntsville and the said Luther Morgan, Samuel D. Morgan, Calvin G. Morgan and Alexander G. Morgan, having failed to pay off the amount of moneys in said deed specified at the time therein specified, and the said William Patton, Benjamin Patterson and George J. Rodgers, having advertised the sale of the above described tracts of Lands for two months, in the Southern Advocate a newspaper published in the Town of Huntsville did proceed on the twentieth day of March in the year one thousand eight hundred and twenty eight, at the Court House in the Town of Huntsville to sell said tracts of land, according to the advertisement and provisions of said deed, and upon said above described tracts of land being offered for sale, the said James Perine and John H. Harris, were the last and highest bidder for said tracts of Land and the same being knocked off to them at the sum of Eight Thousand Dollars, they became the purchasers thereof for that sum.*

The new owners had a dream of making this newly acquired tract into a highly renowned watering place of the Western Country. They styled their resort as "Alabama's Fountain of Youth". The Blount Springs Herald gives them credit for being the first to actually name the place, Blount for the county and Springs for the main attraction of free flowing artesian waters.

Little is known of Harris and Perine but there is no denying the impact they had on the establishment of Blount Springs as an important watering place of the antebellum period. According to *Merriam-Webster*, a watering place is defined as: "1. a health or recreational resort featuring mineral springs for bathing," or, "2. a place where drink is available (nightclub, bar, or lounge)." The former was the main interest, but the latter was quite popular with the patrons also!

Additional cottages were added, the springs were cleaned, and more advertisements were placed in the various leading papers of Alabama and the southeast. Besides the patrons from Huntsville they were able to entice others from the Black Belt of Alabama, notably Tuscaloosa, and even further away. Patrons were limited in their travel accommodations to horseback, wagons and stagecoaches at this time.

In 1830 Blount Springs was given a post office with John H. Harris named as the first postmaster. The venture was finally recognized around the country when it appeared in the 1834 edition of *The Accompaniment to Mitchell's Reference and Distance Map of the United States*. This was quite an accomplishment at the time and assured a good level of success for years to come.

Title Page of the Accompaniment to Mitchell Reference and Distance Map

Some came from as far away as New Orleans to be entertained and cured during the sweltering months of July, August, and September. Refreshing mountain breezes were

Common during those months and patrons enjoyed the pampering they received during their stay.

Quinine was very bitter
carmichael.lib.virginia.edu

It was quite beneficial to the planters living in the Black Belt to leave the malarial river bottomland of the Alabama and Tombigbee Rivers and trade Quinine or "Old No. 6" for a shot of bourbon with a sulfur water chaser. How could that not help your health and feelings?

White, Red, Sweet-Sulfur, and Freestone water were all available in the Spring Yard and just a short distance away were the Limestone and Chalybeate waters, so easily accessible. Besides the health benefits of sparkling, though foul smelling, artesian well water, guests were also able to afford themselves the gentle coolness of the evenings, away from the sweltering summer climate of their home.

It was all the rage for the well-heeled to summer in the valleys and on the precipices of North Alabama. They carefully packed wagons and followed the Huntsville Road to Blount Springs. Whole families would pack for a month-long stay in two or three wagons and bring a household full of accoutrements and servants. When the patrons arrived there was a band playing to greet them and then the first order of the day was to get ready for the walk to the springs.

Clients were lured to spend time here through advertisements placed in newspapers across the South offering the water's curing power for dyspepsia, scrofula, rheumatism, in-fections of the bladder and urinary organs, and other problems. Temperature of the waters never got above 60° which was important in the days before refrigeration and readily available ice.

> The Bank of Mobile has invited a Convention of Delegates from all the Banks in Alabama, to be convened at Blount Springs, on the 17th September, for the purpose of proposing and taking measures for a simultaneous and early resumption of specie payment.

Southern Banner (Athens, Georgia) September 8, 1838

Sulfur is still in use by many natural adherents and doctors also prescribe sulfur drugs for specific ailments. Many skin rashes and other conditions are greatly affected by application of these waters through baths or soaking. Others still drink the spring water for better health and as a curative.

During this time there were many cures for common problems that may or may not have been a factor in the recovery of many sufferers. Now they would be considered quackery but were in general use at that time. At a time when medical treatment was very different from today, the waters were thought to provide an answer to many of the maladies of the day.

Some of the problems of the times were known by slightly different names:

Bilious fever: intestinal or malarial fevers.

Biliousness: nausea, abdominal pains, headache, and constipation

Jaundice: associated with liver disease

Catarrh: inflammation of mucous membranes of the head and throat, with a flow of mucous. (Bronchial catarrh was bronchitis; suffocative catarrh was croup)

Creeping paralysis: a term that encompasses multiple sclerosis and other complications, such as stroke

Dyspepsia: acid indigestion or heart burn.

Effluvia: exhalations. In the mid 19th century, they were called "vapors".

Gout: an arthritic disease marked by recurrent acute attacks of pain, tenderness, redness, and swelling around the joints and tendons caused by deposits of monosodium uric acid crystals.

Scrofula: a tubercular infection of the throat lymph glands.

The practice of medicine was quite different at that time. Bleeding was still used for many ailments and conditions. Some of the medicines used then are now known to cause other problems.

Calomel, a type of mercury pill that stimulated the bowels, was one of the most commonly prescribed medicines during this era.

Soaking in sulfur water can ease inflammation, swelling and pain in the joints due to arthritis and rheumatism. Bathing in sulfur-rich water is therapeutic for arthritis pain because it helps to rebuild the cartilage and synovial fluid found in the body's joints.

Soaking in sulfur water is also beneficial for muscle and joint pain in the back, shoulders and neck. The sulfur minerals seep through the pores of the skin to soothe inflamed muscles and heal joints and bones.

Opium was used to control coughing and diarrhea, morphine to help teething babies, mercury and arsenic were cures for syphilis, heroin for asthma, cocaine for toothache and a host of patent medicines for a variety of diseases and conditions, such as weak hearts, weak blood and liver problems. Some patent medicines were just good for everything such as *Mixer's Cancer and Scrofula Syrup*. It would treat "Cancer, Tumors, Erysipelas, Abscesses, Ulcers, Fever Sores, Goiter, Catarrh, Salt Rheum, Scald Head, Piles, Rheumatism, and ALL BLOOD DISEASES." [sic] from Web MD. Notable among the patent medicines were many targeting the vague category of female complaints.

Hydropathic application, the Half Bath from *Claridge's Hydropathy* book

Some of the most popular cures were through bathing. Bathing at the time was used more often for curing medical problems than for getting clean. Europeans had enjoyed taking the cure at baths since the time of the Romans. On the American Continent Saratoga was the watermark that all other watering places tried to emulate. The closest to Blount was the Virginia Mineral Springs and comparisons were drawn between the two for many years to come. This was a time when Alabama was considered wilderness. Indians still controlled much of the state and were yet to be removed through the Trail of Tears.

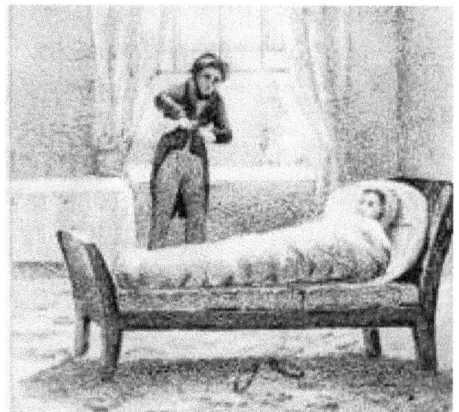

Hydropathic application, the Sweating Bath from *Claridge's Hydropathy* book

This early version of the resort proved to be quite popular and profitable in many ways. A clientele of the wealthy had proven it was worth their time and money to travel two to seven days over rough roads and trails to come and enjoy the waters and the society at the Springs. After a great deal of work, Harris and Perrine improved the resort and brought more acclaim to the benefits of health and fun. The owners paid off their $8,000 debt on the Blount Springs Tract on August 13, 1833 and promptly sold the property for $12,000 to George Mason Goff on August 16, 1833. Things were going to be much different now. A new era was beginning.

3

George Mason Goff

The next owner of Blount Springs was quite imaginative and entrepreneurial. George Mason Goff had quite an impact on the area and the state. Before his purchase he had been a patron of the resort. In fact, his daughter Mary was born there in 1827. He was born in Pomfret, Windham County, Connecticut on February 12, 1798 to Griggs and Esther Goff. As a teenager George moved to New York and then to the newly founded state of Alabama sometime before 1822. In that year he married into the very wealthy Garner family and his success seemed assured.

Riverdale Plantation
Library of Congress

Jason H. Gardner and his wife Polly of Georgia settled in Autauga County in 1819 on a bend in the Alabama River near Mulberry Creek. With Selma a few miles across the line in Dallas County, Gardner made his estate grow quickly. Ultimately he lived on this land until his death.

His daughter Louisa, married George Goff on May 7, 1822. George had acquired the neighboring lands so he moved Louisa into his home and they enjoyed the favor of the Gardners and were doing quite well. But George wanted more.

Four years later, in 1826, Louisa's father died and her 28 year old brother Virgil became master of the Gardner estate. In 1828 he built a new, more elaborate mansion and named it Riverdale. By this time riverboats were plying the waters of the Alabama River quite frequently and they helped his wealth grow to be very large with cheap and convenient shipping available at his doorstep.

One of Goff's first entrepreneurial attempts was to attempt to create a town at the crossroads near his plantation between Selma and Montgomery. His plan was to entice the state to move the capital from Tuscaloosa to his town because he thought it was centrally located within the state. This town was to be named Autaugaville and it was very close to the geographic center of Alabama.

According to the 1830 Census of Autauga County, George and Louisa Goff owned about 50 slaves and were doing pretty well supporting four daughters and five other white workers on their plantation, in addition to the slaves. One of the workers was his brother Joseph Monroe Goff. He had moved in with George and family after another brother, John, died. Joseph was about 14 at the time. The four females listed, aged 0-5, were his daughters Martha, Louise, Elizabeth and Florence.

Col. Virgil Gardner and His Huntsman
Sothby Collection

Dissatisfied with his station in life George moved to Tuscaloosa and opened a store with his much younger brother Joseph. The store proved to be very successful and sales soared but, as was the custom at the time in Alabama, the store offered a great deal of credit to farmers. Small farmers and planters came to town to buy what they needed, often what they wanted, and bought both on credit. Debts were due when the cash crop, usually cotton, was sold. He also bought most of his goods on credit through wholesalers from New York, New Jersey and other states in the northeast.

Florence Estelle Goffe
Ancestry. com

George and Louisa had visited Blount Springs many times during their marriage as it was the place to go for people of their class in the Black Belt. He began to see what a great opportunity it was to make more money by owning the place himself. He decided this would be his way to great wealth.

The 1830s were a time of much land speculation in what was then known as the "Old Southwest". There has been much written about the flush times as evidenced by the substantial growth and speculation in the two states of Alabama and Mississippi. This was considered the frontier since they had only been states about twenty years and were still sparsely settled. People were rapidly moving and fortunes grew large, while others sometimes disappeared overnight.

These are the times Andrew Jackson did everything he possibly could to destroy the Federal Bank. One of his methods was to take government money out of the Bank and deposit it in the independent banks of the Southwest. This only fueled the speculative nature of the area because each bank printed notes as fast as they could and loaned it to most anyone that could manage to get in a bank and ask for it.

Shinplaster was a common name for paper money of low denomination at this time. They were from banks and other entities such as merchants, wealthy individuals and associations. They were basically a printed IOU. This is the basis of the phrase, "not worth the paper it's printed on." Many literally weren't because they might be of the denomination of 3¢.

This practice of loaning money to anyone helped create the climate that caused the Panic of 1837. It caused a major recession that lasted until the mid-1840s. Profits, prices and wages went down, while unemployment went up. Speculation was one of the causes but there was also a drop in cotton prices and too much money was in circulation.

Local Banks Issued Their Own Money
tntcarden.com

On May 10, 1837 New York banks declared they would no longer redeem the commercial paper (shinplasters) at face value. Banks collapsed, businesses failed, prices declined, and thousands of workers lost their jobs. Loans were called in, but most borrowers had no way to pay back those loans. Paper money was virtually worthless.

Receipt to John Cocke from G .M. Goff
The W.S. Hoole Special Collections Library,
The University of Alabama

In 1833 terms, Goff fit in very well as a speculator of the top degree. He was full of ideas and had a great desire to be extremely rich and successful. He had no qualms about borrowing money and trying to do great things with it. After years of attending the establishment of Harris and Perine he saw a way to make more money if he owned and promoted the property so he did not hesitate trying his hand in this venture.

After buying the property in 1833 he began making improvements on this investment. By 1835 Goff was well established in Blount County and was even appointed postmaster that same year. While he and Joe were trying to grow their business in Tuscaloosa he was also seeking to expand his interests in Blount Springs and bought more land there in 1837.

A word about Goff or Goffe: There are many examples of the name as both Goff and Goffe, even from George himself. He signed the receipt above as Goff. Also he signed a letter to the editor of a national magazine as Goff. Yet his wife has written their name as Goffe and George himself signed other papers as Goffe. It could be assumed that both versions are correct.

1837 proved to be a good year for the promotion of Blount Springs. A Professor Brumby of the six-year-old University of Alabama did an analysis of the waters of the resort, in addition to

Front Page of Brumby's Analysis
The W.S. Hoole Special Collections Library,
The University of Alabama

those of Talladega and Shelby Springs. This analysis was a good advertisement for the quality of the waters and did much to increase a desire among patrons to attend regularly.

Goff owned the small lodge and the cottages Morgan, Harris, and Perine built, but Thomas Williams was the official owner of the property the springs were on, due to some fishy business of George Goff, and he asked Brumby to do an analysis to prove the healing powers of the waters. He asked the professor to publish 2,000 copies of his report for the general public and he probably wanted to use all of them to promote that establishment.

In his pamphlet Professor Brumby writes:

> *The ascent continues, however, to the top of the mountain, at the base of which the springs issue. Proceeding about a mile on its summit, over a smooth road, the traveler, exhilarated by the fine scenery and bland atmosphere, begins his descent through a narrow channel, between two steep projections of the mountain, covered with luxuriant vegetation; and though admonished by the strong smell of sulphuretted hydrogen of their proximity, the springs, the buildings, and the clusters of visitors appear before him quite unexpectedly. The springs are situated in a small triangular valley, surrounded by mountains of considerable elevation. The effect of the picturesque scenery is greatly enhanced, when the visiter(sic) is taken into a portico, on the north end of the hotel, whence he looks down into a long valley at the foot of a mountain, not half a mile off, which sweeps boldly across the country from east to west, and presents to his excited imagination masses of rocks, heaped in confusion on its precipitous sides.*

> It is, in my opinion, an extraordinary locality of mineral waters. Sixteen sulphureous springs, differing in a greater or less degree, and many of them essentially, rise through solid rock, within a circle of a few hundred feet in diameter. He who needs an antacid, can drink of a limestone spring of the purest quality; he who wants a tonic, can resort to a chalybeate in the immediate vicinity; and he, whose disease requires, or whose appetite craves, sulphur water of any kind, can find it in the White, Black, Red and Sweet Sulphur Springs, which gush in profusion, and of various degrees of strength, from almost every crevice in the rock.
>
> These names, which are applied to similar waters in other places, were taken, I presume, from the color of the sediment, or some other striking property. Thus, the name White Sulphur is applied to those, which have a milky translucency, caused by a copious deposition of the carbonates of lime and magnesia; Black Sulphur, to those, which yield a copious black sediment of sulphuret of iron; and Red Sulphur, to those, in which the black sediment is covered with a thin red film of bi-sulphuret and peroxide of iron.

**An Excerpt from Brumby's Pamphlet
The W.S. Hoole Special Collections Library,
The University of Alabama**

After spending a month at Blount he had analyzed all the different springs, noting there were 16, and stating that temperatures of the waters ranged from 55° F to 70° F. In his opinion all the springs came from the same underground source but each was changed by the various kinds of rocks they filtered through on their way to the surface.

He further opines this is exactly the

reason they produce such curative effects for a wide range of afflictions and maladies. The various springs produce diverse cures such as antacid, tonic, diuretic, diaphoretic, and in many cases, cathartic effects. They also work to remove "glandular and cutaneous diseases caused by mercurial preparation and in curing rheumatism." Brumby's pamphlet continues:

> *The effects are doubtless promoted by relaxation of mind, agreeable exercise, and the excitements of society; still these alone could not, in a few weeks, enable the crippled rheumatic to dance, the desponding dyspeptic to digest his dinner, nor restore him to sound health, whose debilitated, ulcerated frame had, for years, been the prey of mercurial disease. Such cases have been effectually relieved by the use of these waters.*
>
> *It may be proper to state, that, while at the springs, I conversed with several intelligent gentlemen who had, a short time before, been at the Red and White Sulphur springs of Virginia. They concurred in the opinion that the corresponding Blount Springs are not inferior in any respect.*

Brumby's words were powerful and would be very useful in the promotion of Blount Springs as the premier watering place of the South. Advertising claims of an extraordinary nature are not a new idea of the 21st Century.

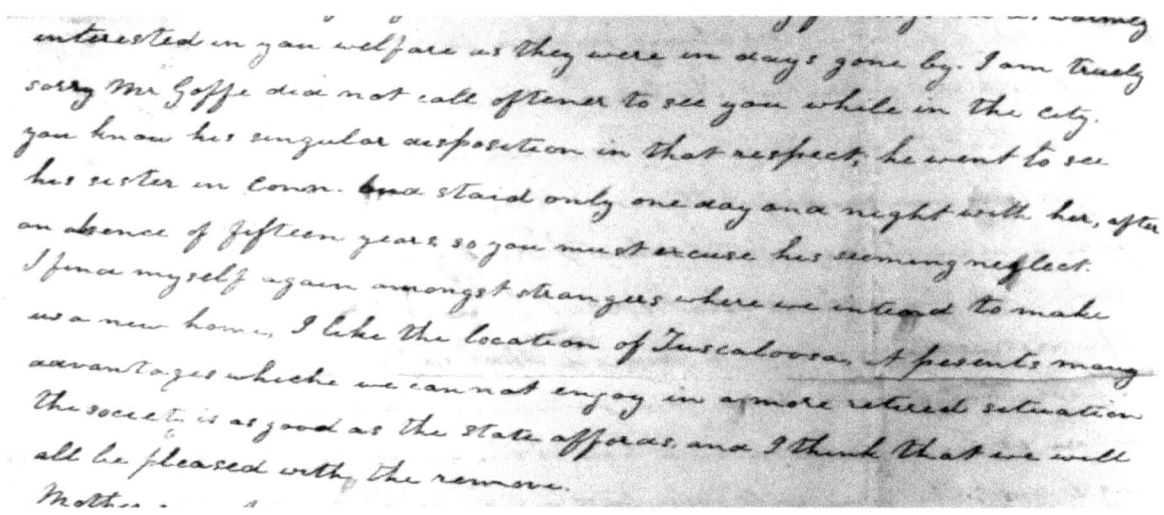

Louisa Goffe letter
The W. S. Hoole Special Collections Library, The University of Alabama

In a letter to her sister Mary, Louisa Goff(e) apologizes for her husband not visiting her family while he was in nearby New York City sometime in 1837. He visited his sister, whom he hadn't seen for 15 years, only a day and night. She also talks of their new home of Tuscaloosa. Her husband was all over the place looking for a way to improve their monetary situation. This was probably a business trip for his store in Tuscaloosa. He was there seeking merchandise and loans for his latest idea of starting a silk farm and also to improve his hotel in Blount County. He was also borrowing more money.

Soon after returning home from New York he built a 40 room, Colonial-style Inn, furnished it accordingly, and named it the Goff Hous, This hotel was near the springs and just above them. He bought land in Huntsville and more in Blount Springs.

> TO THE EDITOR OF THE SILK RECORD.
> Blount Springs, Alabama,
> March 27, 1841.
>
> DEAR SIR:—I have commenced the silk business in this State, and now have about 30 acres in the Morus Multicaulis. They look well, and flatter me with an abundance of foliage this season. I have lately put up a rough and open building, 100 by 28 feet, and nearly filled it with shelving and hurdles, something upon the old plan. But having lately perused one of your publications called the Burlington Silk Record, which contains a description of your improved plan of feeding worms, and which I now think cannot fail of meeting with universal use and patronage, I now want you to forward to me at this office all the numbers of the Record published last year, and continue to send them till ordered otherwise. I notice they are sent gratuitously at present, which I consider a liberal act on your part, and add, that I for one, am willing to make compensation at any time when it becomes necessary for its continuance, or onerous on you. We in this section of country are destitute of late advice as to improvements in this most interesting branch of American agriculture.
>
> Mr. Elam Covington, a neighbor of mine, has also commenced the silk culture upon a pretty extensive scale, and requests me to say to you to forward him some publications, in order that he may understand the principles of your invention in feeding worms, as he has no shelves as yet put up. We two are the only persons here in the mountains that are making any preparations for raising silk, and the people far and near seem to be waiting the issue of our experiments, with much anxiety and solicitude,
>
> Respectfully yours, &c.
> GEO. GOFFE.

Letter to the Editor from George Goffe of the *Burlington Silk Record*, 1841

The imagination of George Goff gave the Mulberry River its name. He purchased several plots of land along the river, planted mulberry trees near the river's edge, and as soon as they were large enough, added millions of silkworms to those same trees. Back at Blount Springs he constructed a silk factory of sorts. For a good while there was a lot of promise for this scheme but it finally proved to be a failure and a great deal of money was lost on this investment. This fiasco may have been the beginning of the end for George Goff.

Sometime in 1939 George sent his younger brother Joseph to Texas with some of his property. It seemed he was trying to get it away from the state before his creditors could get it. This property included slaves and other materials valued at $10,000. Census records for 1840 show him in Blount Springs along with his wife and daughters, with no slaves listed.

To finance some of these new endeavors and keep good credit with his Eastern creditors, he basically sold his interest in the Goff House and the land in Blount Springs for $64,000 to a man named Williams. Or at least that's what looked like he was doing at the time.

Goff's creditors soon discovered what appeared to be an attempt to dodge his creditors. He had sold the Blount Springs land and other holdings to Thomas Williams as a sham to protect his interests in case of bankruptcy.

He had borrowed money from Parrish and Company of New York in February of 1837 and then four more loans in September and October of that year. According to statements made in court he personally owned other property worth $12,000, Negroes worth $13,000 and was owed $10,000 for a total worth of $35,000, plus $30,000 more in business assets. Certainly he had enough assets to secure the loans he was after. Unfortunately much of his wealth was only on paper and his real finances took a downward turn soon after he had secured these loans.

Shortly after he bought the additional land in Blount County, his financial troubles became publicly known. This was 1839. Most of the problems came from his dealings of the previous two years, because he was borrowing more money to finance new plans when he couldn't pay his old debts.

Some of this was due to his Tuscaloosa customers being late or not paying debts at all owed him and his brother Joseph in their mercantile business. By 1938 much more of his debt was due and he lay in default, including the majority of it to Parrish and Company of New York City. Suits were filed against him in 1839 for the payment of these debts.

Section of recording of George Goff Deed
Blount County Courthouse Records

During the time (1837) that he was contracting these large debts he did not disclose that Thomas Williams, Jr. bought 640 acres of his Blount Springs property. Goff sold these holdings to him on credit with the notes payable to his four daughters and finally his wife, the last one due for $14,000. Each of his daughters was to collect $10,000 each, thus taking the property out of his name and not subject to being taken over by his creditors.

Regardless of this hidden transaction, courts found twenty-seven judgments against him. Four of these notes were from February, 1837 and four from September and October. These notes were granted without disclosure of the deed of trust to his wife and daughters concerning the Blount Springs property.

The Blount Springs property was considered to be inconsequential to the Tuscaloosa holdings. The assets of the firm of G. & J. M. Goff consisted of $10,000 worth of merchandise, and $10,000 in debts due them. In the court records it was explained why Goff did not commit fraud, according to attorney representing the defendants.

> *The debts of Goffe (both individual and partnership) according to the testimony of the complainants' own witnesses, only amounted to about $25,000. The first question, then, is fully answered; for there is no conflict of testimony. The allegation of the bill, that the settlement was made to hinder and delay creditors, is fully denied by the answers, and a good reason shown for its being made, to wit, that Goffe, when a poor young man, had married his wife, and obtained by her a considerable amount of property, a portion of which he wished, while in prosperous circumstances, to settle on his children.*

Lawsuits were commenced against him by a large number of creditors, principally Parish and Company, and early in 1839, most of his property was sold to satisfy debts. In 1840 he was alleged to "run off" to Texas with about $10,000 worth of property including cattle and slaves. He went to the southeastern part of Texas around Matagorda Bay.

In the court case "Henry Parish v. Caleb Murphree, Administrator of George Goffe Deceased", there are the names of Louisa C. Goffe, Martha Lucy, Addison Boykin and wife Elizabeth G. Goffe in December Term, 1851.

> *"The bill was filed to set aside a deed of settlement, made by George Goffe, dated the 12th September, 1837, on his wife and four daughters, on the grounds, that it was made in fraud of creditors. At the date above stated, Goffe and wife, by deed of general warranty, conveyed to Thomas Williams, Jr., six hundred and forty acres of land, including the 'Blount Spring Tract,' in Blount County, State of Alabama, for the consideration of sixty-four thousand dollars. To secure the payment of the considerating, on the same day, Williams executed a deed of trust on the same property to Joseph M. Goffe and George Goffe, for which notes bearing interest were given... On the same day, George Goffe executed a deed of settlement signed also by Joseph M. Goffe, by which he appropriated to his four*

daughters, the four ten thousand dollars notes above stated, and the fourteen thousand dollars note to his wife in consideration of 'the natural love and affection he had for them.'..

Finally the Supreme Court of the United States decided for the complainants, Goff's creditors, and the Blount Springs property was turned over to Parish and Company.

One of Goff's nephews made a trip to visit him in Tuscaloosa just before everything collapsed. Upon arrival he learned his Uncle George was in Blount Springs, but after making the difficult journey there he found him to be:

"...very sick with bilious fever at his camp near the shore of Matagorda Bay where he had been herding his cattle. I went to take care of him but he had got some neighbors to take him down on the east side of Pass Cavallo, where the bay joins the Gulf of Mexico. I followed him and found him quite sick and lying in the loft of a warehouse. I was soon taken with the same fever, but having some quinine and blue map, I was enabled partially to break the fever on both of us. ...I never saw him after that for he took a relapse and died in New Orleans as I learned after I got back to Ohio." {George Bolles, 1902}

This visit was about 1843. He probably had a bout with malaria. After seemingly beating that sickness he went to New Orleans where he relapsed. George Goff died sometime in 1844.

Lucy C. Jones was the manager of the Goff House in 1841. By this time the ownership on paper at least had transferred to Williams. The Goffs still acted as if they owned the hotel and Jones had been hired to manage it. During this time he began courting Martha, the Goff's oldest daughter. They were married in 1851 just before the lawsuit was finished.

It was a different time and advertisements often appeared to be more like an article in the newspaper. Here is that advertisement from the *Huntsville Democrat* July 3, 1841:

Blount Springs

This watering place opened on the 13th of May under the direction of Mr. Jones C. Lucy, a young man of much enterprise and industry. He had employed Mr. Joseph Bondurant and lady, lately of Mobile, to superintend the culinary department which is kept in a style highly creditable to him and his accomplished lady. Mr. Lucy has not regarded expense or labor to make this watering establishment comfortable to the sick, and a delightful retreat for the gay and fashionable. The grounds and cabins are much improved since last season; his bedding and furniture are all new. He has for the amusement of his visitors two billiard tables, new tenpin alleys, a number of good guns, and some excellent deer dogs. The bath house is improved and carefully attended to by an excellent servant. For the evening entertainment and for those who like to move "the light fantastic toe" he has procured from Mobile an excellent band of musicians who will perform every evening in the Ball room, and during the day upon the green. The parlor is provided with two Pianos, and he has a good miscellaneous library, the use of which will be extended to visitors. The services of Dr. Smith, an able physician can be procured at any time by invalids who desire his advice and medical aid. The price of board, etc. are very moderate, being reduced twenty-five percent from the rates of last season. Everything that conduces either health or pleasure can be had at these springs, and in a style not inferior to any watering place in the Union. The water is said to be as good as any in the world for diseases of all kinds, and the variety of mineral springs is superior to any place now known, there being some ten or twelve springs, all different in their medicinal properties. The Springs are situated in a wildly romantic part of the country amid high mountains, abounding in great quantities of deer and other game. The roads have been highly improved by the proprietor, so that the Springs can be approached by any kind of vehicles. The mail passes now regularly by the Springs once a week, and will shortly pass three times. All who desire health and pleasure had better give this water place a call.

An oft-told story from around this time is told in *Historic Hotels and Resorts of Alabama* by Sulzby. It concerned a legislator from Morgan County by the name of Charles C. B. Strode. In the summer of 1843 he visited a friend who was staying at Blount. He inquired of his friend about the baths at the resort. The response told of the availability of baths that were hot, cold or tēa-pid (tepid). Being a gentleman he made no mention of his friend's mispronunciation of the word and ordered a warm bath.

During the night he suffered from a severe case of colic (intense pain and cramping within the abdominal cavity). The friend came to be by his side wanting to help him. Strode said, "Oh! What pain; farewell; I cannot survive this attack, I never had such pains before. I am to die in the prime of life. You must pardon my candor in the hour of death. Oh, how sharp the sting! Think not hard of me when I say, you caused my pain, not this infernal colic. Oh, can I have time to tell you what pain you inflicted on my literary taste! Oh, mercy-I shall die, but Milton, you did pronounce that word 'teapid' horribly; I expected better things of you."

After much treatment with hot baths, mustard plaster and stimulants (probably brandy), he recovered and fell asleep. His friend stayed by his side and Strode said upon waking, "It is unworthy of your character. You ought to be a finished gentleman."

Pres. Sam Houston
U.S. National Archives and Records Administration

The President of Texas, Sam Houston, originally hailed from Alabama and naturally, he married an Alabama girl. In June of 1845 he and his wife Margaret, along with their son Little Sam, came to the funeral of his old friend Andrew Jackson at the Hermitage near Nashville, Tennessee. Little Sam was about 1 1/2 years old. Because of their travel distance they didn't make it in time for the funeral but instead spent some time with the grieving widow before going home.

Margaret had asthma and other illnesses that kept her from being able to travel with her Husband on business and she just couldn't shake them. Deciding to visit her parents in Marion, Alabama for a time on their way back to Texas they came through Central Alabama. She had spent many summers at Blount Springs with her parents when she was young and they decided to give it another try for her health.

The stay was quite pleasant for the three of them and they drank the water and saw to Margaret's health. They enjoyed Blount for nearly a month and arrived at her parents September 1st. The time was well spent because it apparently worked. She was able to bear another baby the next year and it was a girl.

Margaret Lea Houston
Sam Houston State University

Billiards were in the basement of the hotel and illegal at the time (1850s) so that made it special. The basement was off limits to children because of the billiards, strong drink, and gambling. The adults called it the Devil's Den. Since it was forbidden, this made it that much more appealing to the young folks. They did their best to sneak a peek at the basement.

The town of Demopolis had long supplied patrons for the Jackson House and some of the cottages. Now, Gaius Whitfield, the wealthiest planter of that city and Marengo

County, was coming. His friend paved the way with a letter of introduction to make sure he was afforded the special attention he deserved and should receive.

W. H. Lyon wrote in June of 1844:

Gaius Whitfield
Ancestry.com

B. Smith Esq.

My Dear Sir,

This will be handed you by the finest of all of us, Mr. Gaius Whitfield. He visits Blount for Mrs. Whitfield's health and his own. I know you and Mr. Lucy will tender his stay comfortable and that Mrs. Smith & Mrs. Lucy will make Mrs. Whitfield so. We will all be on in the course of 3 weeks. Don't let Whitfield leave as I am sure it is the very place for him and Mrs. Whitfield. All that visited Blount last year are away. My wife will be there certainly for 3 weeks. I shall myself come on in July or the 1st of August. Give my kindest works to Mrs. S & Mrs. Lucy.

Truly your friend
W. H. Lyon

Goff had been a major player in the development of Blount Springs and will be remembered for his entrepreneurial feats. He was a product of his times and fully participated in the speculation for quick money that characterized the "Flush Times" in Alabama of the 1830s. He had many ideas and pushed them as hard as he could, but they somehow always went awry. He gave a river its name, operated a store, and a plantation in Dallas County. He was a man of many dreams but not a lot of accomplishment. At the end of the 1840s he had left the scene and others would be taking over as a new decade was ready to begin.

Gambling was always a large part of the entertainment at Blount Springs. The other main entertainment was music and dancing. Now O. J. Noyes was the manager in 1840 when this ad appeared in the May 20th edition of the New Orleans Commercial Bulletin.

Besides running the Waverly House, a popular hotel in Mobile, he was offering first class service also in Blount Springs. Something the resort was always known for was service and hospitality. The copy tells of the waters and the advantages of the countryside of Blount County. As always a new season brings accounts of the many and varied improvements and repairs that have been made to the premises.

In addition to an ample table supplied by the good farmers of the area, it will be supplemented by the many items that come from Mobile, along with an excellent selection of wines from his own Waverly House. Again he refers to the Brumly Analysis as to the particulars of the wonderful waters available for pleasure and healing to all who visit during the upcoming season.

BLOUNT SPRINGS.

THE undersigned (proprietor of the Waverly House, Mobile,) has the pleasure of informing his friends and the public, that he has leased the above establishment for a term of years, and will be ready to receive visitors on the 15th of June. The premises are now undergoing thorough and complete repairs, and many extensive improvements are also being completed.

It is deemed unnecessary to say any thing of the efficacy of these waters. There is, perhaps, no place in the world, where so great a variety of mineral waters can be found. Sixteen springs gush up out of a rock not more than 100 feet in circumference—seven of these have been analysed, and possess distinct qualities. The white, red, black and sweet sulphers are said to be excelled by no waters in the United States. The country in the vicinity is mountainous and picturesque, and abounds in a great variety of game, fish, fruit, &c. The table will be supplied with the best the country—aided with the Mobile market—will afford A choice selection of wines, being a part of the stock of the Waverly House wines, have been sent to the Springs. The entire establishment will be under the exclusive control and management of the proprietor, who assures his guests that nothing shall be wanting on his part to render this one of the most desirable watering places in the United States.

For further particulars respecting these Springs, the public are respectfully referred to a brief account of the analysis of the Blount Springs, by R S Brumly, A M, Professor of Chemistry, Mineralogy and Geology, in the University of Alabama. Also, the certificates of several of the most experienced and scientific medical gentlemen of the city of Mobile.

m15 w6t   O. J. NOYES.

New Orleans Commercial Bulletin May 20, 1840

4

An Irishman Comes to Town

Another Blount Springs connection to Tuscaloosa was Matthew Duffee. On Christmas Day, 1803 at Sirham Frank, Ireland, Matthew Duhy (pronounced DUH-hee) came into the world. In his own words he tells of how the family named was changed.

> *In December 1821, when my father went to the Custom House in Liverpool, England, to report himself and family as coming to America, he gave his right name, John Duhy, but the Custom House officer he was dealing with would have it as Duffee, saying that was the English way of spelling Duffee. So the names were all entered on the ship's passenger list and manifests as Duffee and when the ship arrived at Charleston, South Carolina on February 4th, 1822, we were all called by the name of Duffee.*

The Bayard
State Library of Queenstown

It took 35 days to reach America on the *Bayard* and about a year later, Matthew struck out on his own. He left on February 1, 1823 and arrived in Tuscaloosa on March 17. Once he arrived he set to work at making a living for himself. He had made the journey with a friend named Gallagher and they rented some land together about three miles north of town. Gallagher had a team of horses and they worked hard and planted 45 acres in corn. After gathering this crop he worked in town digging cellars for $5.00 a day, turning a nice profit, always saving as much as he could.

Early in 1824 Duffee contracted with William G. Parish as an overseer for $200 a year. For the next several years he worked as an overseer for different people, always saving every penny he could. In 1826 he used the money he'd saved to open his own mercantile business in Tuscaloosa. He traveled to New York and bought merchandise to sell in his newly acquired store.

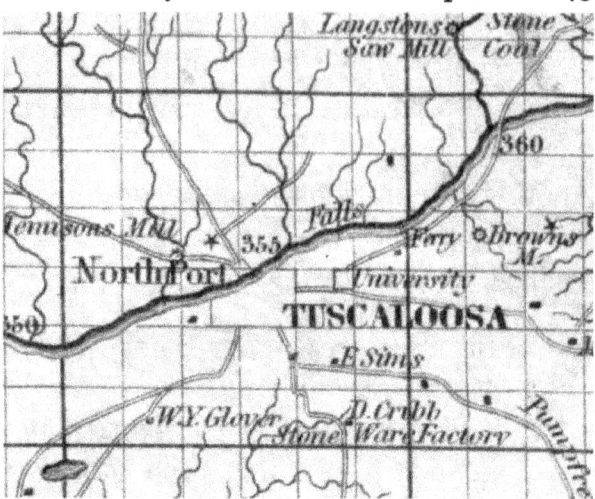

Part of Alabama Map from the 1830s
Alabama Department of Archives and History,
Montgomery, Alabama

A while later he took a year off to return to Ireland, then started another business when he returned in 1829. Making money seemed to come very easily to this hard-working Irishman. It looked like he could be a wealthy man someday if he kept at it.

State Capitol of Alabama at Tuscaloosa
Alabama Department of Archives and History,
Montgomery, Alabama

The Alabama state capital was in Cahaba. The town was located at the junction of the Cahaba and Alabama Rivers and at times legislators were forced to use boats to reach the chambers in the capitol building. In 1826 Tuscaloosa became the capital of Alabama when the legislature voted to move it from Cahaba because of frequent flooding and the fear of malaria. Tuscaloosa became the most important city in Alabama and many flocked to be part of the political scene there. Planters in the area made certain to have an impressive townhouse in the city so they could be part of the fun and frivolity, not to mention the money making opportunities available to those in the inner political circle.

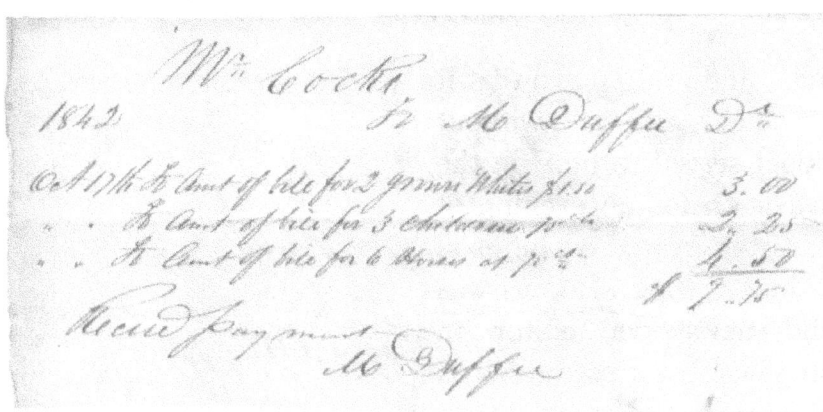

Receipt for William Cocke from M. Duffee
The W. S. Hoole Special Collections Library, The University of Alabama

On February 12, 1832 Matthew Duffee, at the ripe old age of 28, married Martha Allison Gillespie. Martha was the granddaughter of John & Margaret Kerr Gillespie.

Their family had made the long, hard move from Mecklenburg County, North Carolina to Tennessee on pack mules. Andrew Jackson was one of the guards who protected them from the Indians. She was refined, well educated, and a cousin of President James K. Polk.

Their first child, William Henry, was born in December. George Gordon came three years later and John Knox was born in 1837. The last child of this union was Mary Gordon, born in 1844. The Duffees were a happy family with many discussions of politics, religion and other issues of the day at home and especially around the family table.

January 10, 1836 was a big day for the Duffees. Matthew bought the premier hotel in Tuscaloosa, Washington Hall, for $30,000. He would own and operate it for the next 30 years. Washington Hall was located at the corner of Greensboro and Broad St. The First National Bank Building, Tuscaloosa's tallest building, occupies the spot and Broad Street is now University Boulevard. The hotel and bar was the center of the capital city's social and political world.

Legislators from all over the state stayed at Washington Hall when the Legislature was in session and enjoyed the libations available in the Golden Ball Tavern on the second-floor. In later years the ground floor held a saloon and at the back of the lobby was a huge dining room. On the second-floor was an auditorium used for meetings, stage productions and balls and sometimes court. At one time the post office, attorney's offices and a barber shop were in the back side of the building.

Near the entrance a brick pillar was constructed that held a life-size portrait of Washington holding the reins of a gray horse and above was the name of the hotel. It was said that the beauty and fashion of the capital and the state assembled in the ballroom. Truly, this was the center of the political and social scene in the Queen City.

Illustration of Simon Suggs
Flush Times of Alabama and Mississippi

Washington Hall was so popular and well-known that it was where Simon Suggs bolted down, "without mastication, the excellent supper served to him" in the dining room before he sallied forth for an evening of Faro. Simon Suggs was a character created by Johnson Jones Hooper (June 9, 1815– June 7, 1862). Hooper was an American humorist and newspaper editor in Dadeville, Alabama. He wrote several stories and books about the adventures of Captain Simon Suggs. They made him and his work known throughout the United States. It is thought these stories inspired some of the characters in Mark Twain's work. Suggs is often used as the prime example of Southwest Humor.

In 1852 Matthew Duffee bought his first piece of Blount Springs property. He built a small hotel on this property and began a tradition of moving his family from Tuscaloosa to Blount Springs every June to run this new venture. This annual pilgrimage took place until the Civil War.

It was a four day journey on rough roads with only a few houses and businesses along the route. The family and enough servants to take care of them and their guests were in four wagons. Along the way they would camp and stay with friends scattered along the Huntsville Road.

Many years later Mary Duffee would write about these trips in a series of newspaper articles in the Birmingham Age-Herald that would eventually be turned into a book called *Sketches of Alabama*. This would be the only book written by her, but her writings would be prolific and appear in many forms.

Duffee's advertisement in the *Jones Valley Times* of August 31, 1854 listed his rates at $1.00 for all guests over 10 years old and 50₵ for children, servants and horses. It also mentions a stage leaving Elyton every Tuesday, Thursday and Saturday morning and arriving at Blount Springs the same day. Running from July 10th to October 1st, the hack will bring guests to enjoy the medicinal waters and entertainment.

Mary received her early education at the Tuscaloosa Female Seminary. This school was housed in the former capitol building after the state government moved to Montgomery in 1847. Her mother believed women should be well educated because she was highly educated and a lady to the manor born, sensitive and proud. Mary was then sent to New York State to matriculate further. She was shy and a little homely and did not make friends easily. A love of nature led to her writing a series about the varied flora and fauna of West Alabama which became a series of published articles. Because of her writing she was sought after by those that admired her talents. She was inspired by the attention and concentrated on her studies and her writing.

Mary wrote many poems and prose all her life. During her stay at school in New York she met people that were able to help her acquire avenues for publication of many of her works over the years. She also contributed articles to several out-of-state newspapers, wrote guide books, advertising copy, and poetry.

The family continued their annual trek each year, enjoying Tuscaloosa most of the year and then Blount Springs during the "season" that usually lasted from July through early September. In 1858 Matthew bought the land that would come to be called Duffee's Mountain. The foot of this mountain is marked by the present day location of the Top Hat Restaurant. Getting to the top involves an arduous climb up the side of the mountain.

Jones Valley Times
August 31, 1854

The family built a small cabin and he continued to buy more land in and around Blount Springs. During the Civil War the family took refuge in Blount County. Washington Hall was used to house prisoners and also as a hospital. When Gen. Croxton came through during the last month of the war he burned the building to the ground because of its use as a military prison. Some accounts say Mary was in Tuscaloosa when the Yankees came through and witnessed the destruction others say she was in Kentucky spying for the Confederacy at that time.

Matthew Duffee lost all of his Tuscaloosa property because of the war and stayed in Blount Springs the rest of his life. He bought the Goff House and renamed it the Duffee House in 1868, then it tragically burned in 1869. Without insurance there was no money to rebuild.

The Duffees stayed in their cabin on Duffee's Mountain and much merriment went on there and down in the valley below. As long as he was alive he was a large part of the community of Blount Springs. The entire family continued to be held in high regard by the people that lived full time in Blount Springs and the ones that visited. Mary moved away for a time but came home to live the rest of her life on that mountain. Matthew died in 1878, just as a new era of the resort began with the opening of the New Jackson House.

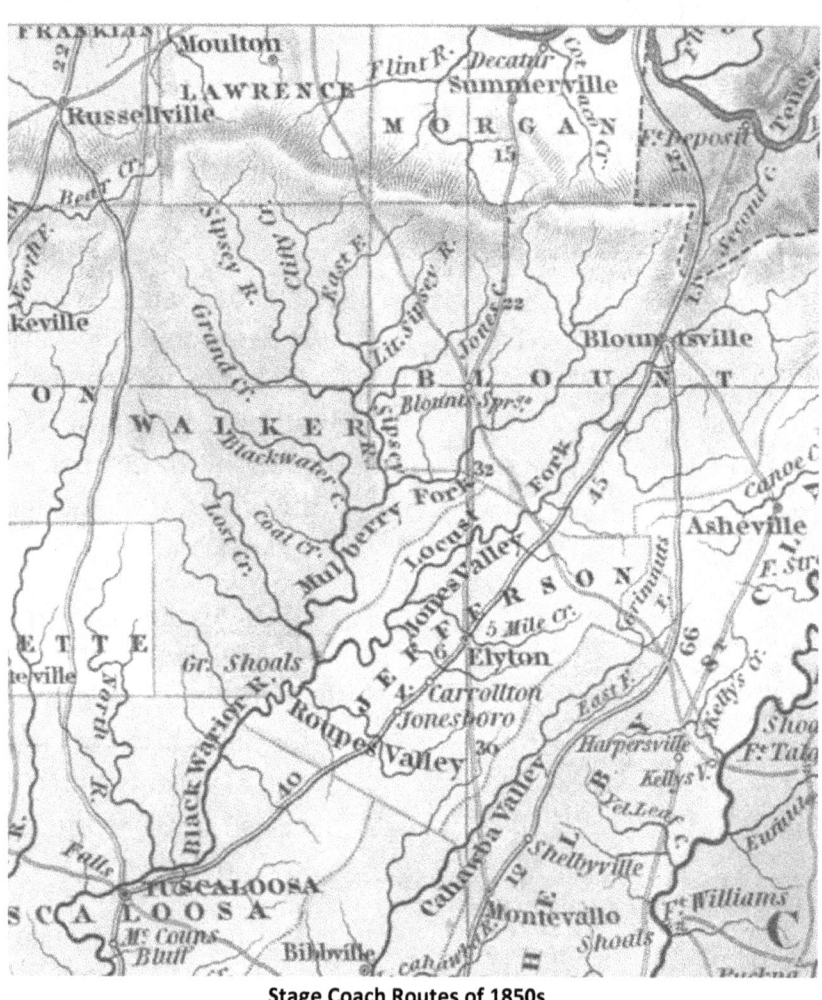

Stage Coach Routes of 1850s
University of Alabama Geography Department

5

Up From the Black Belt

Many of the guests of the antebellum period made a wagon ride that took several days from the Black Belt each summer. It was an arduous journey, but the reward of a month or more of pleasure away from the heat and daily quinine, Old #6, or worse, was worth it. Some came from Forkland where the Warrior and Tombigbee Rivers meet to make it true malaria country. Here the plantations were large, wealthy, and far apart.

Many came from Greene County, one of the wealthiest counties in the United States before the War Between the States. This great wealth was due to its planter society and reliance on King Cotton. The leisure class in these areas had the means and the time to truly enjoy the premiere watering place of Alabama.

Augustus Benners
Disunion, War, Defeat and Recovery in Alabama

Augustus Benners was one of those planters and he was a politician too. He spent the majority of his life in Greensboro, Alabama. Greensboro was part of Greene County but was in the section that would become Hale County after the war. It was a large town for the times and many successful planters, lawyers, and merchants called it home.

He was born Christmas Day, 1819 at New Bern, NC, seven months after the death of his father and 11 days after the birth of Alabama. He graduated from the University of North Carolina in 1839 at the age of 20.

Benners came to Alabama as a young man to practice law with his brother Alfred in Linden, Alabama. Alfred was a few years older and had previously come to Alabama and settled there. Many of the men and women of this area had come from North and South Carolina looking for a new place to start their lives and create a fortune if they could.

Linden was at one time known as Hohenlinden to commemorate Napoleon Bonaparte's battle in 1800 at Hohenlinden, Germany, in which the French were victorious over the Austrians and Bavarians. The spelling was later simplified to Linden. This town was founded by a group of Bonapartists that were given land in Alabama where they formed the Vine and Olive Colony. Members of this group also started the town of Demopolis (city of the people), both in Marengo County.

After a few months Augustus and Alfred decided to move to Greensboro and built their practice into a successful venture. Benners married Jane Hatch in 1846. She was the daughter of one of the wealthiest planters in the region. His name was Alfred Hatch and he lived in mansion on the Black Warrior River named Arcola. The name Arcola also came from the French members of the Vine and Olive Colony who named the little village around the plantation for Napoleon's victory at the Battle of Arcola.

Nine months later Fanny was born on August 23. Two years later along came Alfred, named for his maternal grandfather and eventually they had many more children. Only five would survive past early childhood.

In the 1850s Benners owned two plantations totaling 715 acres and 82 slaves. One of the plantations was known as Walker Place and the other Chaney Place. Of course his cash crop was cotton but he grew severalother crops for the use of his family and servants.

In 1853 he was nominated for the state legislature and the Greene County voters sent him as their representative to Montgomery. He was fastidious with the state's money while he worked to pass legislation that he thought would help Alabama. As the war came on he feared for the state's future but supported the war effort.

He and his best friend, Judge Sydenham Moore began the journey to Montgomery so as to witness the first meeting of the Provisional Congress of the Confederacy. Nearing the city they learned Congress was

The Benners Family at Their Home in Greensboro
Disunion, War, Defeat and Recovery in Alabama

conducting secret sessions and so they turned around and went home instead. Benners and Moore spent a lot of time together, especially long annual fishing trips.

Moore was a graduate of the University of Alabama (1836) and an excellent lawyer that would serve as a judge through much of the 1840s and 50s. Elected to serve the section as a Congressman in 1857 he was one of the Alabama Delegation that came home from Washington, D. C. when the state seceded.

He led the 11th Alabama as Colonel and was mortally wounded at the Battle of Seven Pines in the defense of Richmond. This was the same battle that Joe Johnston was wounded, paving the way for Robert E. Lee to take command of the Confederate Army. Moore died May 31, 1862 in Richmond from those wounds and his body was brought home for burial. Benners mourned his loss bitterly.

Benners was again elected to serve the people and went to Montgomery as part of the Alabama House of 1861, voting against many of the bond issues for the Confederacy. He did believe in the Southern Cause and did many things to support his new country, but he was very careful when it came to spending the state's funds.

The war years were hard in Greensboro as many of the men of the community were killed or wounded. Food became scarce and expensive but the Benners made it through and started putting their lives together again during the Reconstruction Period. Augustus tried to find renters for his land but many didn't work out and finally his sons Alfred and Ed tried to make a go of it, but experienced nothing but hard luck.

Augustus and Fanny in 1853
Disunion, War, Defeat and Recovery in Alabama

Alfred finally chose the law as his profession and struggled through his early life to make a living. He later went on to become a respected judge. Ed wanted to be just like his father and run the plantation but his mental health prevented him from being a success. After much anguish, the Benners finally had to commit him to the State Insane Hospital in Tuscaloosa.

The end of slavery was taken hard by Benners. He had always treated his servants, as he called them, kindly, but some left and some stayed as hired hands to work the land. Some of the most beloved stayed close and never left his side. He grieved when several of them died but the worst was the loss of five of his children. His wife died in 1881 and Ed was ever on his mind. He pressed on but he finally died in 1888 at the age of 69.

A typical trip from the Black Belt was probably like the one described by Augustus Benners he took with his family in 1860. From his journal he writes:

On Tuesday the 24th day of July I started with my family from Greensboro for Blount County. My wife, six children and myself composed the white family[,] Emaline, Celia, Mary, Jenny & Kit the negroes & Ed and Ned drove the wagons, one the six mule the other the two mule wagon and Virgil drove the carriage-I rode in my buggy-The summer had been oppressively hot-and it still continued so. We got off about 7 o'clock-and after a very hot ride got to Turner Harpers 8 miles-where we made our first stop & took our breakfast.

They made another 14 miles that day and on Wednesday night camped near Centreville, a total of 40 miles from home. The Benners were expecting to stay in their newly complete cottage but it took a little longer to build than was expected. It was Saturday by the time they made it to Jonesboro and by very late in the day Monday the family was in Blount Springs.

I found upon arrival that the rooms I had ordered built were not finished - but were nearly so. We got into one of them in about a week and into the other in 3 weeks. Provisions were higher than the year previous chickens 12 ½ & 15 cts- butter d[itt]o- Mutton 6, Eggs 12 ½. The nights were delightful and I never enjoyed walking any where more than at Blount during my stay.

The family did enjoy this trip and stayed through September but then tragedy struck just a few days before it was time to leave for home. Their young son Lucas was struck down with a throat infection that never got better. He died September 19th after being in the bed sick for five days.

Jenny Benners
Disunion, War, Defeat and Recovery in Alabama

Sadly they had to, "leave him behind, his little grave on the mountain's side," in Blount Springs. They started on October 1st for their seven day trip home. Just before they left another son, Alfred started showing signs of sickness but the doctor at Blount advised them to go on home. They all made it safely.

In September of 1867 Alfred, Ed and Henry were at Blount. Benners wants to go get them but needs to stay home to attend a trial he is working. Edward, one of the most trusted servants Augustus Benner ever had, goes the next day. Edward stayed with the family until he died.

November 17, 1868 entry- On 6th July I started with my family to Blount Springs. We geared up the old carriage, my buggy and the two horse *wagon, carried tent for camping, first night we camped at church this side of Carthage—next night stopped out of the rain at Hatters and used his room for sleeping—next night stopped at Vances. Next night at Smiths— next night at Jacks, and next night being Sunday at the C.W/ Hatch houses. Next morning drove to my house at Valley Hill. Livingston who was my tenant at will had cleaned up the house and moved out. We got some corn and fodder & provisions and I felt greatly delighted at my freedom from the routine of cares & brothers at Home. We found that provisions were very plenty and not so high except corn as they were at home. Mutton 6 cts to 8 cts. Venison do[ditto] chickens 15 Eggs 15 to 20 Bitter 20 flour $6 per hundred [wt] lard 20 cts. per pound. I amused myself with walking to Springs occasionally hunting & fishing & roving over the mountains, fine appetites and good fare made an improvement in appearance of nearly everyone. My wife was sick for a week or so. With this exception none of the white folks were sick. Ed would ride in before breakfast and bring keg of water from springs and whenever chance presented the keg went. Fanny Alfred & Ed went to parties at Springs and an occasional picknic(sic) relieved the monotony—the time wore on till Septr. when I left in Major Clarks ambulance with miss Kate Borden for Elyton & Montevallo—reached home on Monday 28 Septr. Maria had the yard swept up and seemed to be looking for me—my family got back on the 2nd November, all well—*

Jenny especially loved it there and would go back many times in her life. Some of the amusements at the Springs during this time period included hunting and fishing, and exploring the mountains and the valley. The social circle never stopped. There was always dancing and music at the hotel and many bridle trails to enjoy.

With many people spending the season at Blount Springs, there was an ever-present social life, fun for young and old alike. Away from the hot, humid river bottomland of the Black Belt, the patrons enjoyed cool breezes, moderate weather, cooler mornings, lots of ice cream, many a game of ten-pins, carriage rides, and dinners with friends.

Early Roads in Alabama
The University of Alabama Geography Department

6

South & North Alabama Railroad

One of the main problems that plagued the South before and during the Civil War was the lack of railroads. True enough, some did exist, but a network of efficient and standardized tracks was not to be had. In the 1850s travel and the movement of goods was very limited and cumbersome. It could only be accomplished by water, horseback or foot.

1856 map showing the Tuscumbia, Courtland, and Decatur Railroad
University of Alabama Geography Department

In 1852 there were only 165 miles of track in the whole of Alabama. Montgomery was connected to West Point, Georgia and a mere 44 miles ran across a portion of North Alabama between Tuscumbia and Decatur. Even less was available near Mobile. Alabama had long been using waterways and a few principal roads, notably the Federal Road, for all its travel and commerce. Travel and extended commerce were extremely limited. Even the mails were limited by the lack of improved roadways and rail.

Many other lines were in the starting phases and a vast improvement of 800 more miles was completed by 1860. Railroads had long been just a few scattered miles of private subscription runs for specific purposes. One such road and one of the first in the state was constructed to overcome the problem of the Muscle Shoals on the Tennessee River. Goods and cotton coming from Huntsville and beyond would have to be unloaded and carted to another boat before it would be ready for passage to New Orleans.

Years ago a decision had been made by the people of the state to concentrate on macadamized roads instead of railways and the dye was cast. A vote of the people in 1840 placed this emphasis mainly because of the excellent amount of navigable waterways throughout the state. The steamboat business was quite large in Alabama. To connect the countryside to ports many roads were built from town to town to accommodate movement of people, crops and goods. They were not built as a way of moving from one area of the state to another.

Throughout the years since the founding of Alabama there was a great divide between the northern part of the state and the southern. In the south was the larger plantation class that basically ruled the

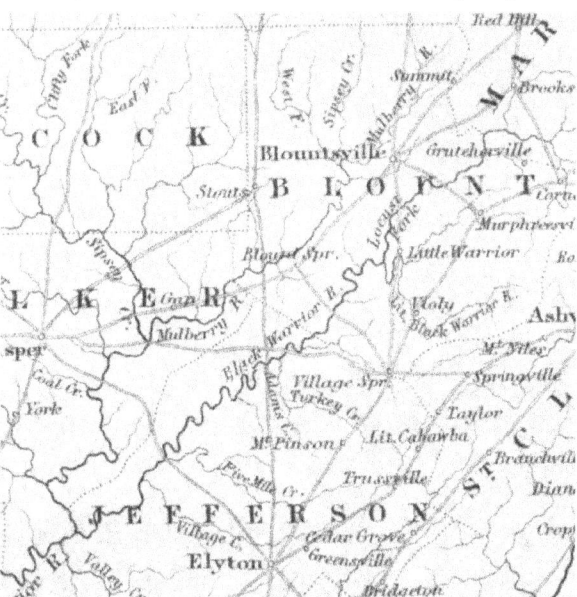

Roads in 1856
The University of Alabama Geography Department

state. In the north were many plantations in the Tennessee Valley, but also a larger number of small farms run by rugged individuals that owned few or no slaves. This northern faction identified more with Tennessee than it did Alabama in many ways.

Iron Ore
geology.com

The north depended on the Tennessee River for connection to the rest of the world. There was no water connection to the Southern half and the roads went through some of the hilliest and roughest parts of the state. This made travel between the two regions difficult and slow. Plans were undertaken to change that situation and exploit the vast mineral resources of Central Alabama to help the people and hopefully to make a few unbelievably rich.

Frank Gilmer was one of those visionaries. He was a wealthy planter and merchant in Montgomery and vividly remembered his trip through the middle of the state as a young man seeking his fortune. As he came through at the age of 21 he noticed the strange red rocks that were everywhere as he crossed a large traveling impediment he later learned was called Red Mountain. He was so fascinated by the strange rocks that he collected several samples that he kept for many years to come.

Indians had discovered the red rocks many, many years ago and used them as one of their dyes for war paint and other decorative purposes. Other travelers also noted the area and thought there was great potential to make a profit if there was better transportation to get the materials out.

By 1850 Gilmer had made his first fortune and, fueled by a recent geological report by Professor Tuomey of the University of Alabama, he began working towards getting a railroad into this mineral rich part of the state. He was not alone in this desire, but he was the driving force behind the creation of what would become the South & North Alabama Railroad. He pushed and toiled for this in much the manner of an Andrew Jackson, with a single purpose of mind and élan that could made things happen.

Prof. Michael Tuomey
W. S. Hoole Special collection
University of Alabama

On February 17, 1854 the Alabama Central Railroad was granted a charter to build the roadway for the South & North. Now was the time to finance this herculean undertaking and barbecues were held, memorials pledged, and speakers went to and fro extolling the virtues and benefits of connecting the state through this new line.

Getting the money to cut a roadbed through this rough terrain was not going to be an easy task. It needed more backing from the state than the mere privilege of a grant, it needed state funds to make the project a success. Previously a bill had passed for the building of the Nashville and Decatur Railroad and one James Withers Sloss was part of that successful project.

A barbecue was held in Blount Springs in the late 1850s to raise subscriptions and cash for the fledgling railroad. Matthew Duffee hosted the affair and opened it to all classes. The fact of the matter was, this project would be of benefit to everyone, rich and poor, industrialist and farmer. Invitations were sent out and lavish preparations were made. Men from all over the state were invited as the success or failure of this event could have long lasting influence on the destiny of the project. Great care was taken in making the event spectacular in all respects.

The Cold Spring was chosen because of its wild beauty and the topography it encompassed. Sands were close to the creek and a terraced hill rose about it as it curved like an elbow. Right at the edge of the mountain beside the creek was a cavern where massive stones parted forming a grotto with large stalactites and stalagmites. This large room, with its constant temperature, had served for many years as a storeroom for beef, mutton and butter that were used in the hotel.

The tables were set up between the entrance to the cave and the spring. The speaker's dais was in a valley near the cave's mouth creating an impressive amphitheater. Orator's voices rolled and echoed throughout the throng gathered there for the fete.

Mary Duffee Gordon was a young girl of 10 on the occasion but later in life she wrote,

> *The day was warm and cloudless. A vast throng gathered there: the yeomanry of the mountains in wagons, on horseback and afoot; the guests of the hotel and the summer cottages in their magnificent equipages. Men from every town in the state met there, listened, and then liberally subscribed to the building of the road.*

It must have been very impressive, especially for the common people. They had come in their simple wagons, carriages, on horses, and some on foot. The guests from the hotel and the cottages scattered about the town and countryside were also impressive in their finery as men and ladies from many towns and hamlets of the state were represented that day. They listened and believed in the new venture. Large amounts were given as subscriptions and much stock bought, along with promises of more for the advancement of the railroad.

Finally through much political wrangling an appropriation was put through the legislature for someone to determine a route for the roadway to follow.

> *Section 7. Be it further enacted, that the sum of $10,000 be, and the same is hereby appropriated, out of the three per cent fund now in the treasury, to be expended and applied, under the direction of the governor, in making a reconnaissance for a route for a railroad from the Tennessee River to some point on the Alabama and Tennessee Rivers Railroad, and to make a survey of the most practicable route to connect the Tennessee River with the navigable waters of the Mobile Bay, with reference to the development of the mineral region of the State, which said reconnaissance and survey must be made in the year 1858, report thereof to be made to the governor, which report shall contain a full statement of the length of the route, grades, cost per mile, together with all the particulars that are usually observed in surveys of this description. Approved, February 8, 1858.*

A young engineer named John Turner Milner was recommended to Governor A. B. Moore as the man for the job and his approval was given. When Milner learned of his appointment he was working on another route south of Montgomery. He immediately jumped on his horse and road the 30 or so miles over rough country to the Capitol. He went straight into the Governor's office, covered in mud and torn clothing. The Governor was impressed by this newly appointed chief engineer in spite of his disheveled appearance.

Milner was a Georgian from Pike County. His father was a railroad contractor in Georgia and Alabama so it was only natural for him to follow into the family business. John's first venture into engineering was the excavation of a gold mine near Dahlonega, Georgia. He and four slaves worked for two months digging until they hit a deposit about 90 feet down.

John Turner Milner
Alabama Department of Archives and History, Montgomery, Alabama

Gold Mining in Georgia
Harper's New Monthly Magazine

From this small fortune he bought two suits and entered college for a specialty in law and engineering. Bad health came upon him in his senior year and he left school planning to finish after his health improved. Instead he began work for the Macon and Western Railroad and moved up through the ranks. He eventually became the first assistant engineer of the Alabama and Florida Railroad Company and worked all over the state in this capacity.

John T. Milner began the reconnaissance work for the South & North Alabama Railroad on March 27, 1858. This was four years after the line had been chartered. He assembled a crew and began making, "His estimates of the quantities of coal and iron that would eventually pass over the road."

He decided that the route would run from Decatur through Blount Springs, Grace's Gap and finally join the Selma, Rome and Dalton line near Montevallo. It would run near Elyton in Jones Valley and Milner considered it the epicenter of the mineral wealth that was to be much of the purpose of the new railroad.

Standing on Red Mountain looking at the farmland of the valley he said:

I rode along the top of Red Mountain, and looked over that beautiful valley where the city of Birmingham lies today. It was one vast garden as far as the eye could reach, northeast and southwest. It was on the first day of June, in the year 1858. Jones Valley was well cultivated then. I had before traveled all over the United States. I had seen the great and rich valleys of the Pacific Coast, but nowhere had I seen an agricultural people so perfectly provided for, and so completely happy. They raised everything they required to eat, and sold thousands of bushels of wheat. Their settlements were around these beautiful, clear running streams found gushing out everywhere in this valley. Cotton was raised here also, but on account of the difficulty of transportation, only in small quantities. It was, on the whole, a quiet easy-going, well farmed, well framed, and well regulated civilization.

The fortunes of Blount Springs would benefit greatly from the founding of the city of Birmingham in Jones Valley and grow quickly along with the fantastic expansion of the Magic City. The citizens knew the benefits of being on the South & North Alabama Railroad and did their part in making funds available to advance the cause of this line.

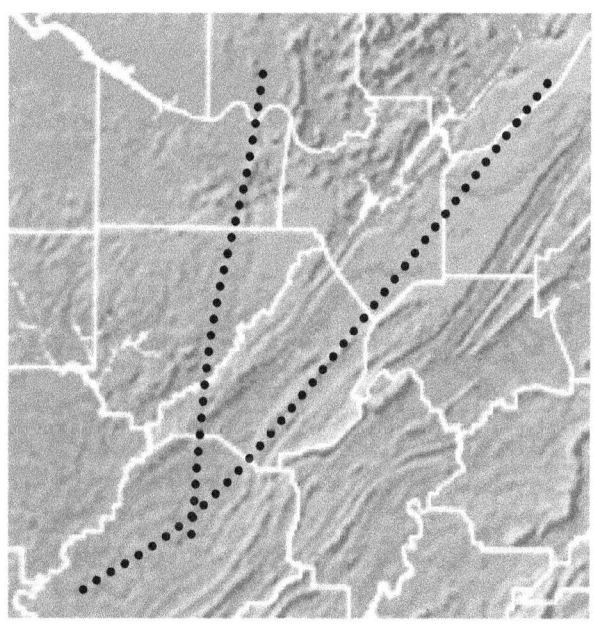

Proposed Routes of the Competing Railroads
University of Alabama Geography Department

The Northwest and Southwest Railroad was also being planned to run more or less parallel to the North and South. It was chartered in December of 1853 by the state and it was to connect Chattanooga and Tuscaloosa. Many feared this would take much of the mineral resources out of the state and prevent Alabama from fully gaining the wealth expected from that part of the state.

After the Civil War the Northwest and Southwest was combined with another group and became the Alabama and Chattanooga Railroad. This union resulted from a group of Boston capitalists gaining control of both companies. By mid-1871 the state seized all the property due to non-payment of the interest on the bonds issued and it was reorganized as the Alabama Great Southern Railroad in 1877.

Milner needed to act quickly and with diligence because the path of the rival railroad would not have the same terrain to deal with as the South and North. His challenge was a series of high ridges, mountains and valleys and the other line would run through a valley without any of those daunting challenges.

His vision was to plan a rail route that tackled the mountains, passed through the heart of the mineral district, and used the valleys as an easy route to develop spur lines to the mineral valleys. This plan would make the needed connection between the north of the state as well as the south, while also providing access to the rich resources in the many valleys along the way.

Roads were normally built with a maximum rise of 6 to 8% but a railroad thought a 1% rise was steep and 2% to be extreme. There was a grade change of 500 feet from Decatur to Montevallo and many hills and valleys in between that could cause concern for keeping the grade constant and workable. It took him several months of evaluation to see the potential routes that could work.

These lines are described in the Report to the Governor of Alabama on the Alabama Central Railroad (Montgomery, 1859) as follows:

> 1. *An "air line" from Montevallo to Decatur*
> 2. *A second line from Montevallo with (?) four alternates:*
> a. *Along and near the stage road to Graces Gap toward Old Warrior Town*
> b. *Near Hawkins Mill on Village Creek*
> c. *Cross the Locust Fork of the Warrior River below the Elyton to Jasper Road*
> d. *Pass near Democrat, Alabama, on the Mulberry Fork of the Locust River, two miles below Hanby's Mill.*
> e. *Then two lines:*
>   1. *One by Stout's Post Office, along the old Stout's Road to a gap in Sand Mountain (S21, T9, R3W)*
>   2. *Up Ross Creek, joining the first survey at Holmes Gap*
>   3. *Holmes Gap was determined to be the best route, and then follow Flint Creek to Decatur. This route came off of Sand Mountain at Wilhoite's Cove.*

Two further choices are of particular importance because they come through Blount Springs.

> *Line 1: Followed the Stage Road to Elyton, then across the head of Black Creek, and then follow Black and Turkey Creeks [north Jefferson County], to Locust Warrior at Minter's Ferry. This line crosses the dividing gap the two Warriors at Reed's(Reid's) Gap, passes by Blount Springs, through Holmes Gap in Sand Mountain and on to Decatur. Milner discusses this as a "compromise" line to "best fit" the goal of passing through the heart of the Warrior basin coalfield and still be practical.*

Line 4: This line was determined to be too costly, passing 5 miles NE of Blount Springs (Byers Gap to Copperas Gap) and then follows a "beautiful valley" to Hagood's Store, having gone 22 miles [up the valley] from Elyton and thus being too far east for access to the coal fields.

It was now in the hands of the Legislature and other events began moving that would complicate matters and prevent the work to culminate in the completion of the North & South Railroad. Work did not begin immediately and in fact it was debated in the Capitol whether the report of Milner would even be published, but due to influential politicians it was and eventually a bill passed granting a loan of $63,135.00 on condition the road was completed in five years.

Frank Gilmer merged his various interests and formed a company to begin the work in 1860 with Milner as chief engineer. Almost immediately, talk of state's rights began to get in the way of the work of laying a route through the piney woods of Central Alabama.

Daniel Pratt
Alabama Department of Archives and History, Montgomery, Alabama

Because of the growing concern of impending war some stockholders wanted out of their obligations to the line. A group of Limestone County stockholders stopped honoring their subscriptions and Gilmer took them over. By the time the Civil War began Gilmer owned three quarters interest in the now named Central Railroad Company of Alabama and he changed the southern terminus from Montevallo to Calera.

He also brought several other investors together including his brother William and other members of the Montgomery stockholders group, most notably, Daniel Pratt. They began the idea of using the ore from Red Mountain to produce the rails and constructed the first foundry in Jefferson County at Oxmoor.

As war clouds blossomed into fruition and the great conflict began they ran out of money. Gilmer appealed to the newly formed Confederate Government and was successful. The railroad was extended from Calera to Brock's Gap which was a sixty-foot cut of solid rock, several hundred feet long, through Shades Mountain.

This was as far as they got. Powder for blasting could not be attained due to its need on the battlefield and workers had to go at it with picks, crowbars, and wedges. This cut would not be finished until two years after the war. Brock's Gap proved to be a very difficult spot on the line. When it was finally accomplished by Col. J. F. B. Jackson it propelled him into the limelight as the bright star in the building process.

7

The War of Northern Aggression

Montgomery is where the Confederacy formed and served as its first capital. Mary Phelen and her family were regulars at Blount Springs and she was at the Capitol when Jefferson Davis was sworn in as President. She tells of what she witnessed in *History Stories of Alabama*.

Inauguration of Jefferson Davis
Alabama Department of Archives and History,
Montgomery, Alabama

On the immense platform, built in front of the Capitol for the occasion, the President's Cabinet and the Confederate Congress met. A seething mass of people from all over the South filled the grounds and the streets nearby. Soldiers were everywhere. Every military company in the South was represented. The cadets from Tuscaloosa especially delighted my young eyes. I thought they presented the grandest sight I had ever beheld.

On a table in front of "The Man of the Hour" lay a big Bible. My father being Clerk of the Supreme Court lifted the Bible. Then, with all the solemnity which this momentous occasion demanded, Jefferson Davis kissed the Book and took the oath of office as President of the Confederate States. Every Sunday after that while the Davis family remained in Montgomery I saw them in their pew at St. John's Episcopal Church. The pew is now marked with a silver plate.

According to Mary Gordon Duffee, "*When the drums beat, and the bugles called for men to march to the front, I tell you old Blount responded nobly, and sent hundreds of her gallant sons to march, fight, suffer and die for the flag that now lies furled forever.*" One of the first groups to leave Blount Springs for the War was the Blount County Tiger Boys. Their official designation was Company F of the 4th Alabama Battalion.

This company was led by Captain Benjamin Harrison Sapp. Sapp was the Justice of the Peace and Postmaster of Blount Springs. Along with his wife Harriett, he also ran the Goff House. Three other companies came from Blount County. The Blount County Hornets, Avalanche Company, and The Phil Weaver Guards were companies B, C, and E respectively. Filling out the battalion were men from Talladega, Barbour and Bibb and were organized together at Montgomery to form the 4th Alabama Battalion in 1861.

Captain B.H. Sapp
findagrave.com

The 4th was sent to help protect the Gulf Coast and were posted to a Camp Pollard and Pensacola. Not much happened during this time and the men grew bored as camp life and drill wore on and they feared the war had passed them by. Two more companies were added in February, 1862 at Pensacola and the 4th Alabama Battalion became the 29th Alabama Infantry Regiment. The other men that made up the unit came from Barbour, Bibb, Blount, Conecuh, Montgomery, Russell, Shelby, and Talladega counties.

During their encampment here they were joined with the 1st, 17th, and 26th Alabama, and 37th Mississippi regiments to form a brigade commanded by Brigadier General James Cantey. Cantey was a lawyer, planter, state legislator in South Carolina and officer in the Mexican-American War before he moved to Alabama. He settled in Russell County and started a successful plantation near Fort Mitchell. At the beginning of the war he served as Colonel of the 15th Alabama. In Ewell's Division, under Stonewall Jackson, he was detached shortly after the Seven Days Battle and sent to Mobile to take command of this new brigade.

Orders were received in July of 1863 to move to Mobile and the brigade was posted to aid in the defense of this important seaport. At Mobile Capt. Sapp contracted smallpox and tragically died December 17, 1863. Because he died of smallpox the railroad would not allow his body on a train to be taken back to Blount County. Hearing of this tragedy, Mrs. Ann Curry gave space in her Magnolia Cemetery family plot in Mobile. His family was never able to have his body brought back home for burial.

The Flag of the 29th Alabama housed at the Alabama Department of Archives and History, Montgomery, Alabama

The 29th was finally posted to Resaca in northern Georgia as part of the Army of Tennessee and consisted of over 1,000 men in

April of 1864. Gen. Edward Asbury O'Neal of Huntsville arrived soon after their move to Georgia to take command of the Brigade and would serve in that capacity throughout the Atlanta campaign. He would later be elected as the 26th Governor of Alabama (1882-1886). He became a frequent visitor to Blount Springs before, during and after his term as Governor.

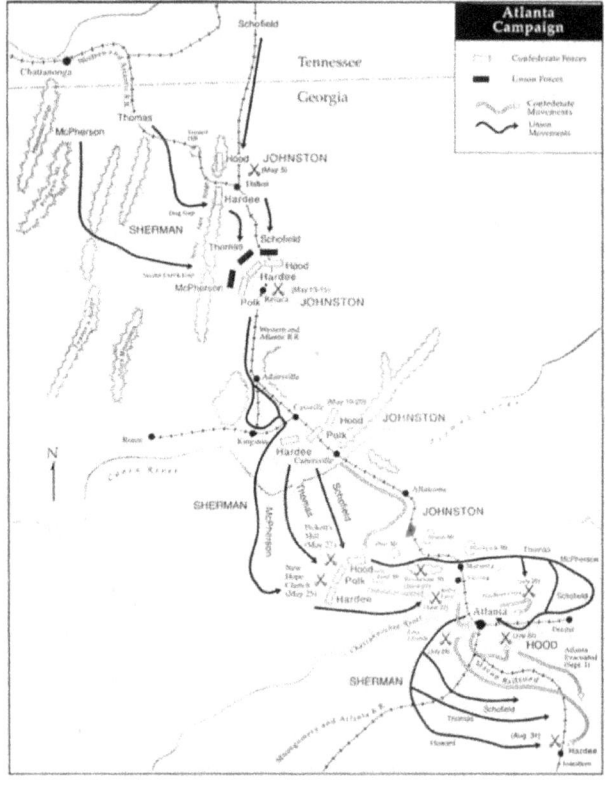

The Atlanta Campaign
americancivilwar.com

About a 100 men were casualties at Resaca, with another heavy loss at New Hope Church. The regiment was decimated at Peach Tree Creek. Shortly after Brigadier-General Charles Miller Shelley of Talladega took command, they moved with Hood to Tennessee. At the disastrous Battle of Franklin they were in the center of the advance of Stewart's Division. Cut to pieces by rifle fire and artillery as they crossed the long open field between them and the breastworks of the enemy, the men bravely met their fate. This movement is known as "Pickett's Charge of the West".

They lost half their men and their flag at this tragedy. It was not returned until long after the War and is now a part of the collection of Regimental Flags at the Alabama Department of Archives and History. Gen. Shelley's horse was shot out from under him and he had seven bullet holes in his clothing by the end of the day. Fourteen Confederate generals were casualties at Franklin. Six were killed, seven wounded, and one was captured. 55 regimental commanders were also casualties. With over a fourth of the Army of Tennessee killed, wounded or captured, this was arguably the most costly battle of the Western Theatre of war.

After more losses at Nashville the men were again under the command of Gen. Joseph Johnston and moved to North Carolina. They participated in the Battle of Bentonville and then moved to Danville. About 90 men were at the surrender at Durham Station, North Carolina on April 26, 1865. Blount County and Blount Springs paid dearly for their country.

The 1860 Presidential Candidate of the Constitutional Union Party, John Bell, was with other prominent Southerners in Alabama to raise funds and men for the war effort. He had fled his Tennessee home as the Northern Army moved in and occupied Nashville. Bell decided to stay in Blount Springs for the summer of 1862.

His wife, Jane Erwin Bell, pled with the Nashville commander to grant safe passage for her husband. After it was granted, she sent Nicholas Davis of Huntsville to let Bell know it was safe for him to return to Nashville. He refused to return under Federal protection and stated he would wait until he could return with safe conduct from Confederates. Later he moved to Georgia to wait out the fighting. After the war he moved back to Tennessee and managed his family iron works in Stewart County. A short time after he returned to Tennessee he died and is buried in Nashville's Mount Olivet Cemetery.

Campaign poster for 1860 U.S. presidential candidate John Bell and his running mate, Edward Everett from Wikipedia

Jeremiah Clemens of Huntsville was a former United States Senator from Alabama before the War and was against secession, but when his home state seceded, he followed and followed enthusiastically. In June of 1862 he went around Alabama stumping for troops and making speeches on behalf of the Confederacy. He also appeared at Blount Springs with John Bell and a Mr. Morgan of Nashville. He had been commissioned a general in the Confederate Army. Sometime after his appearance at Blount Springs he resigned this commission and moved for reconciliation with the North. As the war dragged on, he labored to bring a speedy end to the hostilities. He died in 1865 and was not part of helping the section rejoin the Union.

Jeremiah Clemons
Wikimedia Commons

In 1861 Matthew Duffee was named postmaster for Blount Springs. This led to one of the events that became legendary in the life of Mary Gordon Duffee. Mary often worked with the mails for her father and one day she did something quite extraordinary. In the fall of 1864 a Confederate payroll was sent from Montgomery through Blount Springs. The amount was said to be over $100,000 in Confederate money. When the package failed to arrive at its intended destination, an investigation was launched and it was traced back to the post office at Blount Springs as its last known location.

Right away Mary Duffee admitted that she was the one that took the money. It was suspected by some that she was covering up for someone else and simply took the blame. She had gone throughout the county buying cows, clothing and food for the starving wives and children of the men that were off at the war with the Confederate Army. Mollie (Blount Springs regulars called her Mollie) never tried to hide the money and certainly spent none of the funds on herself. Those people looked upon her as an Angel of Mercy, but the government did not share that view. The Confederacy could ill afford to not prosecute the offender and take the loss of such a significant amount of money without doing something.

President Davis
Alabama Department of Archives and History, Montgomery, Alabama

A regiment of cavalry was sent from Louisiana to arrest her. Once they got there and placed Duffee, who offered no resistance, in custody, they began learning of the sentiment of the community for the ministering angel. Fearing a mob would form and try to rescue her from her oppressors, she was spirited off to Mobile under a strong detachment.

Upon reaching Mobile much influence was exerted to obtain her release. Her father had many friends in Mobile he had made during his former residence there. As quite the friendly and popular fellow he had made many good impressions and was popular with very powerful people. It was argued that she had not acted in greed or for self gain, but rather for the relief of soldiers' families. Finally an appeal was made directly to President Jefferson Davis. After some of Mary's eccentricities were explained to him and with much pleading she was released and returned to Blount Springs.

Another legend involving Mary Duffee says that she was a spy for the Confederacy. The story goes she was staying at Arlington, the home of William Mudd in the village of Elyton after returning from Kentucky on one of her missions. When Union Calvary approached she hid in the attic.

General James H. Wilson was the leader of the largest cavalry mission ever conducted on the American Continent. This command consisted of approximately 17, 000 troopers on a mission to destroy any and everything they found that could aid the Confederacy. They would blaze a trail of destruction through the heart of Alabama. Wilson made Arlington his headquarters after his command arrived and proceeded to make his plans for the rest of his campaign, known to his subordinate commanders. Mollie Duffee listened from her hiding place in the attic.

Wartime Montevallo with the college in the background
elizabethmurphreewilkersonrhodes.blogspot.com

He outlined his route to Selma to destroy the large arsenal and naval foundry. It was one of the largest in the Lower South and one of the last rolling mills still functioning in the Confederacy. He also gave orders for the detachment of a group of troopers for a special mission.

A small cadre lead by General John T. Croxton was detailed from Elyton to Tuscaloosa to burn the University and any foundries they found along the way. With 1,500 men armed with Spencer Repeating Rifles they headed west, reaching the town April 4th.

The Rotunda Ruins sketched in 1866
The W. S. Hoole Special Collections Library,
University of Alabama

Very few buildings survived as the Yankee troops were brutally efficient in their efforts. This unit also burned several buildings in Tuscaloosa that had served military purposes, mainly Washington Hall after liberating the Union prisoners they found there.

Instead of rejoining the main body, Croxton made his way to Georgia, destroying a furnace at Trussville and then occupying Talladega along the way. Croxton planned to burn Talladega because it had been a training center, a Confederate hospital, and rifles had been manufactured there. The town was spared when the mayor came to the General and gave him the Masonic handshake and asked for mercy.

The Brigadier stopped his men from doing any more damage and the next day they again took up the march to Georgia. At Munford they ran into a force of less than two hundred home guard and a sharp fight ensued. Each side lost one man killed. In 1914 a marker was placed by a local U. D. C. chapter to commemorate what they termed the last battle east of the Mississippi River. This was two weeks after Lee surrendered at Appomattox.

After hearing Wilson's plans for his march to Selma, Mary Duffee wandered southward to find Forrest or his scouts. She heard the approach of cavalry as she neared the outskirts of Montevallo. Then, she heard the first shots of a skirmish as the few Confederate Home Guard troops gathered near the depot to oppose the veteran cavalry. The local troops, really just old men and boys, were commanded and organized by Col. John P. West who happened to be in town on a furlough. The modest "Battle of Montevallo" was fought by a few with very limited resources including a canon on a flat car that proved to be as ineffective as the small number of troops. This skirmish was a footnote at the end of a long war and had little, if any, effect on the march toward Selma and its destruction.

In her own words from *Sketches of Alabama* she recounts the events of April, 1865:

> *During March I had passed through Oxmoor, peaceful and hospitable. On the afternoon of April 13 I gazed upon a scene of ruin at this same spot that makes me shudder now as I recall it. It was in Montevallo when the invading army entered. All of my brothers were at the front, my parents at Blount Springs, sixty-five miles away. About sunset rolling drums and prancing horses in a long column approached Montevallo. All night we waited, knowing a battle was imminent as the forces of Forrest and Roddey were on the southern outskirts. Firing began at the depot and a heavy skirmish ensued. Two days afterward, Miss Emmie Bailey and I organized a band of women and children to go down the railroad to Brierfield to search for the wounded and dying.*

Then I resolved to make my way home by foot. I met starvation on every hand and was grateful for the hominy and buttermilk graciously shared with me. After a walk of thirty miles, I reached Oxmoor at the close of a tenderly beautiful day of early spring. There I hoped to receive food and shelter to relieve my hunger and fatigue. As I neared the familiar scene, my heart sank at the strange stillness of the landscape. Here and there a broken-down army horse searched for tender young grass. Wild blue flags and wild honeysuckle bloomed among the rocks. The tranquility was overwhelmingly lonely.

The Bibb Naval Furnace at Brierfield
Alabama Blast Furnaces by Joseph H. Woodward

At last I mustered courage to venture on and found myself standing by blackened ruins, against the wall of the furnace tower. As I contemplated the silent houses up the hill, the deserted road, the awful truth flashed upon me in despair. In bitter despair, blinded with tears, I knelt and prayed.

Rising, I saw smoke issuing from a chimney at the summit of a high hill. Wearily I climbed the steep and rugged path to this sign of security. I did not presume to ask for food, only a sleeping place on the floor. The kind head of the family was a son-in-law of old man Moses Stroup, the pioneer iron-maker. He and his family welcomed me graciously and shared with me what little they had.

Refreshed by a night of unbroken sleep, I bade these blessed friends adieu at an early hour and wended my solitary way to the wretched ruins. The morning sun shone from a cloudless sky, and I lingered long amid those mournful scenes, then pursued my journey up the road, past the silent homes, only one or two of which were left to greet me.

On the summit I stopped to view the grave of a child of Mr. Haynes, a scientist. To my horror a wayfarer told me that stragglers from the army had broken the marble stones and dug into the grave in search of treasure. I hurried away...

The following morning through a lane of mud and water I made my way to Elyton. But ere I retired that night I knelt and dedicated my future life to the glory of my native state.

As she began walking home to Blount Springs from the battlefield, she came across the smoldering ruins of the Oxmoor Furnace in the twilight. Mary, at the ripe old age of 21 was hungry, tired and ready to give up when she saw light in the cabin of Moses Stroup's son-in-law. He offered her a meal and a place to sleep for the night. This made all the difference in the world to the spirits of the young girl and gave her hope. The next day she made it to Elyton. A few days later she made it to the shelter and safety of home on Duffee's Mountain and their beloved hotel.

Col. Abel D. Streight
Library of Congress

The years of the war were not great at Blount Springs but no actual fighting occurred in the area. The closest would be Streight's Raid through Alabama as it came through Blount County in April of 1863. Abel Streight was given the mission of cutting the railroad leading to Chattanooga to weaken the Confederate forces holding that city by cutting their supply lines. His goal was to destroy the rails at Rome, Georgia.

It had been decided the expedition would be benefited by using mules instead of horses over the rough terrain of North Alabama. Actually, this turned out to be an impediment instead of an advantage. Streight entered Blount County with Forrest contesting their advance at every turn. Just north of present day Hanceville, the Union force of just under 2,000 men turned towards Blountsville and was finally forced to give battle near that town. The Union force kept moving towards their goal after the engagement just north of Blountsville.

Forrest finally captured Streight's Mule Brigade using a trick. With a force about one half the size of the invaders, he marched his one canon and a few men past the same open area several times, convincing Streight he had a much larger force. The Unionists were within a few miles of their objective but were not able to achieve their goal. When he learned how he had been tricked he demanded his weapons back. Forrest did not agree that this point of honor should change the way things were and the entire force remained his prisoners.

A three man group of Yankee soldiers were also captured by the Murphee sisters around this time also. The three had been sent looking for horses in the countryside of Blount County. When they found the Murphee farm they forced Ceila, twenty-one, and Winnie Mae, eighteen, to make them mint juleps. What the soldiers didn't know was that they also added large doses of toothache medicine in their drinks.

It was probably morphine and after their second one the men lay down and fell asleep. A little later the men awakened to the barrels of their own guns pointed at them. General Forrest was impressed as the two marched the soldiers into his camp as their prisoners. A reward was forthcoming for the lady warriors as the General bestowed two freshly captured horses on them along with his undying admiration.

When Lee surrendered at Appomattox Courthouse the Cause was lost. The people of Blount Springs were sad they had lost this war, but relieved it was over. There were many other armies and units that would still carry on the fight for a short time, but this virtually ended the war. The last to surrender in Alabama was Gen. Richard Taylor's Army that had attempted to defend Mobile. They capitulated in the little town of Citronelle.

The many survivors of the Confederate Army made their way home to Blount County the best way they could. Most walked home from the site they surrendered, hearts filled with sadness and wonder about what the future would bring. Much hardship and suffering was coming for many in the South, but the people of Blount Springs felt hope and believed things would be better in the next few years. Money would be tight for several years to come.

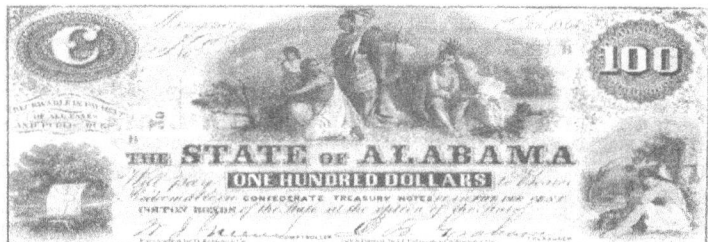

Confederate Money Issued by the State of Alabama
deerrunmercantile.com

8

Devastation and Rebuilding

War had brought destruction and devastation to Alabama and the South and it would take a long time and much hard work to recover. Even the timing of the end of the war worked against them. For many of the soldiers that surrendered in April and May it took weeks to get back home because most had to walk to Alabama from Virginia and North Carolina. That was the time to plow the land to get ready for planting. As the soldiers got home, they plowed and planted as they could. Crops would be late and thin in 1865.

President Andrew Johnson proposed a plan for the reorganization and re-admittance of the Southern States. He appointed John Parsons of Talladega as provisional governor and called for a state convention in September of 1865. Once the convention met they declared the Ordinance of Secession null and void and also abolished slavery. It provided for a governor and legislature to be elected by the voters of Alabama and ready to be recognized as a state in the Union.

The Radical Republican Congress refused to seat the delegation of legislators sent to Washington. In Alabama the state legislature ratified the Thirteenth Amendment. Even though they were not represented in Washington, the state went on with business as normal expecting things to go as the President wished. Johnson was trying to follow what he thought were the wishes and plans of Lincoln, but Congress would have a different agenda.

The Carpetbag Legislature of Alabama
Alabama Archives and History, Montgomery, Alabama

Many of the newly freed slaves left the plantations and headed for the towns and cities of Alabama. The Legislature passed what became known as the Black Codes to control these newly freed men and their idling about the streets. This new behavior was much to the consternation of the white populace and was not going to be tolerated.

By 1867 the Radicals were in complete control and placed Alabama under a military rule. Freedmen became voters for the first time and the only whites allowed to vote were those swearing an oath to the United States. They had to swear they never voluntarily supported the Confederacy. This immediately disenfranchised almost everyone in the former ruling class of the state. The whites in the northern hill counties of Alabama had insisted on this idea so that they would have more control of the government.

This change resulted in 96 or the 100 seats in the Constitutional Convention becoming controlled by Republicans. This group was made up of freedmen, Scalawags (Union sympathizers), and Carpetbaggers (Northerners who had come south for less than honorable intentions). When the convention met in November of 1867 it produced a document that served the special interests of those represented and took actions that would keep most of the former leaders out of any significant official office for many years to come.

Acts like these across the South were the reason the region became known as the Solid South for many decades to come. It also produced the idea of "Yellow Dog Democrats" that most Southern voters became. It was said they would vote for a yellow dog before they would vote for any Republican.

After this Constitution went into effect, the Republican Congress voted to re-admit Alabama to the United States in June of 1868. Things seemed in disarray to the former rulers of the state and many new institutions and taxes were enacted and much public debt was built up because of the many social programs that were created such as hospitals, orphanages and railway bonds. This was the climate for business and life during this dark period of Alabama's history.

Carpet Bagger
Harper's Weekly

With the initial shock of surrender and subjugation fading, harsher realities set in as military rule, carpetbaggers and scalawags took over the state government. The Freedman's Bureau became prominent under the steerage of General Wager T. Swayne. Swayne was in many ways considered to be the military governor of the state.

Early in the war Matthew Duffee sold his interests in Tuscaloosa and moved his family to Blount Springs full time. They had their small hotel and their cabin on Duffee's Mountain and had weather the storm of civil war fairly untouched. Business had not been much during the conflict but being in the isolated hills of Blount County prevented any intrusion by invaders into their lives.

Oldest Known Photograph of Blount Springs in 1866
Alabama Department of Archives and History, Montgomery, Alabama

Few of the Black Belt planters or Huntsville regulars were able to make the trip for pleasure to Blount Springs, but some still did. The hotel business certainly wasn't booming, but the doors did stay open. John Smith was the village blacksmith and had his shop at the foot of the hill in front of the Duffee House. Smith and Rueben Ward, who ran the livery stable, provided music for dancing at the hotel and house parties. Fiddles were the choice instruments of the day and both men were very accomplished at that instrument, as well as a few other string instruments. Dancing had always been one of the most popular activities at the Goff House. Many came for the curative properties of the waters, but many also came for the entertainment and social interaction available at Old Blount.

In 1868 Matthew Duffee became the owner of the Goff House and he and his wife were determined to improve the property. His daughter, 23 year old Mary Gordon, served as the entertainment director and Old Blount became a lively place indeed as a contrast to the drab of the war years. The first thing he did was to change the name to the Duffee House and start a new era of the resort. Other improvements were forthcoming and business started picking up as the planter class was trying to get back their pre-war lives.

Business wasn't great immediately after the war, but as time went on everyone was ready to get back to life as they knew it before the horror came into their lives. The construction of the North & South Railroad was seen as one of the best hopes of using the vast mineral resources of Central Alabama and starting again was crucial to the survival of the entire state. When the first legislature met they made aid for such projects available.

Frank Gilmer had lost almost all of his fortune during the war but he was determined to continue pursuing building the road and fortunes of Jefferson County and Central Alabama. The big money of the company had disappeared and even the stockholders could not pay, but hope continued to exist concerning taking the venture to completion.

Strict Reconstruction laws were passed by the Federal Congress in February of 1867 as they took more power away from President Andrew Johnson. More and more impediments were placed in the way of success for the railroad. John C. Stanton of Boston became the leading figure in the Carpet Bag legislature that took office in June, 1868. All matters concerning railroads went through him and he pressed for the Meridian to Chattanooga line in which he had a personal interest. He got what he wanted and that line was completed to the detriment of all others.

From nearby Forkland came the Randolf family. Carter Randolf was the first to build his own cabin at Blount Springs and generations enjoyed the waters and social life for years afterward. The home was about four miles from the hotel and was located by the Chalybeate Springs. Later the Drennen's summer home was there also. He, like most men that built a cottage or home at Blount Springs, brought a group of servants to stay year-round and maintain it for the family's enjoyment. They were hand-picked and not only kept up the house but grew lush gardens for the family to use.

Many other families availed themselves of the joy of the village such as the Cresswells and Webbs. Greensboro and Greene County (one of the wealthiest counties in the United States during the Ante-bellum period) were also well-represented at the Springs. Lemuel Hatch, uncle of the wife of Augustus Benners, was one such example.

In a 1932 article in The *Birmingham News*, Mrs. John B. Reid recalled her first trip with her father, Brett Randolf, in 1868 when she was 10 years old. They went from Forkland over rugged and narrow road in canvas covered wagons. It was a trip that took several days and very they camped along the way. They would travel in a caravan of wagons carrying the family and servants. Supplies for the two month stay were also pulled along.

Her cousin, Richard R. Randolf, married Florence Goff and carried her home to live in Greensboro. His father was Dr. R. E. Randolf, brother of Carter. This was just one of the marriages that occurred through meeting at Blount Springs. Between the daily promenade to the spring yard and walks to Pivot Rock, many a family had its beginnings at the resort. Mary Hatch Married Thomas Watt after they met here and later even managed the hotel together. Another couple was Carrie Hatch and Jesse Bealle.

Mrs. John B. Reid in 1932
The Birmingham News

Notables of this period include Judge Augustus A. Coleman and family of Livingston. Malvina Phares Coleman was the queen of Blount Springs and was well known for her excellent skills at horseback riding. This was one of the favorite pastimes of the era. Phares Coleman was their son and ran around town dressed ala "Little Lord Fauntleroy" in curls and frilly shirts. He also later became an influential judge in Alabama as well as an important lawyer in Birmingham.

> *The young women, I remember were dressed in beautiful evening gowns, whith huge puffed sleeve s and bouffant draperies, and long curls depending from their headdress. They were the quaintest and loveliest looking young women I ever saw. I was just a child then, but I remember so distinctly the lovely gowns they wore, and I admired them extravagantly, and was greatly interested in their beaux.*

Reid was there when Matthew Duffee and his wife Mary took over ownership of the Goff House and changed it to the Duffee House. They had a small hotel they'd operated since the early 1850s and brought new life to the big hotel. She marveled at the 23 year old Mary that took over as social director and made everyone so happy putting events

Mollie Duffee at 23
Tuscaloosa Magazine

together for all to enjoy. The ten year old idolized Mollie Duffee and tried to be around her as much as possible and enjoy her company.

Sometime after the hotel burned the Duffees sent their youngest child to New York to finish her education. Much of this is shrouded in mystery, including the name of the school she attended. This was when Mollie made many of her connections for her writing career. She made have gone up north after her trip to Forkland in 1870. It cannot be verified, but legend has it that she rode a horse from Blount Springs to visit some of the families that frequented Blount Springs from that area. This trip happened in the spring of the year. She would have been 25 at that time.

Mary's life was full of mystery and not many knew all the details of her adventurous life. She was very intelligent and her writing was admired by many people around the country, but most in Blount Springs would know her as just Mollie Duffee. Mollie was popular for interesting conversation and good company until around the time her mother died. After that she became more legendary to the younger people as she was forced to stay on Duffee Mountain because of her infirmities.

It was around this time the stories circulated about her being a witch and a recluse. Some thought her brother Knox had died in the house and his body was still sitting in his room. Others would climb the mountain and sneak a peak in a window at the old witch on a dare from the other youngsters.

Mary did little to dispel these growing legends as she was quick to speak her mind and refuse an audience with anyone she did feel like talking with and would quickly send them on their way. Old friends and relatives were always welcome at her humble home that was slowly deteriorating through the years. Only the chimney stands there today, along with a marker approximating where the location of the family graveyard.

9

Col. J. F. B. Jackson

One of the most important figures in the promotion of Blount Springs was Col. Joseph Franklin Ballenger Jackson of Murray County Georgia. Not only did he play a large role in finishing the railroad through the town, he also was instrumental in making it the showcase it became.

Born in Franklin County Georgia January 31, 1830 to William Jackson and Lucy Morris, he was one of thirteen children. Six of his maternal ancestors served in the Revolution and his three names came from them. He was the second son and sixth child.

In 1848 the family moved to Murray County and settled on 160 acres at the foot of Foot Mountain. By this time, Frank, as friends and family called him, decided that farming was not the vocation he wanted to pursue and in 1850 he went to work for an uncle who was a merchant. He enjoyed this for a while but then decided he should be in the larger town of Dalton.

Frank Jackson, taken in Dalton, Ga.
murraycountymuseum.com

Dalton was a town with a railroad, the Western & Atlantic Railroad, and was fast becoming the financial, commercial and transportation center of Northwest Georgia. With two other uncles and his brother John, he set up a new store in Dalton and the business thrived. They branched out with their earnings and tried other ventures, including land speculation, and made even more profits.

Frank became sheriff in 1856 and served for two years in that capacity. He was 26, successful and ready to start a family with his new wife whom he married October 12, 1858. Matilda C. Morris was from a very prominent family of North Carolina.

In just a couple of years his estate was valued at over $20,000 and he was a well-established merchant and slave owner, holding title to eleven slaves. Politics weren't really a part of his life other than running for sheriff the one time and he was personally opposed to secession and the coming war. The only strong feelings he had concerned continuing his success in making money and having a better life for his wife and young family.

Northwest Georgia wasn't suited for the large plantation style farming that the South was known for, so most farms were hard-scratch and small in the area. Sentiment generally went against leaving the Union because they saw nothing to gain and much to lose through a war with the North. They were akin to East Tennessee and were a part of the Nickajack proposal to become a separate state and stay in the Union.

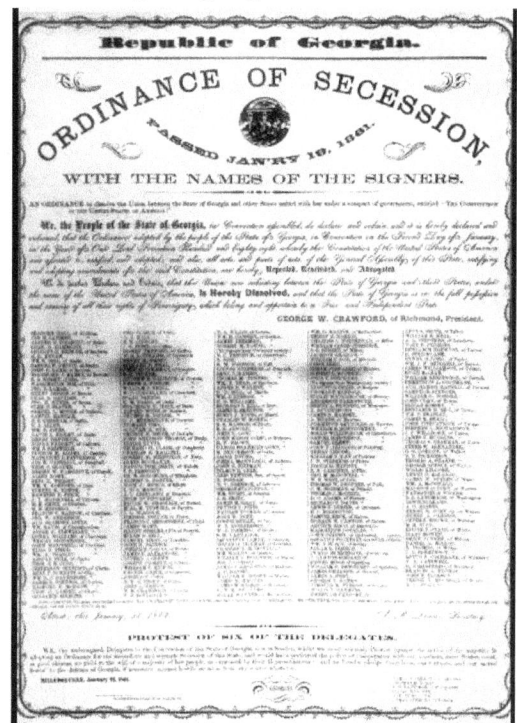

Georgia Ordinance of Secession, 1861
University of Georgia Special Collections Libraries

Frank's brother, John, was the Whitfield County representative in the State Senate and voted against secession at every opportunity. When the state voted to secede all of the Jacksons joined in the cause and followed their state like so many opposed to the move did all over the South. Alabama passed the ordinance by a very narrow margin also.

Georgia began deliberating secession on January 16, 1861. Alexander Stephens, future Vice President of the Confederacy, led the cooperationists in the state and represented the minority of mountain counties in their desire to avoid war and stay in the Union. On January 18 the vote was 166-130 for a resolution for immediate secession. On the next day they voted 208 to 89 to adopt the ordinance and it was officially signed on the 21st.

Before the war a group of young men in Dalton had started a militia company as was the custom across the South and the North. The Dalton Guards began drilling in 1859 and Frank was elected 1st Lieutenant with a Mr. Cook as the Captain. The group worked at drilling and became the toast of the town. On April 12, 1861 the war began and the group was mustered into service on June 11th as Company B of Phillips Legion.

The group saw their first action at Cheat Mountain Pass and a few other places while a part of the Army of Kanawha in West Virginia. By the time they were removed to South Carolina in the late part of the year Frank had been promoted to Lt. Colonel. It seemed he had considerable military ability.

The 39th Georgia was recruiting back in Dalton in the spring of 1862 and Jackson was able to be transferred to the new regiment as second in command. They went to Knoxville and were attached to Stevenson's Division. Immediately they went into action in Kentucky. Soon thereafter they were moved to help defend Middle Mississippi and Vicksburg.

His regiment fought well at Champion's Hill where he was in command of nine companies of the 39th that served as skirmishers during the attempt to turn Pemberton's flank on the Raymond Road. Fully 10,000 Yankee troops poured towards the Angle that three Georgia Regiments, Waddell's Alabama Battery, with five Alabama regiments on the left, were left to defend.

Because of the nature of the terrain and some confusion of the commander of this wing of the army, Gen. Cummings, the troops got to within 50 yards of each other before they knew the other side was there. This precipitated a withering fire from both sides and provided for a "very hot time of it" to all the troops involved. The 39th's leader, Col. Joseph T. McConnell, had only served as the elected commander of the Regiment for two months.

Gen. Carter L. Stevenson
Wikipedia.com

When the battle became hand to hand he got the men to stand firm as they stabbed with bayonets and clubbed each other with the butts of rifles. It was at this point that some unknown Yankee leveled his piece and hit the Colonel in the thigh, taking him out of the action. He would receive a mortal wound at Missionary Ridge just six months later. The command then devolved upon Lt. Col. Jackson as McConnell was taken from the field.

Champion Hill: Decisive Battle for Vicksburg
by Timothy B. Smith

The weight of numbers finally was taken to advantage as the 1500 or so of the 39th and 34th Georgia gave way to the division of Union men of near 10,000. The two regiments fell back to reorganize behind the line of nine companies under the command of Lt. Col. Jackson. These troops had been unable to get back in the line due to confusion of the ground and the movement of troops to form the Angle that had been over-run. The skirmishers had taken shelter on the Middle Road just back from the crest of the hill. It was partially sunken and provided cover for the small group.

As the enemy approached they stood up and delivered a withering fire on the advancing Indiana and Ohio troops. They were the only organized troops between the Yankees and complete victory over the Confederate Army. The line could not last long but it gave those behind them a chance to recover and reorganize. After a few volleys they had to retreat from the hot spot they were in, but the juggernaut had slowed as it also needed a moment to pause and catch its breath.

The tide had been turned after the reorganization and the Confederates advanced, retook part of the field, were stopped again, and the battle was virtually over. Jackson had been through a hot time and stayed cool under the intense strain of battle and helped prevent a total collapse.

He was also involved in several other small engagements with the Union forces under Grant, including the defense of Vicksburg. He was part of the surrender of July 4, 1863 commanding the regiment of 33 officers and 521 enlisted men (1 Colonel, 1 Major, 11 Captains, 20 Lieutenants, 60 Non-Commissioned Officers, and 461 Enlisted Men) on July 8th at the official paroling.

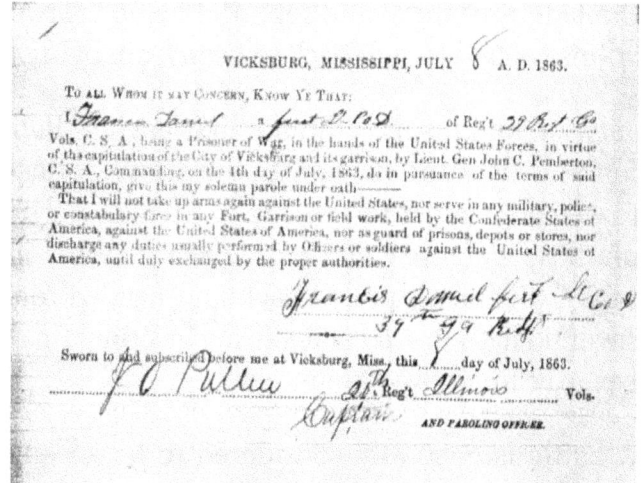

Parole Certificate from Vicksburg
National Parks Service

After leaving Vicksburg Jackson's troops gathered again in Enterprise, Alabama and were soon paroled. They were exchanged and the 39th was back in action again in November of 1863 at Missionary Ridge where they lost Col. McConnell to a mortal wound. Jackson took command and remained in that post for the duration of the war. A notable movement of the regiment on Missionary Ridge was a charge into a ravine that netted many prisoners.

Retreat from Chattanooga brought them home to Dalton, Georgia and a bittersweet reunion for some. The hated invader made a small demonstration against them on February 25, 1864. The Army of the Tennessee stayed and fortified their position while politics came into play with the removal of Gen. Braxton Bragg as overall commander. He was replaced, much to the relief of the majority of the soldiers, by Gen. Joseph

Johnston. Johnston was a very popular choice and was the fourth ranking general in the Confederacy behind Samuel Cooper, the deceased Albert Sidney Johnston and Robert Edward Lee.

While the 39th was stationed in Dalton, Frank Jackson ran for a seat in the Georgia Legislature. He won that seat and resigned his commission April 29, 1864 in order to serve in the Georgia State House. Before his resignation could be accepted and finalized, Sherman moved south with about 110,000 men toward Dalton on May 4, 1864.

Bragg had started building a defensive position in the hill country and Johnston strengthened it. He prepared for Sherman's onslaught even though he believed his army was greatly outnumbered. Johnston wanted Sherman to come straight at him and attack this strong position but Sherman thought otherwise. He sent Thomas to hold the Confederates there and sent McPherson through a gap in the mountains toward Resaca. Johnston had to pull back to keep from being flanked by the Union Army.

Jackson and his men did not like leaving their family and homes undefended but had to follow orders and move with the army. Johnston found a favorable position near Resaca to defend against the enemy. Sherman hit him in the middle of those defenses while McPherson went around his flank again. Johnston pulled back and headed for Cassville. After several chess moves and skirmishes they finally met for a real battle at Kennesaw Mountain.

Gen. James Birdseye McPherson
Public Domain

A battle is generally considered to be an engagement of two armies for an extended period of time, often an entire day, or in rare cases such as Gettysburg, three days. An action is when troops meet each other and fight but do not stay engaged for an extended period of time, such as a few hours. A skirmish is noted when two opposing forces clash accidentally and this does not bring on a general engagement.

On June 22nd the Regiment, with Jackson as its leader, lost about a third of their number in the desperate defense of Kolb's Farm before Kennesaw Mountain. The Battle of Kennesaw Mountain occurred the morning of June 27th as Gen. William Tecumseh Sherman threw his Army at another of Johnston's entrenched and elevated lines. By noon Sherman knew he'd had enough and withdrew his troops for a Confederate victory, but it was short lived.

More maneuvering and skirmishing occurred over the next few days and on the 30th of June Jackson received his fourth wound of the war in one of those skirmishes around Marietta, Georgia. This one was severe enough to send him to the hospital for recovery and ended his military career. The war had been very costly to Jackson and his family. He lost his wife Matilda sometime during the war and three of his brothers were killed while serving the Confederacy.

On November 23, 1866 he married Sallie Elizabeth Hoke of Greenville, South Carolina. He farmed in Dalton, Georgia for a time and invested $30,000 to help organize the Peoples Savings Bank of Dalton in December of 1866. He had other investments but he finally took a job with the railroad. He worked as an agent for the Chattanooga terminus of the Western & Atlantic Railroad. This line was the State of Georgia road.

Major Campbell Wallace had been superintendent of that line at one time and was now the general manager of Tom Tate and Associates. This company was contracted to build the South & North Alabama Railroad from Montgomery to Decatur. The work was starting again after construction had stopped because of the War. It was 1868 and Maj. Wallace brought Col. Jackson to work with him due to the good association they'd enjoyed at the Western & Atlantic. All the engineers and some workers were moved into a camp of small, cramped quarters in the Jefferson County town of Elyton.

Convict Labor Working near Helena
helena-alabama.blogspot.com

The company of Jackson & Wallace were given the contract from Calera to Montgomery. Further, they had the contract to build the road from Pea Vine Creek north to the crossing of the Alabama Great Southern. This was fifteen to twenty miles and went over Red Mountain.

Brock's Gap was a special problem because of the rock that had to be moved or blasted out of the way and John D. Gray had that contract. Frank Wadsworth was the engineer of record for the southern section and John A. Milner, brother of John T. Milner, was over the northern part. The Gap and the twenty miles to Decatur had to be completed by a specified time or bond payments set for those sections would be forfeited.

In the summer of 1869 Jackson brought several hundred hands, mostly convict labor, to Jemison. His first order of business was to organize and build a camp for the workers to live while they started clearing and grading that line. A road had to be cut to this new village and a commissary and cabins built for the workers. They were crude buildings but served the purpose. Convict leasing was used to save labor costs and was really a form of post war slavery. Prisoner labor was leased to private parties such as the Pratt Mines, Tennessee Coal and Iron Company and in this case, contractors such as Col. Jackson.

The company or individual that leased these convicts was responsible for feeding, clothing, and housing them also. There were annual inspections of the facilities used to house the workers but there was much abuse in the system. Many black men were arrested on trumped up charges and sometimes mass arrests were made because labor was needed by one of the companies that regularly leased prisoners. The system finally ended in 1928 under a cloud of misuse and abuse of both men and women in the convict leasing system.

Convict Labor built the South & North Alabama Railroad
from racialinjustice.eji.org

In the 1880s Jackson was the largest individual user of convict labor in the Alabama. He used them on his farm and at the limestone quarry at Blount Springs. In practice the workforce was almost entirely made up of African-Americans. This proved to be a very lucrative practice for the state and the men that leased the convicts. Many fortunes in the industrial district of Birmingham and elsewhere in Alabama were made on the backs of men trapped in this cruel machinery.

A child was born to the Jackson's in 1868. They named her Elizabeth. Mrs. Jackson and Elizabeth stayed in Georgia until arrangements for a decent home in Alabama for the family could be made. During November Mrs. Sallie Jackson and daughter Elizabeth, paid a visit to the camp to see the progress. Major Wallace and his child also came along with them and they all moved into the little camp at Brock's Gap. The Jacksons were in the Brock home.

Jemison and Thorsby were growing rapidly because of this new construction. Seeing how well this work was moving along, Wallace asked Jackson to move to the Decatur site to make sure it was finished. He wanted to make certain the bond money would not be lost by missing the deadline there. If the bonds were lost their contract would be void and they would lose all their money and hard work already put into the project. Jackson was a man that got the job done, and more importantly, on time.

Jackson agreed and took two hundred men with him. He completed the work but it was down to the wire finishing in time. For two weeks the men labored through sleet and snow, finishing the work with but three hours to spare. Tate and the Governor of Alabama signed the bonds that night and the transaction was complete.

Gray could not complete the cut at Brock's Gap and Jackson was sent to finish that job, continuing to build his reputation for getting results. Frank Wadsworth was engineer in charge and a Mr. Edwards was the assistant engineer. Col. Jackson was the man in the field that made things happen. The railroad was depending on Jackson to get them through Brock's Gap and back on their timetable.

Frank Wadsworth, moved into Robert Brock's old home at the gap and lived there through the completion of the work along with Elizabeth and Sallie Jackson. The state helped this project by sending the entire convict labor force to work on the cut. This force was sick and undernourished. Dr. Mortimer Jordan came from his home in Elyton to help bring the convicts back to health so they would be able to work. Many convicts died before they did any work at all, but most recuperated and the job was completed on time because of their hard work.

The cut through Brock's Gap was the first project attacked and after it was finished Jackson moved his men to finish the line from there into Birmingham. In September of 1871 the first train made it to Birmingham with Dock Rosser as the locomotive engineer. The train ran from Montgomery to Birmingham amid much fanfare.

New life was being brought into Alabama by the creation of Birmingham. This was a city being built where the South & North Railroad would cross the line to Chattanooga. Plans were for the rich mineral resources to the city's north to be brought in for use in the furnaces that were to be constructed in the next few years. The Oxmoor and Irondale Furnaces were being rebuilt for the production of iron pigs to ship to rolling mills. If the South & North did not get finished on schedule, the city could collapse before it ever really started.

The State of Alabama had indorsed the mortgage of the railroad bonds in the amount of $2,200,000 to build the road to Birmingham. It was now in operation to Birmingham and actually finished all the way to Blount Springs. There was still a gap between there and Decatur that had barely been even touched. There was a very real fear that the minerals of Central Alabama could end up being sent to Chattanooga instead of keeping them in Alabama for use in Birmingham.

Vernon K. Stevenson
L & N RR

Pressure was being applied to the South & North owners to turn their railroad over to the men who held the bonds since they were not going to be able to finish construction on time. A meeting of the board was demanded by V. K. Stevenson, president of the Nashville and Chattanooga, and Russell Sage. Sage was a financier, a railroad executive and a Whig politician from New York. Both had much to gain by obtaining control of the South & North and funneling everything to Chattanooga. After their heated meeting it seemed to the Alabama men that all was lost. Besides Alabama's future interests, the fortunes of the railroad men were tied not only to the railroad, but to the future of the new city.

Russell Sage
Univ. of Florida

The next night a miracle occurred that would save the day for the South & North RR and Birmingham. Albert Fink, vice-president and general manager of the Louisville and Nashville Railroad brought another proposition to John Milner and his associates. Actually it was the proposition of James Withers Sloss. Colonel Sloss was the president of the Nashville and Decatur Railroad and the South & North's success was tied to his own. He stepped into the middle of a bad situation with a plan to benefit the ailing railroad and also his own fortunes.

Sloss was a native of Tuscumbia and would grow into one of the great players in the success of both Birmingham and Blount Springs. From the age of 15 to 22 Sloss worked as the bookkeeper for a butcher near Florence, Alabama. Daily he walked several miles to do his job and used every spare minute he had to study and read.

At 16 he decided he would marry Miss Mary Biggar and it happened, just as he planned, on his 22nd birthday. He bought a small country store from his savings and began another success in Athens. He invested only in what he thought were sure things and his fortune would grow with each investment.

By the 1850s he owned several fair-sized plantations, was a big influence in politics in his part of the state, and had acquired the honorary title of colonel. This title was often given to men of high standing in the South. He would continue to be called Col. Sloss for the rest of his life.

Col. James Withers Sloss
Public Domain

He bought part of a railroad that was organized January 1, 1867 by the consolidation of the Central, Southern, Tennessee, and Alabama Railroad companies. These groups had owned different parts of the 119 miles of track that ran from Nashville to Decatur. Twenty-six of those miles were in Alabama. The success of this line depended on linking with the South & North. When he learned of the plan of Stevenson and Sage to take control of the South & North and channel all the mineral resources to Chattanooga, he formed his own plan.

Sloss hurried to Louisville, Kentucky to enlist Albert Fink and the resources of the Louisville & Nashville Railroad. He proposed that the L & N should lease the Nashville and Decatur for 30 years, take up the bonds of the South & North, then complete the gap from Blount Springs to Decatur. This would give the L & N a complete line from Nashville to Montgomery where they could connect to other lines and give them the ability to go all the way to the Gulf of Mexico.

Albert Fink
L & N RR

The Louisville & Nashville line had gotten very wealthy during the Civil War transporting men and material south to the front for the Union military. They enjoyed this great wealth and invested more and more of it into improving their road and acquiring more lines to add to their business. This new move would be very good for the company with the addition of new markets as well as prevent the growth of the rival Nashville and Chattanooga. If this move to help the ailing South & North Alabama Railroad did not come through, they could lose the entire state of Alabama and a direct route to the Gulf to their competition.

Albert Fink decided to act fast and proceeded to Montgomery to stop the move of the Sage and Stevenson takeover. The day after the heated meeting of the two groups, Fink met with the South & North group to let them know he was planning to force his board of directors into action for them. He invited them to Louisville to meet with the board of the L & N and possibly void the threats of the Nashville & Chattanooga group.

A group representing the S & N RR went to Louisville a few days later to meet with the directors of the L & N. These men included Frank Gilmer, Bolling Hall, E. K. Mitchell, and John Milner. Sam Tate was also going because he was the contractor in charge of all the construction work. Col. Tate was the man that built the Memphis and Charleston Railroad and was a well-known promoter of railroads in the South. That line was enjoying the highest volume of traffic in the entire South at the time and was a formidable force. Tate was its president and very powerful in his own right.

Fink met Milner at the station and invited him to his home for a preliminary talk about what was needed to keep the S & N RR alive. Milner, ever the enthusiastic salesman, painted a profitable picture of the mineral district and Birmingham that fired the imagination of Fink. Fink then met with Mr. Newcomb who was the president of the L & N and held the deciding vote as far as extension policies were concerned. A meeting was called for that evening of the L & N directors and the S & N committee.

The Louisville & Nashville group was divided, three for and three against. Discussion started and things were going very pleasantly for about an hour with the lines still holding at three to three. At this point Colonel Tate stood up and announced that his company held the construction contract and demanded a $100,000 bonus for surrendering the contract.

This was a shock to both sides and caused the meeting to turn dramatically. Col. Newcomb jumped up and said in a strong voice, *"D'ye think I'll stand for any highway robbery!"* Apparently Tate took great offense at the statement because he ran towards Newcomb and raised his cane at the man but fell short of hitting him. Tate said he wasn't going to waste his cane on him and that he had already arranged a deal with Sage and Stevenson. Newcomb was enraged and went after Tate. While they wrestled in the middle of the boardroom Fink struggled his way in between them. Fink was not only big in the business world, he was just big. At 6' 7" he towered over everyone he met.

The Story of Coal and Iron describes the scene:

> *Though both Colonel Tate and Colonel Newcomb were tall men, Albert Fink towered head and shoulders over both. He laid hands on their shoulders and succedded in partin them, sayin in his broken English: "Colonel Tate, you stop this! Colonel Newcomb, you come along with me," and he got Newcomb out. Milner remarks at this point, "The fat was then all in the fire."*

It did look like things were very bad. Major Hall tried to reason with Tate, but he wouldn't change his feelings. Fink returned to the room and rang a bell. His servant came and Kentucky Whiskey was ordered for all. Order was restored over a few sips and the meeting was adjourned until the next day. All the parties parted feeling a little better.

After the meeting Fink immediately telegraphed Sloss. He quickly wrote up a contract leasing the Nashville and Decatur to the L & N and brought it to the meeting that was held that next afternoon. All parties agreed to the terms and the deal was struck. The contract included a $75,000 payment to Tate. It was signed by H. D. Newcomb and approved by F. M. Gilmer, Bolling Hall, Sam Tate and Associates on May 19, 1871. Gilmer had a large disagreement shortly after the signing and the L & N directors removed him as president. J. W. Sloss took his place and then relocated to Birmingham.

The L & N toyed with changing their name after buying S & N A
The Louisville & Nashville Railroad, 1850-1963

Immediately all the camps were moved north so the work could continue. The goal was for this work to be done by September of 1872 and this timetable had to be met. Finally, just before the deadline, the last spike was driven at Blount Springs and there followed a large celebration. People came from all over the state to join in this celebration hosted by the South & North Railroad and the Blount Springs community.

Jackson stayed for a time in Blount Springs during the construction of this northern part of the road and saw the great potential for investing there. He more or less had inside information as to details of where the route would run and where the depot would be built, so he acted accordingly. He bought the land that the Goff House had occupied and the land adjoining the not yet built depot.

Soon after he purchased the land he began construction of a temporary hotel and named it the Jackson House. It was within 1,000 feet of the depot so many of the workers used this hotel until work was completed. Since the tracks were finished from Birmingham to Blount Springs already, many patrons started returning to enjoy the resort once again. This building would stand for six years as the seat of Blount Springs society for all that time.

After the last spike was driven and the great celebration faded, the task of making the Springs the center of society for the newly founded city of Birmingham began. Jackson did everything he could to encourage the well-heeled of the foundling city to spend as much time as possible in the cool air and rejuvenating feel of the village and of course, his hotel.

Jackson also had a large part in creating new business in the city of Birmingham. He was one of the founders of the Birmingham Gas and Illuminating Company and later the Director of the Tennessee Coal and Iron Railroad. He ran for mayor against the incumbent Thompson and lost in 1888. In 1895 he became the president of Baxter Stove Works and stayed in that post through 1897. In 1899 he was named supervisor of Jefferson County Public Roads.

He never completely left Blount Springs and maintained his cottage for as long as he could. Sallie and his adopted son Starks stayed with him there most of every season until health and finance forbade it. He was always revered for his part in making Blount Springs what it was after rescuing it from decline.

Col. Jackson was considered a great judge of horseflesh.
The W. S. Hoole Special Collections Library,
The University of Alabama

Mary Gordon Duffee wrote of the debt owed to Col. Jackson in one of her articles for the *Birmingham Age Herald*. "Summer Home: Blount Springs and its Rare Environs" was written August 17, 1887. She spoke of Col. Jackson and his wife in glowing terms.

> *Here may they rest in the calm repose they have both earned conscious of duty well done by their adopted state, and reap the reward of great works and self-sacrifice; of wide-spread charities and generous ministration, often falling sweet "as dews upon Hermon." The day that Col. Jackson arrived at this place it was Jeremiah's idea of "the abomination of desolation." And now may he find for many a long year, and many a happy one to come, the "rose above the mould," growing beside his pathway.*

10

A New Hotel, Cholera, and the Press

The 1870s dawned at Blount Springs much as it did across the South. People were confused, downtrodden, and generally hurting from the effects of the late war. Military districts were the order of the day, with carpetbaggers and scalawags running the government, both local and state, in almost all cases. Farmers were having a hard time getting a good price for their crops on top of either too much or too little rain.

To add insult to injury, Blount Springs had just suffered a catastrophic loss with the tragic and accidental burning of the Duffee House in 1869. This also affected everyone in Blount Springs, because as the hotel went, so went the town. Most businesses depended on guests at the hotel and cottages. Without guests coming to town all the other businesses suffered right along with the Duffees.

Building a railroad somewhere in Alabama
L & N Railroad

One bright spot on the horizon was the building of the new South & North Railroad through the town of Blount Springs. In 1871 that line was finished from Blount Springs south and opened a larger market for guests to come from the southern part of Alabama and many other far-away places. This direct connection to the fledgling Birmingham looked promising. The businessmen of Blount Springs were just waiting for the line to Decatur to be finished and open up easy travel for an even greater number of patrons.

With the bright promise of coming prosperity and commerce the little town started waking up from its inactivity. There was no hotel, but there were still cottages that individual families owned and some of these were rented to workers that were busily constructing the railroad. It took another miracle for the South & North to get finished

Chapter 10 - A New Hotel, Cholera, and the Press

and that miracle was supplied by first, James Withers Sloss and then by Albert Frink of the Louisville & Nashville Railroad.

With the L & N backing the construction it appeared things would move more quickly and the connection would be completed by the September, 1872 deadline. Col. James Franklin Ballenger Jackson now appeared in Blount Springs with an energy and determination that would affect the community for many years. Besides his work on the railroad he saw the great potential in the resort. He bought property in Blount Springs, notably the site of the burned Duffee House, and construction for a new hotel began. Located about a 1,000 feet from where the depot would be, it served many of the workers for the railroad.

The Relay House, Birmingham's First Hotel
Alabama Department of Archives and History, Montgomery, Alabama

By 1872 guests were able to enjoy the springs both medically and socially. This new hotel was named the Jackson House. Jackson planned this building as a temporary hotel because he had grand plans for a bigger and better hotel. It was to be located adjacent to the depot that was now under construction as the line was nearing completion to Decatur.

Mrs. Sallie Jackson and Elizabeth stayed in Birmingham at the Relay House during this time. The greatest tragedy imaginable for the Jackson family occurred in 1872 when Elizabeth contracted a sickness that finally ended her life at only three years of age. She was the first white child to die in Birmingham. There was great sadness in the Jackson household. They would never have another child by birth, but would later have a nephew they adopted and raised as their son.

Through his hard work and engineering skills, the last spike was finally driven in at Blount Springs just hours before the deadline was reached. People from all over the state came to take part in the celebration. It was the first of many great events that would be held in Old Blount during this new era. The finishing of the railroad would change Blount Springs for many years to come.

Times were hard for a while after the Duffee House burned in 1869, but with the coming of the railroad new life came to the Springs. In addition to his temporary hotel Col. Jackson built a cottage nearby. His family included his wife and nephew George Morris who they called Sparks. He would be the light of Frank and Sallie's lives.

A store was constructed and owned by James H. McCary and Lee Bivings. Dallas Brown had charge of the livery stable and also served as the master of hunting and fishing. He supplied horses for the many strategically placed bridle paths that ran through the hills and valleys. The little town showed more and more life and more people were coming.

It had always been a place for the gentry to assemble, to see and be seen, but now it might be a little more open to other classes because of the better transportation with the advent of the South & North Alabama Railroad. The new town of Birmingham became the leading supplier of guests and cottage owners for Blount Springs and the two would be intricately linked for the rest of the century.

Birmingham was expanding rapidly and near the end of 1871 the population was counted by the Elyton Land Company to be 900 souls. The Alabama Legislature granted a charter to incorporate the City of Birmingham. They elected a mayor and aldermen and the city continued to grow at a quick pace.

An event almost stopped the growth and caused the near death of the new settlement. This was the Cholera Epidemic of 1873. A group of excursionists from Birmingham came to Blount Springs for a day of picnicking and dancing. They seemed to enjoy their time of revelry immensely, but on the train ride home one of them exhibited great distress. He was taken to bed upon his return to Birmingham and died the next day. This was in the middle of June.

Dr. Mortimer Jordan
Public Domain

There was immediate alarm as a doctor declared he was stricken with cholera. Since he had been at Blount Springs the day before it was linked to the outbreak and quickly the town was deserted. Many suspected this was the place that the malady originated until further investigation. This investigation showed the gentleman had lately moved to Birmingham from Huntsville. The bedding that was shipped to him from that town was found to be the actual carrier of the infection. Blount Springs was cleared and some of the guests returned.

Cholera rapidly spread through the city and the doctors of the town were very busy coping with the outbreak. Many that could, fled Birmingham and some of those sought refuge in Blount Springs. Others went as far away as Montgomery. That day became known as "Blue Monday". With a shortage of nurses willing to work with the victims, a local Magdalene, Lou Wooster, stepped in with her girls and attended to as many as they could. Magdalene was the nice word of those days for Madam.

Dr. Mortimer Jordan was charged with writing a summary of events during the infestation and he noted the heroic work of these women:

> *Before closing this paper, justice demands that we should briefly allude to the heroic and self sacrificing conduct, during this epidemic, of that unfortunate class who are known as "women of the town." These poor creatures, though outcasts from society, anathematized by the church, despised by women and maltreated by men, when the pestilence swept over the city, came forth from their homes to nurse the sick and close the eyes of the dead. It was passing strange that they would receive no pay, expected no thanks; they only went where their presence was needed, and never remained longer than they could do good. While we abhor the degradation of these unfortunates, their magnanimous behavior during these fearful days has drawn forth our sympathy and gratitude.*

Lou Wooster was the leader of that group of women of the town and proved to be quite an interesting person. She was a prominent citizen and highly regarded for many years in the city.

Louise Wooster was born in 1842 to William and Mary Wooster in Tuscaloosa. Her father died when she was only nine years old and her mother was forced to remarry to support the family. Her stepfather ran off a few years later with all their money.

Mary Wooster died in just a short while after he left leaving Lou and her older sister as orphans and destitute. They were living on the mercy of relatives and the girls suffered much distress and abuse. The sister became a prostitute to support them while Lou worked for a time as a seamstress. Lou wrote in her autobiography that she was turned to prostitution slowly, step by step.

She worked for a while in Montgomery, saving all the money she could. Eventually moving to the new city of Birmingham where she opened her own house. She saw a way for her to earn her way to a respectable life in this new city. Always using her keen business sense, she wisely located near city hall. Her clients were not the common man, although they were certainly welcome, but instead she specialized in the elite business and professional men of the community. Politicians were a large part of her clientele.

At her death a strange tribute was paid. Since a gentleman could not be seen attending the funeral of such a woman, many of her admirers sent their carriages in honor of the woman they could only secretly admire and honor. The funeral cortège was said to be over a mile long with carriages occupied only by a driver with no passengers.

At the conclusion of the epidemic, 28 people lost their lives, but many more were affected by this dread threat. Oak Hill Cemetery had to be enlarged to make room for the many victims and Lou Wooster and others were praised and regarded with pride for their roles in saving the city. Wooster was a frequent visitor at Blount Springs. She even owned several lots in the ill-fated L'Orient addition.

Another eye witness was Mrs. Susan Dillard Luckie, wife of Dr. Luckie. In 1916 she wrote an essay titled "The Cholera" for the Pioneer Club for their book, *The Early Days of Birmingham*. She mentions some of the people who contributed to ending the scourge and helped the city survive, plus, thrive afterwards.

Dr. James Buckner Luckie
Public Domain

> *I cannot pass this period without making honorable mention of the heroes who stood the test, the acid test during this trying time in 1873. Some of these were Dr. M. H. Jordan, Dr. J. W. Sears, Dr, Crawford, Dr. Parker, and Dr. Luckie. Dr. Taylor worked in concert with his co-laborers until stricken down, and as soon as he was strong enough left for Montgomery. One of Dr. Tucker's sons also had cholera. Mr. Bonner helped to nurse the sick, doing what he could.*
>
> *It was three weeks before Drs. Jordan and Luckie removed their clothing for a nights rest. As they had been going night and day and were so worn out, they said that if they did not take a little rest they could not be of further service to the sick; so they slipped away and managed to get a few hours of sleep.*

After the epidemic Blount Springs once again became the center of the social universe for many of the important people and founders of Birmingham. The "Duke of Birmingham", Col. James Powell, was a frequent visitor as well as William S. Mudd, James Gilmer and Samuel Tate. Many of these men maintained private cottages and conducted some of their business from them. Col. Jackson was also a great investor in early Birmingham and kept the Jackson House at a high level, ready for all his friends and business associate's pleasure and comfort.

Col. James Robert Powell
Public Domain

Mollie Duffee had been sent to New York for more schooling and experiences. She began her writing career at school when she had several poems published. As her writing skills increased she was offered more chances for publication. Becoming friends with newspapermen and other publishing professionals made possible her desired career of writer. During the Cholera Epidemic of 1873

Duffee came back to Blount Springs to live. She stayed there until her death in 1920.

Promoting Birmingham and Blount Springs were always on the mind of Col. Powell. In 1873 he wrote to the New York Press Association and offered the new city of Birmingham for their annual convention. When they accepted his invitation lavish plans were made to ensure the success of their visit, with an eye towards promoting his young city. Many businessmen were willing to put on a good show for the visitors.

Mayor Powell decided they should be wined and dined on the trip as well as the destination. He met the 70 or so newspaper men in Louisville and they began their excursion to Alabama together. There was a stopover in Blount Springs for lunch, drinks and entertainment. A band met them at the station and paraded them to the well decorated Jackson House. Much fanfare was heaped upon the group and they were thoroughly impressed. Powell supplied the train and Dr. Constantine supplied the food and drink. Champaign and other delicacies were the order of the day. Much toasting would follow. Dr. Constantine was a Birmingham business man that was also promoting land in Blount Springs.

> *Such a glorious day as we did have, such a lunch, with champagne in the greatest profusion and everything, just such as you know a Frenchman would provide. The Press was so pleased they spread the fame of Birmingham far and wide.*

From *Early Days of Birmingham*

Mary Gordon Duffee had been engaged to give a welcoming address and promote Birmingham and Blount Springs as she socialized with the dignitaries. She is often regarded as an eccentric and a hermit. She was far from that. Eloquent and entertaining would be much better words to describe this intelligent, well-read, and witty sophisticate. She began her address to the group with lines that sounded much like they'd come from one of her melodic poems.

> *It becomes my pleasant duty, gentlemen of the Press Association of New York, to welcome you to Blount Springs, Alabama, long and well known throughout the land as "the Saratoga of the South" and, like that famous resort of your own state, situated between two beautiful rivers, surrounded by a combination and variety of landscape as matchless as it is grand and beautiful.*

She spoke in glowing tones of the marvels of Blount Springs, of the waters and their curative powers, of their comparison with the watering places of the Americas as well as those on the European Continent. Then she listed the many important people of Alabama that had given testimony to the miraculous waters and their healing powers. Among them were Vice President William King, Senator and Presidential Candidate John Bell, President of Columbia College F. A. P. Barnard and Vanderbilt University Dr. L. C. Garland.

By the time the party was over and the gentlemen boarded the train to continue on to Birmingham, the die was cast. An overwhelming feeling of goodwill pervaded the group and the fame of Birmingham was spread far and wide by the Press of New York. Powell, Duffee, Constantine and many others had done his work well and succeeded in advancing the cause of the city.

Popularity of the resort grew also and the hotel became known for its excellent accommodations and service. At this time W. C. Morrow and his wife were the managers and did much to promulgate the growing impression of luxury for the country hotel. Many compared it favorably with the best hotels of any American city. There was a big push to get business from cities like Memphis now that rail service was available. Sam Tate was influential there and would become an agent for the hotel.

BLOUNT SPRINGS!
The Great Alterative, Tonic and Aperient.

THE JACKSON HOUSE, AT BLOUNT Springs, will be ready to accommodate the public by the **First of June**. The rates of board will be $50 per month, $17 50 per week and $3 per day. Table board (without room), $35 per month. Children under ten years of age and colored servants, half price. White servants, three-fourths price. A discount of 10 per cent. will be made on all bills from $300 to $500; on all over $500, 15 per cent.
These Springs are situated on the South and North Alabama Railroad 130 miles north of Montgomery. A great many improvements have been made, with a view to health and comfort, since last season.
Those who patronize the Jackson House will get the worth of their money. Cheaper board can be obtained at private houses. THERE IS ROOM FOR ALL! We expect a large crowd at this fountain of health and pleasure. W. C. MORROW.

Memphis Daily Appeal
May 23, 1874

The railroad made travel much easier for people and more came from further away. Newspaper advertisements began to appear in places like the *Memphis Daily Appeal*. This one was from the May 23, 1874 edition. Advertising was more about careful placement of praise instead of an ad like those of today. Those were also used but an endorsement from the newspaper or a specific columnist was considered to be even better.

A letter from Julia Wynne to her fiancée tells about the goings on in 1874 at the hotel.

Dr. Scott,

Your letter was received yesterday saying that mine after much delay had reached you. I'm sorry you were caused a moments uneasiness. Hope this will reach you much sooner. We are having quite a gay time this week. Yesterday the Democratic meeting came off. There was not quite so large a crowd as was expected; the weather being so unbearable prevented a great many from attending. Great many able politicians were here and a number of fine speeches were delivered so I heard. I didn't have the pleasure of hearing these as the speaking was some little distance from the Springs. We had the balls every evening and I danced no little. I do dance a great deal, but it does not seem to hurt me; think I am looking better than when I left home. We still have quite a number of gentlemen. Some of my best friends leave this evening and tomorrow. I have ever so much foolishness to tell you when I get home. I had quite a gay time. exploring that cave I spoke of. It is almost a half mile long and the rocks inside are beautiful, it is quite a curiosity. Thought I was getting near the lower regions when in the cave. It was lit safe by lamps but still it was not light enough to dispense with candles. Some places would be so steep that it was all we could do to keep from falling. Expect I will see you before a great while, think we will leave about the tenth of Sept. Won't you be sorry when that time comes! Believe I would like right well to see you. Anna was at the springs. I would like to have seen her, and talked over old times.

Advertising was always a big part of letting people know about the wonderful advantages of Blount Springs. Ads would run in many different papers in cities all over the South. Memphis, Nashville and New Orleans were some of the major towns that were used, but smaller towns also got their fair share of advertising. This same ad ran in several different papers in the region for several months announcing the new seasons. Often the only difference would be the layout used by different papers. Apparently Mr. Morrow and Col. Jackson saw the advantages of a media blitz.

Pulaski Citizen June 3, 1875

April 1, 1875 a new manager of the Jackson House was announced to be J. D. Towner. More advertizing for the Jackson House was now appearing across the South. Finally a new advertisement for Blount Springs formally noted it as the "Saratoga of the South", recalling Mary Duffee's pronouncement to the New York Press.

Informally they had been compared to the great resort of Saratoga, New York many times. The State's Vice-President King had been one of the first to favorably compare the two and now this was being used to draw more patrons. The railroads made it easy for people to come from Memphis and Nashville and enjoy the resort from farther away. The L & N was a great company to encourage travel.

Not only was special attention paid to invalids at the resort, but hunting, fishing, riding and carriages were at the beck and call for guests. Towner welcomed all to come and benefit from the waters to help with: *Blood, Bowel and Liver Affections, Rheumatism, Nervous Diseases, Dyspepsia, Scrofula, Debility, and Uterine Affection of Females.*

The official season started July 1st and rates went up accordingly. From $2.50 to 3.00 a day and $12 to $15 per week with board extra were the going rates. A doctor and druggist were available and more able staff, including Mr. E. C. Paynter, head clerk, insured the best enjoyment of a stay of any length at the Jackson House. Service was becoming more and more legendary at the Springs!

Great Southern Summer Resort.

THE JACKSON HOUSE, AT BLOUNT Springs, Ala., will be opened on

Thursday, May 20th, 1875,

And remain open for the accommodation of guests during the balance of the year. Special attention given to the wants and comfort of invalids.

The water from these springs are highly recommended by eminent physicians and chemists to those suffering from Bowel, Liver, and Blood Affections.

This water purifies the blood, invigorates the feeble and debilitated, and for Rheumatism, Nervous Diseases, Dyspepsia, Scrofulous Diseases, Debility, and Urine Affection of Females, etc., it is unsurpassed.

Good fishing and hunting ground is quite accessible. Good livery turnouts for riding or driving can be had at moderate rates.

These springs are on the South and North Alabama Railroad, 53 miles south of Decatur, Ala., and 32 miles north of Birmingham, Ala., in a high and romantic part of the State, mountain scenery beautiful, location healthy. Visitors step from the cars to the platform of the hotel, and avoid the fatigue of a long ride in a stage or private conveyance across the country.

If you wish to regain your health, have a jolly time, or a pleasant and quiet retreat from business cares, you can accomplish your object by spending the summer at Blount Springs.

Rates of Board Up to the 1st of July.

Board and Lodging by the day $ 2 50
    "   "   "   week   12 00
    "   "   "   month.   40 00
Day Board without Lodging, per
  month   25 00

Rates after July 1st and for the balance of the Season.

Board and Lodging by the day $ 3 00
    "   "   "   week   15 00
    "   "   "   month,
  2 or more in one room   40 00
Board and Lodging by the month, 1
  person in a room   50 00
Day Board without room or Lodging 30 00

Ample and comfortable rooms furnished either in cottages or hotel by
may8 tf   J. D. TOWNER,
                              Proprietor.

Pulaski Citizen **May 13, 1875**

11

L'Orient, a Ghost Town Within a Ghost Town

Many years ago on the European Continent, Napoleon Bonaparte fought and lost the Battle of Waterloo to the British and Austrian forces under Wellington. After this defeat coalition forces inside France were able to restore Louis XVIII to the throne and exile the dictator to Saint Helena. This created a backlash in the higher ranks of Napoleon's Army and a great many officers fled the country for asylum in the Americas.

Napoleon Bonaparte in Exile
Wikimedia Commons

One of those groups was granted land in what is now Marengo County. They established Demopolis, City of the People, and proceeded to create the famed Vine and Olive Colony. A log cabin was constructed that served as a museum to their general and the past glory of arms raised in the name of France as Napoleon almost conquered Europe. Inside were flags, equipment, swords, and other souvenirs surrounding a bust of the Emperor Napoleon.

Vine and Olive Colony Panel Detail
Alabama Department of Archives and History, Montgomery, Alabama

The United States Government was glad to grant the land to the émigrés as a means of possibly securing that region for the country. This was the Mississippi Territory at the time and the southern portion was under the control of Spain.

In 1817, prior to the creation of the Alabama Territory, Congress gave the Frenchmen four townships (92,000 acres) with a stipulation they would cultivate it in grapes and olives. The Choctaw

Nation had given the land to the US just the year before. There was also a two year grace period before the cost of $2 per acre was due.

General Count Charles Lefebvre Desnouettes was one of those colonists and worked hard to make it a success. He was a personal friend of Napoleon Bonaparte, a General of the French Army, a Count of the Empire and leader of the Vine and Olive colony that founded Demopolis in 1817.

Gen. Count Lefebvre
Wikimedia Commons

Only about 150 of the original 347 grantees ever made it to Alabama. Many of the others had already established themselves at other points in the nation such as Philadelphia, a place where many Frenchmen settled, and felt no need to travel further. The legends have long been told of the men working the fields in their resplendent uniforms while the women labored in their finery of hoop skirts and petticoats. A series of four paintings commemorating the colony are in the possession of the Alabama Department of Archives and History in Montgomery.

One of the panels depicting the Vine and Olive Colony
Alabama Department of Archives and History, Montgomery, Alabama

These murals currently reside behind the closed doors of a conference room at the Archives building. This is an attempt to help preserve them. The years have not been kind to the pieces. Viewing is allowed only by request. They are always available unless the conference room is in use.

After much hard work was put into building a new city on the white bluffs of Demopolis, a survey found they had worked the wrong land. This mistake allowed speculators to move in and take over the plots they had developed. This forced the Frenchmen to move further inland to their real grant where they founded Aigleville, named in honor of Napoleon's ensign, featuring an eagle.

The vineyards they planted would live a year or two and then die. They never planted the olives so the colony finally went bust. Most survivors moved away to New Orleans or other areas with a French concentration. The few that did remain were absorbed into the community and little is left to show for the grand experiment.

Postcard of the last remaining building of the Colony
Card Cow

In *Alabama: Her History, Resources, War Record, and Public Men From 1540 to 1872* the author describes the settlement:

> *There were but few settlers in the region, and it was a vast wilderness. But the French made little progress in agriculture. The vines (the Cataba) would grow only a year or two, and the olive they did not plant. They were very industrious, but their time was frittered away on trivial things. There were several prominent men among them, and others who had been wealthy in France. These spent the greater part of their time in social pleasures, and the others were not slow to follow their example. They made no wine, but they drank all they were able to import, and carried into their humble pioneer homes all the charms and graces of their native country. Thriftlessness was their error, not idleness; for the hands that had "flashed the saber bare" at Borodino and Austerlitz were not slow to mix the mud which daubed the chinks of their log cabins; and dames who had made their toilettes in the chambers of St. Cloud readily prepared the humble repast of the forest home.*

The Fighting Kentuckian with John Wayne
Republic Pictures

An interesting side note for the Vine and Olive Colony is a visit by John Wayne's character in "The Fighting Kentuckian" (1949). A group of buckskin clad volunteers are making their way back home after helping Andrew Jackson stop the "bloody British in the town of New Orleans" and dally in Demopolis for a few days to gather supplies. Wayne's character falls for a local girl and they stay long enough to learn of the rough treatment some of the locals have been giving the colonists. They lend a hand in stopping the trouble. Some "Tuscaloosa River Rats" are plotting to steal the land of the Bonapartists, so John Wayne and company help them defend themselves. Oliver Hardy serves as Wayne's sidekick in the feature.

Francis Louis Constantine was the 14 year old son of Major Marshall Dominique Constantine, a decorated officer of the Army of France. They settled in Demopolis with the others but soon the young Constantine moved to the town of Erie several miles to the north on the banks of the Black Warrior.

Location of Constantine & Dupuy
The Birmingham News

A little later Constantine moved to Eutaw, truly establishing himself on his own and began creating his estate. He became a farmer and in addition, started a medical practice. He married Clementine Hamlett on March 27, 1827 and began a family. The couple would eventually have eleven children, all still living in 1891.

After having lived in Eutaw for almost 50 years they decided to move to the newly founded city of Birmingham. At 65 years of age, Dr. Constantine became one of the earliest merchants and cotton buyers in the city. For many years he was a partner in a clothing and grocery store at 20th Street and 2nd Avenue North, Constantine and Dupuy. The 20th Street storefront was groceries and the other was dry goods.

Back in Erie, one of his neighbors was another doctor by the name of Herndon Beverly Robinson. He had moved to Birmingham about the same time as Constantine and they remained friends. He also sought the healing waters and cooler climate of Blount Springs to avoid the epidemic.

Dr. Robinson
Tuscaloosa Magazine

Dr. Robinson was instrumental in the care of Cholera victims during the epidemic of 1873. He worked tirelessly to minister to the sick and was a major factor in bringing Birmingham through the tragedy. After it was over he decided to leave what he termed the "petulant nature" of Birmingham and enjoy the healthier climate of Blount Springs.

He went a step further and established the first hospital in Blount County. It was located on his property on what would become known as Robinson Mountain. It was an L shaped affair of ten rooms opening onto a shared porch. The building was modified later when the back wing was torn down and turned into a home that was used for many years. Now the entire building is gone but the home of Dr. Robinson is still used by some of his descendants.

Dr. Robinson was a firm believer in and practitioner of hydropathy. Britanica defines hydropathy as *"a therapeutic system that professes to cure all disease with water, either by bathing in it or by drinking it."* Blount Springs offered an excellent location for him to practice hydropathy, or hydrotherapy as it was called at the time. He began experimenting with innovative treatments. He was well respected in medical circles and quoted in journals of that era as to the treatment of diseases.

Dr. Robinson's Hospital on Robinson Mountain
Blount County Museum

In an 1889 State Board of Health document he is cited as a noted proponent using creosote to treat Pulmonary Phthisis.

> *The experience of Dr. Beverly Robinson with creosote in the treatment of phthisis is very encouraging. He gives it both internally and by inhalation, and says "the frequent or prolonged topical application of creosote vapors to the respiratory tract, in a considerable area, is of undoubted utility."*
>
> *He recommends the following formula for internal administration: Creosote (beechwood), six minims; glycerin, one ounce; whisky, two ounces. Mix, and use as directed.*
>
> *The daily amount of creosote prescribed by him for adults has varied usually from three to six minims, and continued frequently many months without increase or interruption, or any evidence of intolerance.*

A minim is 1/480 of a fluid ounce and Pulmonary Phthisis was defined as a wasting or consumption of the tissue; also known as tuberculosis.

Constantine saw the potential for great profit by investing in the town of Blount Springs.

He had an idea of setting up another town as a suburb of Blount Springs. This suburb would serve as a home for workers of the resort town to live. There was a renaissance of sorts going on that year, in spite of the Panic of 1873. The Panic held the entire country in fear of losing everything they had so many were holding their money and investing was slow.

Dr. Francis Louis Constantine
Ancestry.com

All along the new railroad line more and more small villages were starting up, directly encouraged by the L & N RR. Gilmer was already a fairly large community. Farmers had moved into this part of Blount County before the Civil War and there were a few merchants setting up shop there also. A man named Col. Cullman was working with the railroad to sell land a little further north of Gilmer that would become the town of Hanceville in just a few years.

Constantine bought the land just north of Blount Springs, laid out streets and named it L'Orient, after the town of his birth in France. Many of the streets were named for Confederate leaders such as Stonewall and Beauregard Streets. Other streets were named for people he admired, such as, Jefferson and Hamlet Streets. There was even one named Duffee Street. L'Orient was located in the SW1/4 of Section 1, Township 13, Range 3W and SW1/4 of Section 6, Township 13, Range 2W.

Early in 1874 it served as the post office for Blount Springs with Constantine himself as the postmaster. The first man to buy a lot in his new town was Phorandor H. Kinney. He needed a place to live since he was a merchant up the road in Gilmer. Wanting to better establish his store, he applied for a commission to open a post office in it. When he submitted his application for the post office commission he learned there was already a Gilmer in Alabama. Because of this the town had to be named something else. Kinney named the young town of Hanceville in honor of his father, Hance Kinney.

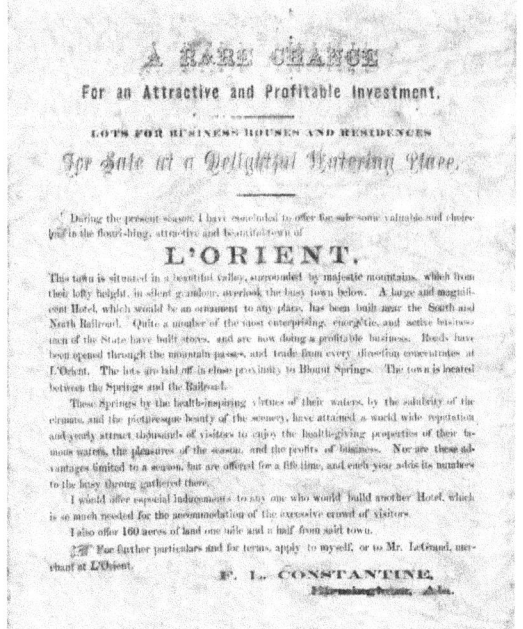

Advertisement for L'Orient
Wallace State Community College Genealogy Department, Hanceville, Alabama

He bought lots 6 and 7 on Washington Street.

Also on Washington Street there was a lot purchased by the notorious Madam of Birmingham, Lou Wooster. Others that bought lots included Mr. McPherson, who bought close to twenty lots, a Mr. Gamble on Jackson Street, along with Mr. Green, Mr. Sinclair and Mr. Haynes on Cedar and Stonewall Streets.

Lou Wooster was a frequent visitor and loved to roam the hillsides and valleys of Blount Springs. She enjoyed the beautiful nature when she could get away from the rigors of her profession. Probably she was able to move more freely amongst the people there because most probably had no idea who she was or what she did for a living, or more importantly, the female patrons had no idea who she was or what she did.

In *Autobiography of a Magdalene* Wooster writes:

> *Nature's works are grand. Man is the spoiler of the powers to love nature's works. "I have often spent the day wandering over the mountains at Blount Springs, Ala. I would become lost in thought, in admiration of the beauties of nature around me. Blount Springs is but a poor, little, almost unknown village in Blount County, yet some of the scenes there are grand, and well worth the notice of fine artists.*

She was very good with money and made many wise investments. L'Orient appeared to be one of them because it had to be a success because Blount Springs was certainly a success. Lou Wooster amassed a sizeable fortune and was an independent businessperson when it was very much frowned upon for women to take the lead in commercial ventures. There were many properties she acquired throughout the city and state. By investing in Blount Springs she was not only using her business sense but was also buying into the society of Blount Springs. Wooster was always quite resentful and bitter when people avoided her in the streets of Birmingham. That is, they avoided her until they wanted a contribution for one of their charities. In spite of the way many of the upper class treated her, she was quite generous with her money.

> A SPLENDID CAKE.—A few days since one of the gentlemanly attaches of the firm of Constantine & Dupuy, entered our office with a package which we were sure contained something nice. And it was nice! A magnificent cake, beautifully and deliciously iced and frosted, and on its side, in elegant raised letters, was the word, "L'Orient." The fair hands that made that delicious piece of confection are certainly expert in the art. We return our grateful thanks to the donors and drink to them this old toast of Rip Van Winkle: "Here's to you and all your families—may you live long and prosper!"
>
> **Birmingham Iron Age March 5, 1874**

Lou Wooster died in 1913 of Bright's Disease, a degenerative kidney disease. In death she was the equal of all and she would have been amused about lying for eternity amidst the movers and shakers of Magic City Society and the captains of industry at Oak Hill Cemetery in downtown Birmingham.

Because of her work in the Cholera epidemic, her charitable work with the poor, and contributions to places like Hillman Hospital, there is now an award to recognize individuals, groups, or organizations who are unconventional public health heroes. It is called The Lou Wooster Public Health Award and presented by the University of Alabama in Birmingham School of Public Health.

Promoting Birmingham and Blount Springs were always on the mind of the good Dr. Constantine. When Col. Powell invited the New York Press Association to come to Birmingham for their annual convention, Dr. Constantine provided the food and drink for the party they were given in Blount Springs. This was to give them more reason to enjoy Birmingham. The food was exquisite and the Champaign flowed. No doubt there was quite a bit of promotional talk between the press and Dr. Constantine about L'Orient and his plans for the development.

The "Marquis of L'Orient" continued to conduct business in Birmingham and sell lots in his town. For a while it seemed his town would thrive as Blount Springs became one of the South's leading health spas. During this period there were eight hotels, a legal casino, seven mineral springs, bottled sulphur water, and thousands of patrons each season. A large amount of workers were needed for such a large clientele but many lots went unsold in L'Orient. Few homes were ever constructed and the town faded away.

Around 1880 Constantine retired from the mercantile business and moved with his wife to Atlanta. In 1887 they celebrated their 60th wedding anniversary. He was one of the last survivors of the Vine and Olive Colony and died in 1891. Both are buried in the famed Oakwood Cemetery among governors, Confederate generals. Bobby Jones and Margaret Mitchell also rest there.

Right to left Dominique Francis Constantine, Henry Hamlett Constantine, Henry Hamlett Constantine Jr., F. L. Constantine
Ancestry.com

Sadly his town never really made it and most of the land stayed in the Constantine family for many years. It was all eventually sold to others, notably George Sanders, and now there is nothing to show that it ever even existed.

12

Press, Picnics, and Politics

Many varied groups came just for the day to enjoy the wonders of Blount Springs. These included Sunday Schools, fraternal orders, company parties and some events sponsored by the hotel. On the 12th of May around 700 people rode the morning train from Nashville and arrived around 10:00 AM. Mr. Towner and his assistants, Dr. Oates and Mr. Paynter, made certain that all was readied for their day and met them at the depot with fiddlers. These same fiddlers walked the guests from the depot to the dining room where a dance had been prearranged for them. Food and drink were abundant and everyone was highly entertained.

A few weeks after the grand excursion there was a humorous event that occurred near town when a donkey was on the tracks and would not move. The Accommodation came along blowing its whistle and trying to slow down but the donkey would not move. The story is told that the animal was caught up by the pilot (some call it the cow catcher) on the front of the engine and carried several hundred yards. All this time the train was slowing and when it was about to stop the stubborn one jumped off and scampered into the woods, a much wiser beast!

A few years before there had been a grand reception for the New York Press Association on its trip to their convention. What a grand and profitable success that had been, so another was planned by Capt. Towner for the benefit of Blount Springs. This time Newspaper correspondents from all over Tennessee were invited to take the ride south for the pleasures of music, dancing, and some special events before the season opened for 1875.

> **A DAY AT BLOUNT SPRINGS, ALA.**
> To the Union and American:
> The excursion to Blount Springs on the 12th inst., was certainly a most pleasant affair. About seven hundred visitors from Birmingham, whose numbers increased with recruits along the route, arrived at the Jackson House about 10 o'clock, and were received by Capt. Towner, the urbane proprietor, who with his assistants, Dr. Oates and Mr. Paynter, vied with each other in welcoming the guests to their hospitable house. The commodious dining room opened wide its doors, and before long frenzied fiddlers plied their well trained bows and fair women and brave men soon mixed in the mazes of the dance.
> The Jackson House presents many and varied attractions, and promises to be exceedingly popular with summer pleasure-seekers.
> Blount Springs is now all that could be desired as a summer resort. The waters are unsurpassed in mineral virtues, the scenery is grand and beautiful. The proprietor is the right man in the right place, and all connected with the house are well fitted to make guests feel at home. The visitors on the 12th will long remember with pleasure the day spent in the halls and beneath the shady groves of Blount Springs, and never forget the genial hospitality extended to them by all with whom they came in contact. VISITOR.

Nashville Union and American, May 18, 1875

The Jackson House offered a full evening's entertainment on the first night for the

Tennesseans and some special invited guests. Among those special guests were the Hon. Thomas J. Judge, sitting Justice of the Alabama Supreme Court, the Hon. Abner Nash Ogden of New Orleans, former Justice of the Supreme Court of Louisiana, Mrs. W. H. Graves of Montgomery, Mrs. Whitfield and her daughter Florence, other locals and assorted state and local governmental officials.

Mr. Brown was steward in charge of the first event, a banquet and did an outstanding job. Throughout the feasting there was much laughter and many entertaining stories traded. As the banquet was ending several toasts were offered and responded to by various reporters and guests. Finally, the last one was drunk to the health of Col J. F. B. Jackson.

Major Sidney Herbert, Master of Ceremony for the evening, then began introducing the evening's entertainment. Mrs. Whitfield sang several songs and then the Decatur Amateur Dramatic Company performed two farces, "New Sausage Grinders" and "The Nitroglycerine Doctor". Their performances brought the house down with laughter and they received rousing applause from the audience. Dancing followed as they drank and danced into the early hours of the morning.

The next few days were filled with walks along the cool mountain trails, horseback rides, and the daily promenade to the spring yard. The springs and bath house were enjoyed and then there was an excursion to the Great Southern Cave up the road in Bangor. The cave was always a popular trip for those visiting the resort.

Blount Springs and the Great Southern Cave were happy places and this trip left an extremely favorable impression on the Tennessee Press. More excellent advertising came of this as the reporters talked well of it through many articles in the future. One reporter remarked in his paper that it was, "One unceasing round of pleasure." More guests came to know the resort and started coming from Pulaski, Nashville, Memphis and other Tennessee cities and countryside homes.

In July the season opened and another group made the short trip from Birmingham to the Jackson House in a special first-class car provided by the South and North Alabama Railroad. Capt. Towner, ever the promoter, reduced his rates for the party through an agreement with the Committee of Arrangements for the un-named party. An article from the July 27th Birmingham Iron Age continues the story:

> *This house presents every convenience that could be desired by the most fastidious seeker of health or pleasure. E. C. Paynter, the obliging head clerk, and his active assistants show their guests all the attention in their power. A glance over the well-filled register that not only Alabama is*

> *represented, but surrounding states themselves containing noted mineral waters and summer resorts, this seeming to verify the prediction that Blount Springs will soon be the Saratoga of the South.*

At 9:00 dancing began in the well decorated dining room. It lasted until very, very late. The special train arrived in Birmingham at 4:40 AM. Apparently a good time was had by all!

The Mobile Register writes of the wonders of Blount Springs in an article reprinted in the *Birmingham Iron Age* of June 18, 1874:

> *Since the opening of the South and North Alabama Railroad these springs have been improved to a considerable extent. A commodious and very pretty hotel called the Jackson House has been erected immediately upon the Railroad; and large, pleasant cottages back of the hotel upon the mountain side; there are capable of accommodating a large number of people and making them very comfortable. Good bath houses; which are very accessible and supplied from the springs, have been put up, so that visitors may have their option at any hour, whether they will have it hot or cold, common or sulphur. These sulphur baths are delightful and healthy to the utmost degree. They will sweat disease out of the thickest skin and start the most sluggish liver agoing(sic). The scenery around Blount is beautiful, and as mountain after mountain breaks upon the gaze of the astonished visitor as he thrusts his head out of the hotel window "next morning," a delightful sense of being shut out from the cares and heat of the world, amid woodland dells and rustic glens, playing fountains and rippling waterfalls, steals over and thoroughly soothes him.*

The fountain mentioned is one that George Montague of Birmingham constructed on the lawn of the Jackson House.

Everyone that came to Old Blount wasn't there for a party. A more sober crowd was the Quarterly Conference moderated by the Rev. Dr. West. There were also many Sunday School classes from a variety of churches that made Blount Springs and the Great Southern Cave regulars trips for picnics and events. Several different years the Alabama Druggists Association would meet there, or if meeting in Birmingham, have an excursion for a daytrip included in their activities.

Mrs. R.H. Pearson explains in *Early Days of Birmingham* how the social life of Birmingham was intertwined with that of Blount Springs. Major Thomas Tate built "Sublett Hall" for Major Sublett of Mississippi as a place to host theatricals. The operetta "Bo Peep and Her 19 Sheep" was presented twice in Sublett Hall and then for a third time in Blount Springs. The production netted $250 which was used to buy the first sterling silver communion service for the Church of the Advent. Mamie Pearson Pike starred as Bo Peep and was 6 years old at the time.

The Louisville & Nashville Railroad controlled the South and North Alabama line due to the bailout of 1871 that allowed for the completion of the road. They often made special rates for the regular runs of trains from Birmingham to Decatur. At times they added special trains that ran just from Birmingham to Blount Springs or from Decatur to Blount. During the early 1870s they sold land along the line to increase their ridership and profits.

Cullman, Alabama came into being due to the hard work and salesmanship of Col. John Cullman, late of Bavaria. He brought German colonists that had emigrated to Cincinati to a part of Blount County that was unsettled along the tracks of the South & North Railroad. The majority of these families and men were from the Rhine River Valley. They created a town from scratch and made it a great success.

Col. Cullman (left) with a group enjoying a picnic
Wallace State Community College Genealogy Department, Hanceville Alabama

Out of this settlement more towns were either created or grew. One of these was new towns was Vinemont. The Germans needed vineyards to produce the wines they loved to drink and thought the plateau above Cullman would be the perfect spot to start growing grapes. On down south on the S & N, Gilmer experienced growth because of the railroad as did Garden City. When Gilmer applied for a post office it was learned another Gilmer already existed. The man applying for the post officedecided to rename the town Hanceville after his father, Hance Kinney.

More people quickly moved into the area and finally the population warranted the creation of a new county. Cullman County was created out of Blount in 1877 and

Cullman became the county seat. The county line was set near the present day Johnson's Crossing but was moved to the Mulberry River in 1899.

It took a few years after the Civil War for Southern militia to be allowed to organize once again, but when it was allowed, it flourished. The Montgomery Greys was one such unit and they had a military ball at the Jackson House on August 11th that was a great success. Because of the huge group that would be making the trek, the South & North put extras cars on the train to make it a comfortable ride for all.

The mix of the uniforms of the militia and the beautiful gowns of the ladies presented quite a spectacle for the eyes of the guests. A great variety of dances were performed by the company and all was fun and frolic until 11:00. At that moment the strains of Dixie filled the room and the men fell to attention. A member of the Montgomery Cadets, J. W. Oates, presented a flag to the Greys. Solemn remarks by Captain Winter ended the ceremony and the dancing resumed. The party continued into the early morning hours as did so many fine evenings at Blount Springs.

Gov. John Calvin Brown
Tennessee State Library and Archives
Nashville, Tennessee

This was certainly not the last ball of the year as a Grand Dress Ball was announced for Thursday, July 29. It was a grand ball and was planned by no less than former Tennessee Gov. John C. Brown, J. N. Brooks and Robert Meek, the Superintendent of the South & North Alabama Railroad. They were looking to have about 400 guests. It was also a success in all respects.

Besides these grand events daily life at the hotel was filled with entertainments such as music, dancing, ten pins, and cards. Gambling was always a mainstay. Besides cards, there was roulette and slot machines. A new ten pin alley had been built by Alexander Simpson to replace Dr. Constantine's that was destroyed by a tree falling on it during a storm. Each day the ladies and gentlemen made it a point to promenade to the springs in their finery for all to see.

Advertising was written in the style of a news article explaining the virtues of the "Great Southern Health and Pleasure Resort" and the many benefits of going to the hotel. The Jackson House is praised along with a recommendation for the medicinal properties of the waters and the many maladies they will cure or curtail.

Now it was possible to reach Blount within 24 hours by train from New Orleans. This timetable is quite a change from the seven day trip by wagon of the Benners from Greensboro less than 20 years before. Possibly the most striking part of the article is the testimonial given by the Very Rev. O'Callaghan, *"...well pleased with the accommodations, etc, and strongly endorses everything that is claimed for the waters of the springs."*

> THE GREAT SOUTHERN HEALTH AND PLEASURE RESORT.—We refer with especial pleasure to the card of Mr. J. D. Towner, Proprietor of the Alabama Blount Springs, which we publish in another column of to-day's paper. The waters of these springs are justly celebrated for their medicinal properties, which innumerable instances of cures in cases of rheumatism, neuralgia, gout, eruptive diseases of the skin, etc. prove. Competent judges, among whom are a number of physicians, pronounce them equal to any known waters of the kind either in this country or Europe.
>
> Another strong point in favor of the Blount Springs is the fact that the Jackson House and surrounding cottages afford the most ample and pleasant accommodations for visitors, and that the fare is first class, including everything desirable from city markets, together with the best fruits and vegetables from the surrounding country.
>
> Blount Springs are in the mountainous mineral regions of North Alabama, 150 miles north of Montgomery, and passengers from New Orleans are landed there inside of twenty-four hours after departure and without changing cars. It will be interesting to our readers to know that among the visitors at Blount Springs, just now, is the Very Rev C. T. O'Callaghan, the present distinguished Vicar General of the Diocese of Mobile, who is well pleased with the accommodations, etc., and strongly endorses everything that is claimed for the waters of the springs.

Morning Star and Catholic Messenger
July 1, 1877
New Orleans, Louisiana

New Orleans had long supplied guests for the Jackson House and even further back in time for the hotel and cottages of Harris and Perine. More Creole and French influence would be coming to Blount in the next decade as sweeping changes and upgrades were made.

September 17, 1876 was a day long remembered by the people and guests of Blount Springs for the heinous act that occurred and the manner in which it was committed. Not only was the crime against one of their own, but it was done in a way that was cowardly and callous.

J. S. Mayberry lived near Blount Springs and was the owner of several properties, most notably a saloon. Being a well-respected member of the community, he was thought of as kind and generous. For the last few years he had worked all over the state and the Southeast as a United States Government detective. One of the cases he worked on resulted in the arrest of a group of three counterfeiters that operated in Huntsville and Southeastern Tennessee. He had conducted a thorough investigation of their criminal activity and was one of the main witnesses against them in the case pending before the United States Courts in Huntsville.

On that September night, a man crept towards an open door and fired one fatal shot, striking Mayberry in the head. About 8 PM on that Saturday night the guests at the Jackson House heard a loud pop that sounded like a gunshot. As the men rushed towards the direction of the sound they found the lifeless body of the detective lying behind the bar of his saloon. The men examined the body and found seven buckshot in the victim. His skull was fractured and he was probably killed instantly.

There were no clues to implicate anyone and most people thought the murderer just walked away in the darkness. Since it was dark there was no chance of forming a posse to track him. There was no trail to be found after daylight arrived. From all appearances the shot was fired from outside in the dark, still night. Coming through the open back door into the lighted saloon, it was an obvious murder.

After the coroner investigated, he turned the evidence over to the grand jury and they ruled Mayberry had been murdered by a person or persons unknown. The only people that would wish him harm had to be the counterfeiters or someone they had hired to do the job.

The conclusion was drawn that this had to be to prevent the testimony he was scheduled to give. That week he had been making his preparations to remove himself to the courtroom in Huntsville to speak against the three counterfeiters. One week previously his nephew, a Mr. Bolton of Tuscaloosa, had been brutally murdered in that city. He had assisted Mayberry in gathering evidence and arresting the trio. He was to be a witness for the prosecution and they were immediate suspects in his case.

Wallace W. Gordon, a West Point graduate, Henry M. Neil, James R. Neil and Andrew J. Edwards, all of Tennessee, were arrested by officers of the Secret Service in 1875 for dealing in counterfeit money. Indicted for conspiracy by a grand jury in the United States District Court at Huntsville, they were tried in April of 1876 in that same city. The government was represented by Ex-Governor of Alabama Lewis E. Parsons. Seven attorneys formed the defense team and were able to keep their clients from being convicted in this initial trial. Eleven jurors voted to convict and one was a hold-out for acquittal. After this first trial the witnesses started being killed.

The case came up for retrial in April of 1877 and only Henry Neil was convicted. Yet again, the jurors could not agree on a verdict. After this trial more murders followed. Thomas Maxwell was a Huntsville merchant who testified to the fact the men had passed counterfeit bills to him in his store. He was poisoned. A man named Dill was stabbed to death in Tuscaloosa after testifying. Joseph I. Davis, the Mayor of Tuscaloosa, was poisoned within a few weeks of the others. Davis was a former Secret Service officer and had helped arrest the men.

In May of 1977 it was announced that a new kitchen and other renovations had made the Jackson House the model of neatness and convenience. The new kitchen was 50 feet by 22 feet, whitewashed and a convenient distance from the dining hall. New cooking ranges, of finely tempered iron, with all the modern conveniences were installed. The main one was connected by pipes from the well in the courtyard to furnish warm water for the entire hotel. A smaller range was connected to the main one and was to be used to cook vegetables and keep dishes warm. It was estimated that the kitchen could easily cook for 400. These new appliances cost the unheard of price of $500.

In an article from the *Birmingham Iron Age* of May 23, the story continues of the renovations at the Jackson House:

An example of a commercial cook stove of the 1870s
ebay.com

> *The next feature claiming our attention was the new cottages that have been erected within the last few months, adding 20 more rooms to the lodging capacity of the hotel. They are all within a convenient distance of the Jackson House. Another neat, two story cottage is being erected immediately in the rear of the hotel, between Capt. Graves' and Col. Jackson's cottage.*
>
> *The improvement most likely to claim the attention of the invalid perhaps, is the new furnace for heating the sulphur water for the bathhouse. It is built of stone and of ample size to furnish hot water almost continually. It is supplied by a pipe from the red sulphur spring.*
>
> *There is a very fine vegetable garden, run under the auspices of the Jackson House, cultivated by a skillful German gardener, and from its flourishing appearance an abundance of fine vegetables will be served up at the tables.*
>
> *The dining room is now under the stewardship of Mr. O. L. Smith, a nephew of Capt. Towner. He is young in this capacity, but thoroughly understands his business, to which his well kept tables, polite and orderly waiters and the general neatness of the dining hall can fully testify.*
>
> *The office is still under the supervision of Mr. R. T Bugg, chief clerk, and the guests may be sure of excellent treatment at his hands, for he is well acquainted with all the details of the office, and will leave nothing undone that will tend to their comfort and convenience.*

Chapter 12 – Press, Picnics, and Politics

A listing of businesses in Blount Springs in the late 70s to early 1880s included a wide variety of ventures. E. S. Bettus and Company, W. G. Byars, J. E. DuBois, J. M. Foust, Samuel Foust, James Cox, John H. Hamilton, J. G. Harkins, J. J Suydam and Company selling general Merchandise. W. C. Hanlin listed his business as fancy grocer and confectioner, but another grocer was Hester & LeGrand. A Mr. Hood and I. Graves were blacksmiths, while John R. Perkins ran a cotton gin, James Poe was a harness maker, and William P. Turner was a shoemaker. S. H. Estell was a druggist. Dr. John C. Lee was the hotel physician and also had an apothecary in the town.

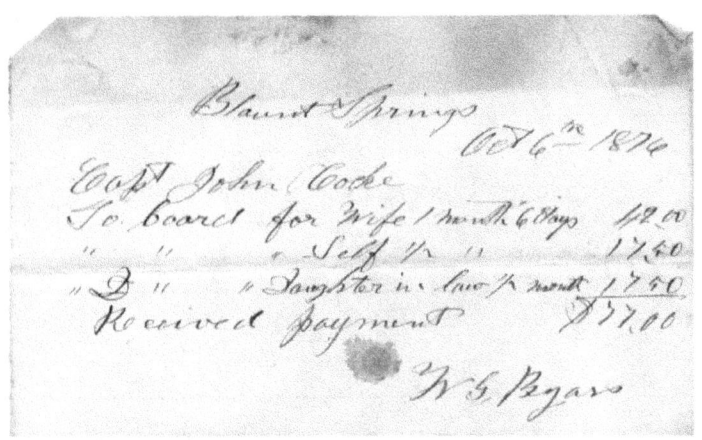

Receipt of Capt. John Cocke from W. S. Byars
The W.S. Hoole Special Collections Library, The University of Alabama

The largest business in town was the Blount Spring Hotel, and there was a smaller hotel owned by C. E Smedes. Jackson also ran horse sales, a livery and feed stable, a saloon and the Jackson Lime Company. His quarry had one of the largest convict labor forces at around 100 in the entire state. He supplied lime to Sloss furnace and was closely associated with their success.

W. G. Byars also ran a hotel for many years along with a livery stable and his general merchandise store. His mother had a boarding house she operated until she was 100 years old. Byars was a lifelong resident of the area, born there March 6, 1826 (he also died in Blount Springs May 16, 1902). His father was Jonas Byars who immigrated to Blount County from the Spartanburg district of South Carolina in 1818.

Reuben Smith ran the livery stable for Col. Jackson
Mrs. Evelyn Howell Sapp

Jonas sent his son to the only school around, a one room log cabin that served the frontier area very well over the years and produced many students that helped build the county of Blount. William grew up on the farm and married Mary Thomas in 1854.

They had eight children, four of whom lived to adulthood and grew to be a minister, a physician, and merchants. William, Jr. went into business with his father in Blount Springs.

W. G. served as Justice of the Peace, Postmaster for Blount Springs and County Commissioner besides running his varied business interests. As early as 1872 there was a strong chapter of the American Bible Society in Blount Springs and Byars served as Treasurer. At one time he even ran the Blount Springs Hotel.

In early September of 1877 Blount Springs hosted the State Agriculture and Industrial Convention of Alabama. Sen. John Tyler Morgan was one of the main sponsors of this meeting and hoped it would bring white workers back to the South. Several prominent men spoke to the gathered interested parties. Among the speakers were Col. George B. Clitherall, C. C. Langdon, and others. The aforementioned men spoke on the idea of increasing fruit production in Alabama. Several representatives of the burgeoning industrial town of Birmingham also spoke on their interests. As a result of a resolution from the conference, Senator Morgan proposed a bill for an appropriation for the improvement of the harbor in Mobile Bay in the Senate. It was the consensus of the convention that this was necessary for the general improvement of both agriculture and industry in Alabama.

Joseph Adrien Nunez
vermilionhistorical.com

Politicians even tried to run for office while attending to their health and pleasure at Blount Springs. On August 10, 1878, an article ran in the *Meridional* (Abbeville, La.) where Frank R. King, an attorney from Abbeville, La. railed against Adrien Nunez, state senator for Vermilion Parish, for giving his vote to the neighboring parish for an appointment of another State Senator in Louisiana. King wanted to make sure that everyone knew he was the man for the job and not Nunez. He said, "I am at these springs at present for my health, but will return to Louisiana by the first of September, and will canvass the district before the election." The September 10th *Meridional* reported he did go home and campaign, but he lost to Nunez who served until 1884. Nunez proved to be virtually unstoppable and served many terms as representative and senator before and after this challenge by King.

Mrs. Reid, in a1932 interview for the *Birmingham News,* told of the popular trend of building cottages in the 1870s. Some of these were built by Col. W. H. Graves, Ellie Matthews, Virginia Gunster, and Col J. W. Sears. On the mountain were the cottages of the Hadens, Ploattenburghs, Hoopers, Harrels and the Tiptons of Selma and Dallas

Chapter 12 – Press, Picnics, and Politics

County, along with the Gid Nelsons of the newly created Hale County. Among the regulars at the hotel were the Thompsons, Davenports, Willoughbys, Porters, Fausts, Livingstons, McAnallys, Bakers, Byars, McPhersons, Rices, Corneliuses, LeGrande, Hamilton and the Whaleys.

The Moores built a home on top of Robinson Mountain. She was the daughter of Dr. Robinson. Others living there were Dr Cora Arthur, Mary Steif and Sarah Brainard of Little Rock, Arkansas.

So often present at the hotel was the family of William Rufus King of Selma. They were stalwarts of Blount Springs and spent a great deal of time there over several decades. King himself was gone. He had been one of the most important politicians of his day, serving as a U.S. Representative from North Carolina, Senator from Alabama, and Minister to France. His greatest political accomplishment was becoming the 13th Vice President of the United States. Unfortunately he only held that post for about six weeks before his death in 1853. His family continued their patronage after his death and continued to be very popular when in attendance.

Vice-President William Rufus King
Alabama Department of Archives and History

Often in the 1840s he would stay at Blount Springs for his health. For years he suffered with breathing problems and finally died from tuberculosis after only 45 days as Vice President. He held the highest political office of any Alabamian in American history.

Other important patrons of the area were the Fitzhugh girls, Lizzie, Fannie and Grace. Their father was a very important man with the railroad and built Glenwood in 1877 for his family to live in while he was on the road as an engineer. They settled there because of his friendship with Col. Jackson and Jackson's commitment to the town.

It stills stands today and was built facing the old stagecoach road. Today most people know the back of it since that is what can be seen from US Hwy 31. Fitzhugh would become the chief engineer for the Louisville & Nashville Railroad in the 1880s.

He traveled all over the Southeastern United States for his company and consulted with other rail companies also. His wife and three daughters remained at home while the captain was away. The family became well known for their house parties. Everyone wanted to be invited to these events.

13

A New Partner and a New Hotel

Jackson had used his temporary hotel for five seasons and a big renovation on that temporary building, but it was not enough. He knew he needed to build a permanent hotel but he didn't have the available cash to do it right. If he could build his dream hotel he knew he would have more guests, make more money, and make his town more prestigious than before. All he needed was an investor, or maybe a partner.

Henry DeBardeleben was the son of farmers in Montgomery County. His father died when he was ten and he eventually found his way to becoming the ward of a family friend. That friend was one of the wealthiest men in Alabama, Daniel Pratt. Pratt owned the largest factory in the state and had a hand in many other business concerns.

After a stint in the Prattville Dragoons during the Civil War, DeBardeleben resigned from the army and eloped with Pratt's daughter Ellen. He ran the family machine shops for a time and then after the war was over he and Pratt rebuilt Oxmoor Furnace and went into the iron business. Pratt died in 1873 and at that point everything came under the control of DeBardeleben. He went on to become one of the founders of the Pratt Coal and Coke Company, with J. W. Sloss. He developed Alice Furnace, naming it after his daughter. Birmingham's growth was directly tied to both of these projects and they made him a very wealthy man. Another of his projects was the founding of the City of Bessemer.

Henry W. DeBardeleben
Public Domain

By 1877 DeBardeleben was well established as a friend of Jackson and a regular at Blount Springs. DeBardeleben loved Blount Springs and wanted to invest in some good money maker. Col. Jackson gave him a very good opportunity to do just that. It was only natural for him to become a partner in helping build the new, improved version of the Jackson House. Putting up the money for the construction seemed like an excellent idea. It seemed an excellent investment and it would be entertaining to have a hand in a place like Blount Springs. Construction began with the hope the new hotel would be ready for the 1878 season.

Chapter 13 – A New Partner and a New Hotel

Exciting events were not exclusive to the hotel construction and also afoot during the summer months was a plot that was very secret. A man was planning to rob one of the payroll trains that regularly came through Blount Springs. The train came from Nashville, paying employees of the Louisville & Nashville and South & North Railroads all along the line. A local man, W. C. Reid of Reid's Gap, was recruited to help in this robbery by a shady character, but Reid had another idea.

Around the 15th of July a man who identified himself as Sherwood asked Reid to help him with his plot. He planned to cause the payroll train to jump the track and then rob it during the ensuing confusion. It didn't bother him if someone was killed when the train wrecked, that was just something that didn't concern him.

Reid listened to the plan, agreeing to be a part of this conspiracy. As soon as he left Sherwood, he went to some of his friends and neighbors telling them about this strange man and his plan. Those friends told him he should act like he was willing to go along with the plot so that he could get more of the details, then do something about it.

He kept his friends advised of what was going on from time to time and the exact plan was finally revealed. Sherwood said he had a gang of ten to fifteen men who would place some kind of obstruction on the tracks in a deserted place between Blount Springs and Reid's Gap. Sherwood would hide near the obstruction and shoot the engineer so that he couldn't stop the train and all aboard would surely be killed in the wreck. During the confusion the others would rob the train, make off with the loot and make their way into the mountains for their getaway.

Heading for Reid's Gap
Miss Irene Reid

Knowing now how the plan was to work, Reid went to Judge Moore of Blountsville and gave him the details. He'd already made the judge aware of Mr. Sherwood and the plot. The judge informed the railroad authorities and Sherwood was arrested. Detectives questioned him and he quickly broke down and told more of his plan.

It seems he was just getting his gang together and the arrest made further organization impossible. He stated that if he'd had enough time to get them together he would've made a "big haul" and gotten away with it. This did not sit well with the railroad men or the people of Blount County.

Sherwood was an alias and the man had Jones tattooed on his arm. He was about 30 years old and it was obvious from scars on his ankles that he'd worn shackles sometime in the past. The man was assumed to be someone who lived by crime and had moved about frequently so that he could get away with this way of life.

Reid's Gap Depot
Miss Irene Reid

Unfortunately he had committed no felonious crime and could only be slightly punished since he'd been stopped before any true mischief was accomplished. Mr. Reid was hailed as a hero in the community and there was much excitement and conversation generated by the events of midsummer.

Every season had its share of balls and dances. Every meal, except breakfast, had the resident band playing for the enjoyment of the guests. Often they played concerts at the spring yard on Sunday afternoons and other times. In 1978 a grand ball was put on for the opening of the season and the opening of the new Jackson House Hotel. That was not the only big dance, such as the Midsummer Hop that occurred at the Jackson House August 15th.

More than 500 were present for this dance which was a grand masked ball. The large ballroom was crowded and even overflowed onto the porches and grounds of the Jackson House. Ladies toilets (outfits) were described as "unsurpassed in variety, beauty and elegance" by the *Columbus Sunday Enquirer*. As always there were many celebrities in attendance.

Gov. Houston   Gov. Cobb   Gen. Walker   Hon. H. A. Herbert

Alabama Department of Archives and History, Montgomery, Alabama

Among other important persons at the ball were Gov. Houston, Governor-elect Cobb, Gen. Pope Walker, former Secretary of War for the Confederacy, and the Hon. H. A. Herbert, Congressman and Chairman of the Committee on Naval Affairs and United States Ambassador. There were very few dull moments at Blount Springs!

Business suffered greatly as another scare of fever occurred after several children died in Blount Springs. Immediately Montgomery's Mayor and Board of Health declared a quarantine against the town without any real evidence. This action hurt business dramatically. Soon it was learned the problem came from elsewhere and the ban lifted.

Many important people made appearances at the Springs for their health throughout the years. Josiah Gorgas had been the President of the University of the South at Sewanee, Georgia until July of 1878. While he struggled to keep the school financially afloat, his health failed, and the trustees blamed him for the school's difficulties. He resigned and came back home to Alabama.

In August of 1878 he came to Blount to seek relief from a chronic pain he felt in his left side. His family was so affected by his troubles that he came to Blount alone, stating, "I can bear it better in solitude." While he was at Blount getting better he was elected president of the University of Alabama.

Josiah Gorgas
Public Domain

In September he moved into the President's Mansion on campus. A few months later his family joined him. His wife was the former Amelia Gayle, daughter of Gov. Gayle. She was a well known belle in Tuscaloosa when her father was governor and the capital was in the Druid City. Throughout Alabama she was popular and Gorgas was well-known for his role as Chief of Ordnance for the Confederacy.

Gorgas started his new job with a will to improve the school and continue its recovery from the war. Unfortunately he suffered a massive stroke on February 23, 1879 and never fully recovered. He resigned as president in July and the trustees created the post of University Librarian expressly for him. The house they were living in was given to the family and still is called the Gorgas House. The main library of the University is located on the northern edge of the Quadrangle and is named the Amelia Gayle Gorgas Library.

Although people came to Blount for their health, sometimes they left in a very unhealthy state. One case in point was Captain Charles B. Church of Memphis. Church died from a stroke in 1879 while visiting Blount, mostly for relaxation.

Church was born in Ohio and showed quite a knack for machinery and engineering. As a young boy he took to the water and started working in the engine room on steamboats plying the Tennessee, Mississippi, and Ohio Rivers. Quickly moving up the ladder of command he was given his own boat at an early age. Before many more years he was able to buy interest in the boat he captained and eventually achieved complete ownership.

Captain Charles B. Church
historic-memphis.com

In 1839 Capt. Church had a son with Emmeline, a mixed-race slave he owned. According to family accounts, Emmeline was the daughter of a white planter from Lynchburg, Virginia and a "Malay" Malagasy princess. The child was named Robert.

When he was older, Church took him aboard his steamboat to serve as his cabin boy.

Chapter 13 – A New Partner and a New Hotel

Wreck of the Bulletin #2
Public Domain

This proved to be a good resolution for both Robert and his father and they served together for many years. In 1855, on a trip downriver on the *Bulletin #2*, they encountered tragedy. On the way to New Orleans somehow the steamboat caught fire near Vicksburg and sank. The Captain acted coolly under pressure and saved many lives, including his son and some very influential men from Memphis.

Church continued to command steamboats and started buying more boats for others to captain. He started amassing more capital, but then talk of war with the North began in earnest. Life went on as normal until fighting began. At this point, Church quit the river and began buying property in Memphis.

Robert had proven himself and worked on other boats. He was finally captured by the Yankees while serving as a steward on the steamer Victoria .and he became a fugitive slave behind the lines. A little later he became a freedman and returned to Memphis during the occupation, staying after the end of the war.

He had also worked hard, saved his money and used those savings to invest in a saloon on DeSoto Street in the Black business area of town. With his success there he continued to open new businesses including a hotel. This venture became the only first class hotel in Memphis for blacks and did a phenomenal business. Through hard work and shrewd business deals he turned his investments into a fortune and became a wealthy man.

Robert Reed Church, Sr
historic-memphis.com

Before long he decided more money was to be made in recreation for blacks and he opened Church's Park and Auditorium. Valued at $100,000 and seating 2,000 people, it became the cultural center of the region for African-Americans. William C. Handy, known later as the Father of the Blues, was the leader of the house orchestra and all the big acts of the day played there.

Along with several other men, he helped found the Solvent Savings Bank and Trust Company. This was the first black bank in Memphis since the collapse of the Freedman's Savings and Trust Company Bank 1874. This bank went a long way in improving lives and financial stability of not only Blacks in Memphis and the countryside, but the City of Memphis itself. Some maintain that he was the first Black millionaire in the South.

Church's Park and Auditorium located on what is now Beale Street Park
historic-memphis.com

After Church's death in 1912 his family carried on his legacy. His wife and children worked diligently for civil rights. The auditorium was torn down and the property became part of the Beale Street Historic District. Robert Reed Church is still revered by the citizens in the city by the mighty Mississippi.

Nathan Bedford Forrest
Public Domain

Memphis was one of the cities targeted by S. D. Holt, manager of the Blount Springs Hotel, to bring in more guests. Col. Jackson still owned the property but he would lease it to others and stay out of the day to day operations. Holt visited the city regularly to encourage travel to his hotel and also hired agents there to help in making it easier for guests to make their arrangements. A local attorney, J. P. Houston, was one of those men. Also working with him was Col. Sam Tate. Not only was he an attorney, but he was president of the Charleston and Memphis Railroad, a major player in Memphis and also the line that connected to the South and North Alabama Railroad taking people to Blount Springs.

Col. Tate was a very popular man in Memphis and it didn't hurt Blount Springs' reputation to be associated with him as one of its agents. He was called Colonel because of his wartime service with the Confederate Army. After the war he was able to get control of the Memphis and Charleston Railroad away from the United States Government and put many Southerners back to work and helped the area rebuild.

Chapter 13 – A New Partner and a New Hotel

By associating himself with Nathan Bedford Forrest and because of his own reputation, he wielded a great deal of influence in Memphis and the surrounding countryside. S. D. Holt also associated himself with Tate and many of the elite of the city spent their leisure time in Blount Springs as a result. Somehow it was arranged (could it have been the M & C RR President?) for the Memphis to Decatur train to arrive just in time to coordinate with the South and North train's departure time, insuring no layover in Decatur. Previously there had been up to a 14 hour layover at the Alabama city. This made it almost an express ride to Blount Springs from Memphis.

Blount Springs, ALABAMA.

SEASON OF 1879! NOW OPEN FOR VISITORS! Special arrangements for board at reduced rates will be made with parties wishing to come early. High in the mountains of north Alabama; entirely free from all malarial influences. Best mineral waters on the continent. All chronic diseases successfully treated. Dyspepsia a specialty. The most accessible resort in the south. Less than ten hours from Memphis; one change of cars, at Decatur.
Refer to Colonel Sam Tate, Memphis; J. P. Houston, 89 Madison street, Memphis.
For further particulars, address
S. D. HOLT, Proprietor.

Memphis Daily Appeal, April 26, 1879

Weekly ads appeared in the Memphis Daily Appeal extolling Blount as the place to be and making it an appealing place to travel and stay. In May of that year it was annouced that a popular member of the Peabody staff was now ensconsed at the Jackson House. The Peabody was one of the most elegant and grand hotels in the South. This was no small indication of the quality and service of the accomodations available at the watering hole and was not lost on the targeted clientele of Southwest Tennessee.

Blount Springs.

The waters of Blount Springs, Alabama, have gained a wide reputation for the many wonderful cures they have effected, and the wonder is that more of our citizens do not go there instead of going so far from home. It is very accesible, with a delightfully pure and bracing mountain atmosphere and the best of mineral waters. They are said to be specific for dyspepsia and rheumatism. We learn that round-trip tickets to Blount Springs are only about fourteen dollars and fifty cents.

Memphis Daily Appeal, June 04, 1879

Ho! for Blount Springs, Ala.

The Memphis and Charleston railroad now makes close connection at Decatur with the south-bound trains on the Louisville and Nashville and Great Southern railroad, landing you at Blount without delay. Many of our citizens who thought of going there hesitated because of a lay over of fourteen hours at Decatur, and they will be pleased to learn of this favorable change. Mr. E. C. Bannon, late of the Peabody hotel, and well known in Memphis, is now at Blount and will be glad to welcome any of his friends at the New Jackson house.

Memphis Daily Appeal, May 27, 1879

Several different ads appeared regularly in the Memphis papers in the spring, summer and early fall of 1879. Apparently things did not go as Mr. Holt hoped because he left the hotel after this season to go into the mercantile business in the little town of Verbena, Alabama. Jackson took over the reins of the establishment himself and hired a Mr. Derby as chief clerk for the next season.

As the decade came to a close Mr. D. P. West was the agent for a new concern, the

Blount Springs Natural Sulphur Water Bottling Company. Now you could take the curative water with you and have it available at home.

Young boys boarded the trains at Warrior and Hanceville and sell the water to travelers that may not have had the time or inclination to stop and enjoy the accommodations. It was also shipped to many towns in Alabama and Tennessee. The bottling plant produced both pint and quart bottles. Many families carried a few bottles with them to keep them well after they returned home.

D. P. West presented clients with different cards for different maladies. His water cured anything that ailed you!
Blount Springs Alabama History Facebook Page

The distinctive blue bottles were colored to preserve the healing powers of the red sulphur water. West advertised the powers of the water to cure *"skin diseases, sore eyes, gout, pimples, blotches and ulcers of every description, restoring lost appetites and for paralysis, the water has no equal on the continent."* He further stated that *"Nature, the Great Physician, never intended the sulphur water to be sold on draught. It has to be natural, to be effective."* Quote from *Historic Alabama Hotels and Resorts*

A letter to Col. Jackson offered an explanation for the demise of the Blount Springs Natural Sulphur Water Bottling Company that said, *"I received my sulphur water today and it was in a most stinking and piltrid condition."* Letter reprinted in *The Birmingham News* April, 3, 1958

The Blount Springs Natural Sulphur Water Bottling Company Trademark
American Bottle Auctions

14

The Great Southern Cave

No visit to Blount Springs was complete without a visit to the Great Southern Cave. The Chambliss family operated this attraction for many years. The property remained in the family until recent times.

A reporter for the *Gallatin Examiner* (Tennessee) came to the Tennessee Press Association meeting and filed this report about The Great Southern Cave:

> *Your correspondent, in company with a number of the guests of the hotel, including a fair sprinkling of ladies, yesterday visited "The Great Southern Cave", which is said to rival in the beauty and grandeur of its stalactite formations; the wonderful Mammoth Cave of Kentucky. It is located only 4 miles distant from the Springs, directly on the line of the railroad, and the short ride to it is rendered more pleasant and interesting by some of the most beautiful mountain scenery in the state. The cave is about a half mile in length, and contains 4 separate apartments, viz: "Concert Hall", the "Sounding Room", the "Formation Room", and "Terminus Hall". Concert Hall is arranged for dancers and concerts, which are frequently held in the cavernous depths of the cave. It can be brilliantly lighted, and was at the time our party visited the cave. We yesterday had the pleasure of witnessing a performance by the Decatur Dramatic Troupe in the subterranean hall. "The Path of Humiliation and the Narrow Way" is the name given to the only low, narrow passage in the cave, and through which only one person can pass at a time and then is a stooping position. The titles given to the other attractions in this wonderful little care are "Dona's Pyramid", "Iceburg Hill", Pillar of Plumes", "Scribe's Gallery", Pillar of Herousies", "Cathedral Pulpit", and "Pillar of Clouds". Almost everyone who goes to Blount visits "The Great Southern Cave" and rarely fails to return more than satisfied. There are, also, several smaller, but none the less attractive caves in the neighborhood.*

Blount Springs and the Great Southern Cave were happy places and this trip left such a favorable impression on the Tennessee Press. More excellent advertising came of this as the reporters spoke well of it through many articles in the future. More guests came to know the resort and started coming from Pulaski, Nashville, and other Tennessee cities and countryside homes. A souvenir token was presented to all those brave enough to hazard the trip to view the many strange and beautiful formations found within.

Souvenir Token
Blount County Museum

Near the cave were three springs of freestone and chalybeate waters, plus more natural wonders for all to enjoy. Many of the citizens of the county enjoyed the picnic grounds for church socials, picnics and family reunions. There were walking trails through the beautiful mountainsides and it was all very convenient by wagon or a short train ride from Blount Springs. The South & North Alabama added a spur that came right to the entrance of the park for their passengers to be able to gain easy access.

The park had a place for speakers, mostly political, to extol their ideas and plans they would enact if elected by the fair citizens of Blount County and the State of Alabama. Many of the South's greatest orators spoke there or at Blount Springs during their many years of operation.

Sen. John Hollis Bankhead   Sen. Oscar W. Underwood   Gov. Thomas Goode Jones   Rufus N. Rhodes
Alabama Department of Archives and History, Montgomery, Alabama

Many politicians spoke on the grounds of the Great Southern Cave. Just a few include: Governors Jelks, Brown, Seay and more, Senators John Tyler Morgan, Oscar Underwood and B. B. Comer. William Jennings Bryan spoke at Blount Springs during a tour of the South and even Teddy Roosevelt visited in the early part of the 20th Century.

The Blount County News and Dispatch in 1896 reprinted this article that came from the Decatur Advertiser giving a thorough picture of the cave and grounds:

Chapter 14 – The Great Southern Cave

Here in this quiet nook in Blount county, half a mile from Bangor and thirty-six miles north of Birmingham, on the east side of the Louisville & Nashville track, is situated one of the most picturesque and lovely spots in the South, if not in the whole country, connected with which is one of those grand and stupendous works of nature which when once seen is ever after present to the memory.

The climate is pleasant, the heat of the summer sun being tempered by the cool breezes blowing through the mountain forests. The winters are mild; from the hillsides about there gushes numerous bold springs of delicious water which runs over rocky beds to form some of the many mountain streams that abound here about. The people who reside in the vicinity of Bangor are such people as you would expect to find in such a place. They are rugged, healthy, hard working men and women, boys and girls. They show the effects of breathing the pure fresh air of the mountain home in their ruddy faces; while their wiry frames, large hands and brawny limbs show that they and toil are not strangers.

It is not on its fruitful valleys, its many mountain streams, its towering mountains, or its hardy, happy, laboring people that the country about Bangor rests its claim to the attention of the people of this State. Such conditions, qualities and people are found in many other localities in Alabama. Just north of the station there stands a spur of Sand Mountain, rearing its rock-crowned head high in the air.

You follow a rocky and indistinct road from the station, around the foot of this spur until it brings you to a beautiful grove surrounded by a whitewashed fence, and which is used now as a picnic ground. On the mountain side facing this grove an opening between massive boulders, which leads into a cavern, or rather a series of caverns, for there are five chambers extending into the heart of the mountain for a distance of about one half mile, which form what is known locally as the Great Southern Cave, and is probably the most extensive known subterranean cavity south of Kentucky's wonder. The cave was visited in company with a gentleman from Montgomery. We called at the house of Mr. James H. Chamblee, the owner of the property on which the cave is situated, and his son, Mr. Tillman Chamblee, a representative young man of this section, became our guide. The cave is entered through an aperture about three feet wide by six feet high, which was found closed by a roughly constructed gate, fastened with a padlock and chain. The entrance sloped downward until, , when the floor of the first chamber was reached, we were about six feet below the level of the point of entry. At this place Mr. Chamblee provided himself with material for a light from a large pile of split pine, and with a flaming pine torch in hand, he led the way through the first chamber, which is about thirty feet long, closing at the further end to an opening about six or eight feet wide, which is the entrance to the second chamber.

The ceiling of the first room is about twenty feet above the floor and is almost a well defined arch in shape, falling gradually to the floor at either side. The second chamber is probably a little larger than the first and except that the ceiling is higher above head and its arch more symmetrical presents no new feature until the point of entering the third cavern is reached. Here the walls of the cave come within three or four feet of each other bearing a narrow but high passway.

The face of one side of this passage attracts attention because it appears to be a series of massive scalloped or shell shaped stones piled one on top of another until the ceiling is reached. This formation was called by the guide, "Pompey's Pillar," and a littler further on in the passage there is a large opening in one of the walls, in which hang numerous stalactites; this opening is called "the Piano"—probably because it bears no resemblance in the world to that instrument. It would be a stretch of imagination to think that the pendant stalactites resembled the pipes of an organ, but it would be more reasonable to call this point "the organ," than the name it now bears.

The third chamber is a little smaller than the first, nor is the ceiling quite so high. To the right, entering, the ceiling slopes away close to the floor for some distance and the guide says that a dark hole, which can be indistinctly seen, is the entrance to an adjoining and unexplored cave. In the pathway, before the entrance to the fourth room is reached, there stands a rock round in form, about two and a half feet in height and 18 inches in diameter. This is known as the growing rock, and down its body are well defined indentions or rings, showing its height at different periods of its upward growth. The top of this rock is something like the upper portionof a pear and by many is called the "Pear Rock." In the center there is an indentation like that in an apple from which the stem protrudes.

This spot is the point where a falling drop of water strikes the rock and this drop, which gathers in its percolation, through the stone forming the ceiling, minute particles of that stone will, in time, cause this growing stone to be a pillar reaching to the ceiling of the cave. Further on the ceiling lowers and the floor ascends, making the entrance to the fourth chamber so low that you have to stoop almost double in traversing the eight or ten feet dividing the two compartments.

The fourth chamber, which is the largest, is entered by descending a flight of ten or twelve steps cut in the solid (rock). Out of this, natural and easy steps lead the visitor through a low, arched passage, called the "Fat Man's Misery," to Ambassador's Hall. In this magnifcently vaulted chamber are many objects that would delight the heart of the most ardent devotee of paleontology. Here is a Sphinx, with turbaned head, overarched by a canopy of rare tracery and beautiful design. In this hall is Solomon's Temple, a magnificent natural structure, that looks as if designed and wrought by the brain and hand of man.

Passing many curious objects, the Dragon's Chamber is reached by a temporary wooden bridge over a narrow chasm which leads from what appears to be the bed of an extinct lake. Projecting from the roof of this chamber, with most of the body well exposed, is a fossil dragon of immense proportions. A portion of the head, where the jaws were situated is broken off. The balance of the monster is well preserved, even to the wings, flippers, or whatever they might be called, and which gave it propulsive power in the water, or air, or land, wherever its home may have been in the dim and distant Paleozoic age in which it lived and moved and had its being. About fifteen feet in length and six feet in depth of body of this strange and wonderful monster is exposed to view. An examination of this one object alone would create a sensation in Smithsonian circles.

Farther on in this chamber, amid a mass of curious and gigantic objects, is a mammoth and almost perfect elephant in stone. Beyond this is the Boudoir. a small chamber arched over with a ceiling of the most delicate penciling and tracery of pure white. which. resting against the wall at one end, springs in a most graceful curve resting the other end on the opposite wall.

The next chamber is called the Serpents' Den, but timid ladies need not fear to enter as the serpents have been stone for many eons of ages. and lie in a group as quiet and peaceable as possible. On the left side of the chamber, attached to the wall only two or three feet from the floor, is the Condor, an almost perfect gigantic bird, one wing lifted exposing the inner side of that member, while the other wing is stretched downward showing the outside. The head and great beak are perfect except where some vandal broke a small piece from the latter. At the further end of this chamber is an almost perfect Camel, showing head bowed on breast, hump, hip, and side. Beyond the Camel is the post office, showing windows, letter boxes and some fine designs in architecture in the walls and lower structure.

Further on is Sangre de Christo Park, showing that famous mountain range, snow-capped and glittering, to the right. On the left against the wall is the dejected Eagle, with head on breast and wings folded, as if his enforced imprisonment in this subterranean abode had broken the spirit of the proud and lordly bird. At the end of this chamber a pile of debris reaching to the roof bars farther advance. It looks much as if it had been blasted down by the hand of man, and there is an unauthenticated legend that this cave was once the home and haunt of a desperate band of robbers, who, being closely pressed by a body of Creek Indians, then occupying the country, hid their ill gotten booty and barred an entrance to its hiding place by closing the entrance with debris and then fled the country. The park and cave is in charge of Mr. Dilmos L. Duncan, who lives on the place with his family, and who takes great pleasure in showing visitors through the beautiful grounds and wonder cave. When excursions visit the place in summer, visitors are taken to the gates, but if an individual or small party wishes to visit this wonderful place the nearest station is Bangor, one half mile distant, which is also the post office address of Mr. Duncan.

Many people left an autograph in the cave for later generations to see who had come before them. Some used charcoal, others pencils and many used the smoke from their pine knots to paint their name in smoke. Unfortunately most of those are gone now, covered in graffiti and defaced by reckless and irresponsible people on the walls of this privately owned cavern.

In 1937 a new twist was given to the cave when several investors ran a totally different enterprise called the Bangor Café Club. This oft raided club offered a very interested public dinner, dancing, drinks, and dice as there was a casino and bar available. In two short years of operation, it is said they made over $2,000,000 from a $75,000 investment. It is truly phenomenal because they spent the majority of their time closed due to raids.

A concrete floor covered in linoleum was put in along with an elaborate system to keep water from dripping on the heads of patrons. Pine knots were replaced by lighting that showed off the formations and made dining and dancing such a pleasure. Acts from Atlanta and Chicago performed for the large crowds that appeared for drinks and gambling, even though both were illegal in Blount County.

The Bangor Cafe Club just before its opening in 1937
Dr. Rebecca Reeves

15

The Golden Age

Some might consider the 1880s as the Golden Age for Blount Springs. Col. Jackson did a great job of promoting and improving the Springs in the 70s and their popularity was exploding by the time the 80s came along. Many improvements were made and the newly founded Birmingham supplied clientele that swelled the ranks of patrons at the hotels.

BLOUNT SPRINGS, ALABAMA

How to use the waters, and their effects on the system.

Preserve this for future reference

The Great Southern Health and Pleasure Resort

THE WATERS OF BLOUNT SPRINGS,

AND THEIR

APPLICABILITY TO DISEASES,

AS SHOWN BY THEIR ANALYSIS.

1st. SULPHURIC ACID.
Diluted Sulphuric Acid is tonic, refrigerant and astringent. It is given in typhoid and other low fevers, and especially in the convalescent stage. It is employed in calliquative sweats, passive hemorrhages, diarrheas, in gargles for ulcerations of the throat, ptyalism, and as a wash for cutaneous eruptions and ill-conditioned ulcers.

2d. PHOSPHORIC ACID, DILUTED.
Is tonic and refrigerant, and has a direct effect upon the nervous system and is called into frequent use where there is a lethargy or prostration of *nerve* power.

5th. BROMINE
Is an alterative and stimulant to the lymphatic system. It has been employed in bronchocele, scrofulous tumors and ulcers, secondary and tertiary syphilis, arsenarrhae, chronic diseases of the skin, and hypertrophy of the ventricles. It is recommended in cases where iodine has lost its effect by long use.

6th. IODINE.
It operates as a general excitant of the vital actions; especially of the absorbents and glandular systems. Its effects are varied by its degree of concentration, and hence it may prove corrosive, irritant, desicant, tonic, diuretic, diphoretic and emmenagogue.

8th. MAGNESIA
Is antacid and laxative, and is valuable in dyspepsia, sick headache, gout, and other complaints attended with sour stomach and constipation. It is also a favorite remedy in the summer complaints of children, where the prima vie is implicated.

10th. IRON
Is a tonic, and enters into hundreds of compounds, and in fact all, *where there is a demand for new blood, as* in cases of broken down constitutions from almost any cause.

13th. POTASSIUM.
This medicine enters into many of our most popular *remedies*, and used as alteratives, diuretic and diphoretic.

14th. LITHIUM
Has a direct *solvent power over* uric *acid*, hence is used in gout and rheumatism. Where there is a tendency to deposits in the joints of uremic acid it is a fine diuretic and solvent.

From A *Guide to Blount Springs*
Tuscaloosa Magazine

Over the next ten years Birmingham would grow at a magical rate: from 3,086 in 1880 to 26,178 by 1890. This rapid growth was the origin of the famous nickname, the Magic City. Why wouldn't those hard working industrialists want to get away from the rigors of the growing city? The beauty of the area was unsurpassed and the climate was so tantalizing. To those that lived in the malaria infested Black Belt, or bound by the close-quarters of the newly founded and congested Magic City, this beauty had to be visited and enjoyed. Being in a mountainous region meant cooler, dryer temperatures for day and night as compared to the damp and hot Black Belt. Also plantation life was comparatively lonely, dull, and isolated, but at Blount the social scene was extraordinary and exciting.

A Guide to Blount Springs was published in 1880 so everyone knew exactly how to use the various waters for their greatest benefit. They would especially want to go to a place as it was described in this booklet to help them ease the pains and cares of life. The natural beauty of Blount County is described in *A Guide to Blount Springs*:

> *The atmosphere is dry, pure and highly electric, and its invigoration effects are peculiarly grateful to persons having weak or diseased lungs, and to all who are suffering in any way from the influences of a miasmatic district, or the damp chilling winds common to the sea coast. Its hills and valleys washed by numerous streams of the clearest and purest water, such a thing as swamps and malaria are unknown; while the mitigating air of the more southerly part of the State, mingling with that of the mountains, softens the otherwise harsh winds that are too often the disagreeable features of a mountain residence; with a mean annual temperature of 50 degrees, neither the heat of summer nor the cold of winter is felt with the severity of Northern(sic) or Southern climes; while the seasons melt into each other with all the soft enchantment of day drifting into twilight.*

Each spring was noted as to its chemical makeup and recommendations were given as to the best use of each type of water. *The Guide* also specified which maladies each different spring would cure or lessen. In addition to the curative properties to be found in the waters, and they were proven to be of a wide variety, there were many amusements for the patient and the members of their family. The booklet tells more:

> *A first-class Band of Music, and a large Ball Room for dancing every night; Billiard Rooms, Shooting Galleries and Ten-pin Alleys; a good Livery Stable; Daily Excursions to the Mountains; Hunting, Fishing, &c.*

Advertising had always been a vital part of the operation and advancement of the hotels and boarding houses at the healing springs. A doctor was on staff to aid the visitors in deciding a course to follow while they took the cure. There were many different problems the springs were purported to cure. The cures increased the pleasure of those in attendance and still gave many a reason to visit.

At one time during this period, there were up to eight different hotels operating in the town. The largest was always the Jackson House, still owned by Jackson but operated by a variety of managers and others that leased it over the years. For several years J. D. Towner was the man who ran the enterprise. He also was in charge of the Huntsville Hotel at the same time, but on September 9th he died from heart disease while at Blount Springs. Jackson had to take the reins again until he found someone to fill Towner's shoes.

People filled the rooms and many more private cottages sprang up all around the hotel in the valley, on the hills and in mountains. During the season the population would often reach 3,000 and sometimes it even swelled to nearly 5,000 people.

Birmingham's growth figured more and more into the prosperity of the resort. Jackson also joined his partner, DeBardeleben, in buying some properties in Birmingham. He had his eyes set on some property he thought would do well for mining. DeBardeleben sold his interest in the hotel to Jackson and used the money from his share of the hotel business to start production in the Pratt Mines.

Towner managed both hotels
Memphis Daily Appeal., June 01, 1880

This investment proved to be one of the wisest he ever made. The Pratt Mines was one of the most important pieces of making Birmingham the "Pittsburg of the South." DeBardeleben went on to open the Alice Furnace and invest more and more in coal and iron.

Jackson's several new business ventures, included opening a quarry in Blount Springs, supplying limestone to the burgeoning iron and steel industry. Limestone was used as slag that separated the impurities from iron ore and was the third element needed for its production. The other two, iron ore and coke (made from coal), were also abundant in and near Birmingham.

The quarry operated by Col. Jackson was on the northeast side of Duffee's Mountain just above the town. Almost all the workers were leased convicts and there were some dramatic escapes, or at least attempted escapes. Many times the sound of bloodhounds could be heard in the valley as they followed the trail of men trying to get away from the oppressive conditions of the quarry and the convict lease system.

The *Atlanta Constitution* of October 19, 1886 offers the following account of the escape attempt of James Handley. Handley was about to finish a 60 day sentence from Walker County. On its surface it seems foolish to escape when his 60 days were almost up, but he was to be turned over to Jefferson County to face charges of horse stealing after he finished the first sentence.

> *He was working on the top of the limestone quarry, which is one thousand feet perpendicular at one point. The rock stands out a few feet, enough to hide a man from view, which he slipped behind and crawled on his all fours the distance of two hundred feet by his hands and teeth, holding to slender bushes. He was compelled to suspend himself in the air several times to climb up successfully, and at one time he held on by his teeth to a small sapling, because his hands were so blistered. When he reached the top he was exhausted and laid down to rest. He was awakened by the yelp of the blood hounds who were looking for his trail, which they had found but could not follow up the steep limestone cliff.*

An unknown quarry in Alabama
Alabama Department of Archives and History, Montgomery, Alabama

He had gotten about 12 miles from the place of his imprisonment and was on the cliff of Jack Blanket's mountain when he saw two men, James Hanley and William King, on horseback about three miles away. They saw him too and with the six dogs they had with them, he was finally tracked down on the other side of the mountain.

Convict labor is one of the factors that helped many men in Alabama become rich quickly at the sacrifice of many lives. It was used extensively by Col. Jackson and many other industrialists of Birmingham. Mines and quarries were the main places this modern form of slavery existed, but farming also used this type of labor. Jackson also used it on his farm.

Blount Springs had some bad and good things happen at this time too. In the year 1880 much talk was given to Blount Springs becoming a terminal for the Georgia Western Railroad. There was a proposed route from Atlanta directly to Blount Springs. The idea was to link halfway between Decatur and Birmingham. This would create much new trade in goods available to the different towns and hamlets along the line, provide new markets for Georgia and Atlanta concerns, and also give more access to the rich mineral deposits of Central Alabama to more than just Birmingham.

This was the brainchild of some of those involved in running the L & N Railroad that would make them even more money and give them greater control of the market. A preliminary survey of where the line could run was completed by Captain A. W. Gloster. It was estimated it would cost $2,000,000 less than a proposed route directly to Decatur and only be eight miles longer. Another added allure would be the ability to be closer to Birmingham's rails and additionally the Montevallo and Selma lines. It came very close to reality but in the end nothing ever became of this grandiose plan, although it kept the press busy and provided much to talk about in various smoke filled rooms and hotel lobbies.

On August 6th the *Sunny South* reported there were 225 guests at the Jackson House. This was the most visitors ever recorded at the hotel up to this time. Jackson hosted a Grand Fancy Dress Ball for his guests and friends a couple of weeks later. There was a new manager at this time, a Mr. Sherman, and he was did everything he could to make this ball a success. By the next year a change in management would take place.

Judge John Dennis Phelan
Alabama Department
of Archives and History,
Montgomery, Alabama

The *Huntsville Weekly Democrat* reported on May 10, 1882 that Mr. Robert L. Watt, formerly of the Exchange Hotel in Montgomery and the Stanton House of Chattanooga, was taking charge of the Jackson House. His wife, Mary Phelan Watt, served as hostess and came from significant Blount Springs stock. She was the daughter of Judge John Dennis Phelan of Montgomery. The Phelans had been regulars at the resort for many years and were quite prominent there and in the Black Belt where they lived. Because of the political career of the Judge, they also were well known in Montgomery.

Judge Phelan was very prominent in Alabama politics, serving as Supreme Court Justice, Attorney General, member of the Alabama legislature, lawyer and professor at

Sewanee. He held the Bible at the swearing in of Jefferson Davis and worked in the Alabama Government throughout the war. Afterwards he was disqualified for governmental service by the carpetbag rulers of the state. Mrs. Phelan was one of the charter members and first vice-president of the Ladies Memorial Association of Montgomery, organized in April, 1866. This group was partly responsible for the beginnings of Confederate Memorial Day and it later becoming a ritual of the South.

Mary Phelan had been one of the queens of the social life of the resort. She was a trend setter and one of the premier belles of Blount Springs and the Black Belt. Her family was quite large with 5 siblings. Three of her brothers served in the war and two of them died for their country. Robert served in the Confederate Army and lost an arm for the Cause. He had worked with Sidney Lanier in the famed Exchange Hotel of Montgomery.

The Exchange Hotel from a Montgomery promotional booklet

The Exchange Hotel was the pride of Montgomery for many years. It was constructed about the time the capital moved to the city in 1847 and served as the de facto capitol when the original capitol on Goat Hill burned. The Legislature met in the ballroom and much business was and has always been conducted in the lobby and public rooms of the edifice. Jefferson Davis lived in the hotel until a suitable home was found for him and his family and he started his walk to the capitol for his inauguration from there. In a speech from the balcony of the Exchange Hotel William Lowdes Yancy pronounced the importance of the moment when he said, "The man and hour have met".

Watt immediately began work on the property to make it more in line with the hotels he had previously managed. Service would again be the hallmark of the Jackson House, as his reputation was that only the best would do for his guests. In July of that year there were 275 guests at the Jackson House, passing the previous high mark. In time more accommodations would be needed as the hotel kept housing more and more guests.

Some of the fun of Blount Springs can be seen in this letter to the editor of the *Blount County News and Dispatch* from Thursday, May 18, 1882:

> Blount Springs, Alabama, the Saratoga of the Sunny South.
>
> *Mr. Editor*

As one who has been so true to the progress and prosperity of this fine old County of Blount, I feel assured you take pride and deep interest in Blount Springs whose reputation has made Blount County so famous and, I believe you would rejoice to see that fame increased tenfold; nay, one hundred fold. Owing to the luxuriant forest growth immediately surrounding, the Spring is always enchantingly beautiful here, but now that art combines with nature, we are doubly blessed; and never before has the picturesque location, and scenic attractions appeared to better advantage. Much and unwearied labor has been spent upon the streets and drives and they have been set off to marked advantage; the stately hotel buildings and many handsome cottages, all add to the beauty, health and comfort of the place. The prospects for a large crowd are unusually good, and, under the administration of Capt. Robt. Watts of Montgomery, Ala., many who have not visited Blount Springs for years, and others who have never been here, will meet and mingle under the shadows of the grand old beech, and drink from nature's founts of healing and refreshment. Mr. Watt long since won for himself, the reputation of being the most popular and successful hotel proprietor in the State, and to these honors he has added those won in his control of the elegant Stanton House, Chattanooga, Tennessee. Courteous and manly the humblest and poorest will find equal attention with the most favored children of fortune, and the citizens will see him one whose liberal dealings will remind them of happier and better days. His wife is a daughter of the late Hon. Jno. D. Phelan, so well known and esteemed in all parts of this State, and who spent many summers in these grand, old hills. Col. Jackson is doing all in his power to develop and build up the place: at present trade is dull, but with the opening of the season, all will brighten up. Our Debating Society is in a flourishing condition and our school, under the accomplished guidance of Prof. Lovett, is doing finely. At the late municipal election here, a large, and almost unanimous vote conferred

BLOUNT SPRINGS HIGH SCHOOL.

The next session of this school commences on

MONDAY, OCTOBER 6, 1884,

and continues nine months.

Thorough and correct instructions given in all the ordinary branches of an English education, and in the

Latin and Greek Languages.

Tuition and Board (including light, fuel and washing), at from **$12 to $15 per Month.**
The finest Sulphur Water in the South free of charge to students.
For further information or circulars, address,

W. D. LOVETT, Principal,
aug17,sun&wkly-3ms   Blount Springs, Ala.

September 4, 1884
Weekly Iron Age

the responsibilities of Mayor on Mr. W.C. Hanlin, and though in office but a limited time, he has effected marked improvement greatly needed, being fortunate enough to have the indefatigable Mr. George LeGrand on the Street Committee, we can now see the result. Perhaps it is only an act of justice to our Mayor to refer to him as a representative man of the particular class every Southern community needs and welcomes; for coming here a stranger, he has by consistent devotion to his duties. worked his way up, to a very high standard of esteem and good will. As a business man he is a success, and deservedly popular; as a Christian gentleman, foremost in every effort to sustain the morality of the people: as a citizen, prompt and untiring in the performance of duty; knowing his modesty, you will readily know that the office had to seek him; firm in opinion, he has maintained his integrity; and the friends who have voted him into office expect from him a wise and beneficent administration. Personally his appearance is aldermanic, and he is a warm friend of the News. (Another evidence of good sense, properly applied. Passing up Depot Street, you will hardly recognize in an exceedingly neat building, so much changed by paint and other improvements, a thrifty business stand, and likewise the residence of Mr. and Mrs. Cox. The latter the popular industrious and well known "Miss Martha" of the Jackson House, who well remembers you; and when you visit the Springs you must call and get a genuine welcome from her and her liege lord. Then you won't have far to go ere you halt before the handsome establishment of that incorrigible bachelor, Mr. J. Foust. How he has escaped the wiles and nets spread for him, is beyond my ken, but here he is looking younger and better and for years: and ready to enter the summer campaign with renewed alacrity. With his fine business qualities, abundant means, broad acre, flouring mill, and last but not least, his stylish team, he deserved a better fate than single blessedness, and it is to be hoped that, when he least expects it, the silken rein of Cupid will be drawn over his head, and his liberty be at an end. Considering the freedom he has so long enjoyed, it will be a pleasure to see him suddenly relinquish it. He is very popular among the visitors here.

The most cheerful man one meets is Alderman LeGrand. and so far as the town is concerned, he is undoubtedly the father of the place, (Say grandfather, and leave the paternity to Col. Jackson—Editor). He came here when the old buildings were in ruins and the valley a wilderness: he had faith in the future, and embarked his untiring will and means here;

to enumerate his self sacrifice, toil and devotion would fill a volume; but its evidence stands forth in public roads, buildings, and a house of worship; his is a record that will be honored long after he has passed from time to eternity. He served two terms as Mayor, and still labors in the interests of the town; to all he is uniformly polite, and deserved the success of his present business, and the possession of one of the loveliest residences in the valley. To him we are indebted for the location amongst of one of our most useful citizens, Mr. McAllester, and his amiable wife. By the way, we have another rising young man, of whom we are proud, that very successful merchant, Mr. Jno. H. Hamilton, who by habits of strict morality, industry, integrity and economy has worked himself up to his present honorable position. Comparatively young, he has a sweet home, a lovable wife, and a fine store, the arrangement of which is sufficient to impress one with the belief that he had studied merchandising as an art. Long may he be prosperous and happy! Your good friend, Alderman Jno. Crane, is our efficient R.R. Agent, and finds time to make love to the pretty girls; and as his good looks combine with his rare business integrity and qualifications he is as popular with the old folks as their children. And while on the subject of handsome people, let me tell you that the finest looking lady I have seen in a long time, is your valued acquaintance, Mrs. R., nee Miss Augusta Randolph, who is on a visit to her honored parents here.

Occasional

Since it was signed Occasional it could be supposed that this was really a form of advertising used in that day. It certainly promotes the resort and the town in glowing terms, even down to mentioning specific people that will add to the wonder of a stay in Blount Springs.

The *Sunny South* was akin to the social media of today. At that time many young people connected with each other by corresponding in magazines such as this one. Many missives came from writers at Blount Springs as they tried to fill their idle time during the winter months. One of these used the pen name of Timid Alleen. She describes her surroundings in the language of the times in her letter of February 3, 1883.

Night is trailing her dusky robes over the mountains. The shadows falling noiselessly, envelope our quiet valley in the gloomy shades of twilight. Looming up before me, tall and grand is Duffee's mountain. The gaunt, leafless trees, and gray lichen-covered rocks gleam weird and ghostly in the pale uncertain light of the winter gloaming, and fill my heart with a strange, irrepressible longing to stretch out my arms, and puts away the tall, dark wall nature has formed around us, shutting us in from the outer world.

Our little summer resort is completely surrounded by hills and mountains: hence, unless we climb these lofty eminences, we never view the rose-tinted couch here the day-god arises from slumber: or, the glorious splendor of the sunset gates where he sinks to repose.

... And yet there is a subtle charm unexplainable for me clustering around these romantic hills and crags. Not very far away from our vine-wreathed cottage up the mountain's rugged side is a frowning precipice more than a hundred feet high-where, in the dim, mystical years of the "long ago," a dusky Indian maiden with her newly-wedded brave of a different tribe, sought death to escape the anger of pursuing father—but, pshaw! What watering place among the mountains possesses not its "Lovers Leap" whereby "hangs a tale?"

She paints a picture of the beauty and loneliness of off-season, the time without all the parties and gay society for which the resort was known. As a young person the quiet and solitude was not among the greatest attributes of Blount Springs to be admired in winter.

Judge George Hoadly
Ohio Historical Society

In August of 1883 the Alabama State Bar Association held their annual meeting at the Hotel. They elected officers and conducted other important business. Judge George Hoadly of Ohio spoke and the title of his address was "True Limits of Municipal Law in a Democracy". This was a huge coup for the town to get this convention and many more were to follow.

Hoadly was the Democratic nominee for the governor's race in Ohio at the time of his speech at this convention. Several news releases pertaining to campaigning were sent out by him while he was in Alabama. He won the election and served as the 36th Governor of Ohio from 1884 to 1886.

Business continued to be good and the hotel was often sold out. It was decided that an addition was in order and in 1883 a new building was constructed on the hill overlooking the Jackson House. It was named the Mountain House and served as a place to host parties and to let rooms for overflow from the main .hotel. Rates were less at the Mountain House because of the climb to get there.

A storm that came through in May damaged Dr. Constantine's ten pin alley, located across from the main hotel. It had been very popular for many years and was in the L'Orient part of town. A tree crashed through the roof and did considerable damage. It was repaired and ready in time for the new season. In September during that same season, an earthquake was felt in town. It was said oil oozed out of the ground for a considerable time.

An amazing feat was accomplished by a local woman. For the third time in a few years the same woman gave birth to triplets, nine children in three births! Dr. Lee, whose comments appeared in the Blount Springs Guide, said he thought her use of the waters contributed to the amazing births. About two miles south of town something else was happening. Anthony Henderson was stabbed to death by Bill Sanders at a "house of ill fame".

The July 23, 1885 edition of the *Weekly Iron Age* featured the goings on at Blount Springs:

> *The season at Blount Springs is beginning to feature much gaiety and life. The guests are in the happiest spirits and new tenants are being daily added. There are now over 150 daily guests at the springs and Sunday every table in the spacious dining room was crowded. Mr. Hickle, the genial proprietor hovered about the door and smiles wreathed about his jolly face. The crowd was the largest he had entertained this season. An Age reporter was lost in the crowd, and he floated about on a sea of white lawn and gay laughter until one of the young ladies moored him safely to a large rocking chair in a corner of the large piazza and as she waved a large palmetto fan, settled back and exclaimed: "Oh I am so happy, I am dying to gossip and have had no one to join me in a long time."*

The unidentified girl goes on to describe the other girls and women at the springs that July and how they are working the boys with their coquettish ways. She tells of the beautiful married women from Birmingham and other towns. Dancing is one of the chief entertainments and there are some excellent dancers among the guests. The young female patrons are noted and their methods of bewitching the men are listed.

There are notable older folks too from Montgomery, Birmingham, New Orleans, and even South Carolina. The author of Simon Suggs is among the guests this month and so many others. Kids are running everywhere and they are amusing, but the most important guests are the young men, and there just aren't enough of them.

The story continues as the young lady describes a family of young children:

> *There are some bright little children here whose graces and manners are too nice for anything. Among them are little Clara Burnham, Pauline Cameron, Lena Walter and Clara Mae Mason. The little things are quiet, and are the most perfectly behaved children I ever saw together. We have a great deal of pleasure here now, and have a dance every Saturday night. Saturday night the German was led by Mr. W. B. Stard and Miss Bessie Kirkman, of Birmingham. The only thing we need now is plenty of beaux and ice cream occasionally.*

Blount Springs and The Great Southern Cave had long been important spots for stump-speaking and the haunt of many politicians. Governor E. A. O'Neal was a guest when he was interviewed by the Columbus Daily Enquirer. He spoke of the wonders of the iron and steel industry and the many resources of our state, including that of Blount Springs.

Many other Governors made appearances in Blount County, either to campaign or vacation. Some of them included over the resort's long history: Clement C. Clay, John Winston, Andrew B. Moore, William Smith, George Houston, Rufus Cobb, William Oates, William Jelks and others. Senators and Congressmen also made Blount Springs one of their haunts. Frequent visitors were John Morgan, and Oscar Underwood, William Rufus King of Selma, owned a home there hoping to ease his tuberculosis. Not only did he become an ambassador, but he was also Vice President of the United States. His family continued to visit Blount Springs long after his death in 1853. Teddy Roosevelt was perhaps the most famous politician to speak at Blount Springs.

John Tyler Morgan   **Gov. William Oates**   **Gov. Emmit A. O'Neal**   **Gov. William Jelks**

Alabama Department of Archives and History, Montgomery, Alabama

A letter from a guest, Minnie Anderson, to her mother in Ireland reveals a few details about what went on for patrons to enjoy and help them forget about their normal, mundane lives in the 1880s.

> *So H. [Harrie?] brought us all out to this nice & very fashionable Summer resort all hours drive by rail from B [Birmingham?]. It is up in a mountain valley, a small village with mineral springs, a large Hotel with at present 300 people - prittely [prettily?] situated between two hills, surrounded by lovely trees, & having a very wide, shady verandah [veranda?] all round it on which everyone sits & walks - an excellent 'MENU' & nice string band which plays during meals, & after tea for dancing - there are some nice children with whom our young ones play, & the quartette are very much admired, everyone remarking "What fine children! Surely they are not Americans with those rosy cheeks". There is a piano, at which the young ladies play & squall. The mountains rise up all round as, rather hills than mountains. Masses of shelving rock picturesquely mingling with the loveliest foliage - trees of all kinds, oaks, beeches & all the English trees, besides many beautiful kinds which do not grow in England all of them linked together by creeping plants of every imaginable kind & color- no flowers strange to say, but beautiful ferns, harts-tongue, maiden-hair, & all the dear old friend growing wild, the first ferns I have seen since leaving home - a great number of pine trees which scent the air deliciously - in fact a lovely place & so cool, never too hot. The wood rises up just behind the Hotel, & there the children play all day long - they have already an enormous collection of ferns of different sorts curious stones, seeds & berries, & they never tire of gathering others- Oh the delight of it all to them, after the flat hatefulness of Kansas - & to me a perfect feast of beauty.*

Parties of every sort were hosted in various homes as well as at the hotel. There was a big benefit party for the local church in the home of J. E. DuBois. It was the scene of a rainbow party. The mountainside was alight with Japanese lanterns. Young boys singing and playing tambourines greeted the guests and entertained them. A prize of a beautiful white silk handkerchief was given for the best sewing by a man and it was won by Frank Wheless.

Miss Hundley and Miss Fears of Huntsville served as the "angelic hosts" for the evening and were much appreciated by the young men. Some of the older gentlemen included Dr. Foster of Tuscaloosa and Dr. Cochran of Montgomery. The latter was the state medical director. Other ladies were Miss Spratt, Miss Houston and Miss Martin of Birmingham, Miss Graves and Miss Bell of Montgomery and Miss Randolph and Miss Robinson of Blount Springs.

The party lasted until 11:00 and the attendees walked home in the moonlight two by two. These are the times many young men and women found their mates.

Polly Hopkins was a popular character of song and storyies in the Victorian Era across the South and the rest of the country. The song is about a man telling Polly he loves her, but she has no interest in him. Everyone in the 1880s knew who Polly Hopkins was and this fact was telling when someone using that name penned letters to the *Southern World* under a nom de plume.

Library of Congress

Who at Blount Springs wrote using the name of Polly Hopkins is unknown, but she was quite the popular girl among the other writers to the magazine. She is mentioned over and over by writers from across the South and how they enjoy hearing from her.

In her letter of June 15, 1884, she describes her home as a place called "Moss Dale" and tells of her life. Her yard is full of locust trees and she loves to ride her pony. Riding is one of her favorite things to do, but in a later letter she tells of her father having to sell her pony and she has no way to attend Sunday school. It appears Polly is one of the favorite writers and the other writers vie to correspond with her.

In one particular letter she tells of her thrill at riding to the post office and about playing organ at church. There is also a story of going with her sister to Bangor Cave. Her sister met a beau there but Polly did not. Reading her letters will transport one back to a much simpler time in the world.

The weather brought drama and tragedy to town when a railroad bridge was washed out by torrential rains causing a southbound freight train to run into the creek. The conductor, Brascom Donk, was drowned and the engineer and fireman were severely injured. Another accident the year before occurred when two freight trains hit head-on. Over the years there were many train wrecks and other rail related tragedies in this part of Blount County. Perhaps some of these were caused by the need to construct the road bed so quickly. The grade was not always what is should have been and some bridges were not of the best construction and possibly failed due to this.

Enough people lived full-time in Blount for the incorporation as a city to be granted by the state legislature in 1885. The first mayor to serve was James I. Cox, with Thomas Jones as Justice of the Peace. Further, there were two day and two night Marshalls.

Blount Springs also had a high school at this time. Latin and Greek were taught along with the *"ordinary branches of an English education."* W. D. Lovett was the principal and the *"finest Sulphur Water in the South"* was free of charge to students. Tuition of $12 to $15 per month included board, lights, fuel and washing.

The September 25th edition of the *Sunny South* contained a letter to the editor from Mrs. N. L. Kierulff about her recent trip to Blount Springs from her home in Birmingham. She considered the scenery remarkable in the town, but the people she met we more remarkable.

> *As I walked under the archway (surmounted by a indescribable eagle) up to the Hotel Jackson, a colored band was making the rugged hills resound with vigorous strains of music. At first all seemed gay and happy, but very soon complaints were heard on all sides. Everybody was feeling badly. People who had come to Blount well, were now sick, and declared they grew worse every day. I wondered at this, until I went with a party out to visit the many excellent springs of mineral water. Then it seemed wonderful to me that they had been there some weeks, and still lived! They were drowning themselves with sulphur water! Think of one, sweet, pale faced little woman drinking six large sized mugs of water in rapid succession. She sat down breathless, and said she felt worse than she did before leaving the hotel. No wonder, I answered, you are a perfect water monster!*

> *Oh don't discourage me she cried, the water is fattening, and I have determined to go home from here stout!*

> *What inequality in the gifts of nature! How I longed to give her about fifty pounds of what Bill Arp calls, ong bong pong.*

> *In the late afternoon, as I sat on the hotel verandah sketching the castled terraces and clustering trees, I saw a beautiful and stately form approaching me. What grace and sweetness enveloped this human flower, royal as a red rose! The soft, liquid dark eyes, the gentle smiling mouth, the rose-pearl complexion, the curling locks of raven hair, have indelibly fixed themselves in my memory. The voice too, as soft as a dove, fascinated me still more. Pleasant, sweetly flowing sentences came charmingly natural to the ear from this being of beauty. She was from New Orleans. I was very sorry when the horses were brought around, and she left me to join her friends in a horseback ride over the hills.*

The evenings at Blount are delightfully cool, and many of the visitors did not appear until the lamps were lighted, and the band was hard at work, earning its salary. I was glad to see the young ladies less coquettish, and seemingly more indisposed to flirtation, than might have been expected. It may be the proper masculine element may have been wanting, or it may be overdoses of sulphur water indisposes one for emotional amusement; be that as it may, the evenings were pleasant and were passed in harmless amusements. The only objections to Blount Springs this summer were the continual blastings going on on the mountain side, very near, and in full view of Hotel Jackson, and the presence of convict laborers.

Grambs Military Band at the Spring Yard in 1884
Blount County Museum

Many groups came to Blount Springs to have picnics and other daytrips for their clubs and organizations. Pictured above is a Methodist Sunday School group that was entertained by Fred Grambs Military Band of Birmingham. This photograph is one of the most widely known of Blount Springs. Taken in 1884, it became a widely circulated post card. Note the elaborate Victorian gazebo. Grambs is in the foreground standing near one of the springs.

Fred Grambs was a popular coronet player and band leader in Birmingham and Blount Springs. He and his wife Fannie moved to Birmingham from Scranton, Pennsylvania in 1883. They became members of the Church of the Advent where Grambs served as the organist and choir director for 35 years.

For many years he gave private lessons on a variety of instruments to many students. He became known as Professor Gramb and was also the music director for O'Brien's Opera House. O'Brien's was in Sublett Hall on the second floor and had a seating capacity of 1,250. Not only did Gramb lead the eight piece orchestra, he also served as business manager and finally he and B. S Theiss partnered in the leasing of the theatre from Henry Badham and A. L. Fulenwider when they owned it.

Fred Grambs
Birmingham's Highland Park

Besides his theatre work, Gramb wrote several popular songs and was known across the country for his instrument work. He was considered one of the best coronet players in the United States and had a great affect on many players. Possibly his largest concert was at Capitol Park. It was estimated his band played for over 2,000 listeners.

He continued teaching piano and organ until he retired in 1932. At the age of 82 Gramb died in Birmingham, August 23, 1940.

16

The Blount Springs Hotel

Things were about to change at the Jackson House and all over Blount Springs. The Colonel had gone through a few managers and was growing tired of running the hotel and his other businesses too. He had the farm, limestone quarry, horse track and the rest. For many years two of the regulars were James Withers Sloss, his brother Mack, and their respective families. The Sloss Brothers had been very active in the founding of Birmingham. J. W. Sloss had been instrumental in getting the South & North Alabama Railroad through from Decatur to Birmingham and beyond to assure the success of the Cahaba Mineral District.

In 1882 he opened Sloss Furnace in Birmingham, just east of downtown near what is now 1st Avenue North. The furnace, with a second one added the next year, continued to operate in this location until 1971. One of the backbones and marvels of the city, many couples and families would park on the 1st Avenue viaduct to watch a "pour" for entertainment.

Sloss retired in 1886 and sold the company to a group of investors headed by John Johnston and Joseph Johnston. Oddly enough, they were not related. This group went on to change the company to Sloss-Sheffield in 1899. J. W.'s retirement gave him more time to spend at Blount Springs. The next year he and his brother Mack decided to buy out Col. Jackson and take on a new challenge to make it Blount Springs even more of a showplace.

When Sloss did something, he did it right. The hotel was completely refurbished. It was painted and papered and all the furnishings were redone or replaced. In the Salon a Fisher concert grand piano was placed on top of the new mossy carpet. Every piece of furniture in this room was new with curtains and all new accoutrements of the finest quality.

In the dining room particular attention was paid to papering the walls so that it would look right with the new frosted silver and china that was handpicked for the hotel. Only the best servants were allowed in the room. The Mobile Brass Band played for the opening and provided what was considered by some as the best music ever at the resort.

Hanging baskets on the veranda and a fountain in the courtyard supplied by the freestone spring was the centerpiece of the renovations. To provide water for the hotels a system of pipes were constructed and connected to the freestone spring that was above the spring yard.

A range of the highest order was installed in the kitchen, manned by French chefs from New Orleans. The dining hall was full of elegant tables and chairs, and new silverware. The parlor had all new furniture, and a new lighting system was installed throughout the hotel of gas lights furnished by gas works that were located on the hotel property.

The Blount Springs Hotel with the Mountain Hotel in background
Blount County Museum

In addition to refurnishing all the individual hotel rooms, modern ventilation and sewage systems were added for the complete convenience of the guests. Each day and night music was provided by Haecker's Brass and String Band.

Just the hotel was not enough. It was only the beginning. Joseph F. Lux of Louisville, Kentucky was hired to rework and improve the spring yard and the grounds around the hotel. He was a landscape gardener of the first degree and brought in carpenters and laborers to beautify and build every known and modern artifice for the enjoyment and edification of everyone that used the springs and the area around them. This is when the curbing around several of the springs were poured. The spaces between the various springs were covered in gravel. The trees were trimmed and underbrush cleared.

Nothing short of fantastic was the impression the decorations made on the regulars at "Old Blount". To top it all off the name was changed from the Jackson House to the Blount Springs Hotel and the Mountain Hotel.

A Curbed Spring
Photo by the Author

Regulars of this time were listed by Mary Gordon Duffee in one of her many newspaper contributions and included:

> *Sam Robertson of Birmingham, W. W. Woodward of Wheeling, Al., Fannie Linn, Dr. John Davis and his mother, and niece Miss Josephine Latham, all of Birmingham. A Mrs. Green was often there from Memphis, Tennessee, sisters, Misses Acklen of Huntsville and Mrs. Gen. Rucker of Birmingham.*
>
> *Fred Sloss, wife and daughter, Fred Averitt, Col. J. F.B. Jackson wife and son (he still maintained his cottage there), Sam D. Block, L. Hammel, Miss Bertha Block of Mobile. J. J. Braun of New Orleans, R. H. Rose from Nashville, B. Sloper, NY, D. S. Green and J. C. Jernigan, Nashville, R. R. Sturdivant, Talladega, S. A. Manlove, M. Keith, J. W. Gayle, B'ham, Ed Mason, Athens, J. R. Gresham, Huntsville Beaux of Blount, D. Mac Drennen, finest looking man at the springs, Hugh McNutt, Sam Perry, Jr. all of Birmingham, Jap Faust, boarder of the hotel, also F. L. Bivings, T. W. Hansel and D. G. Brown. Mr. Bayne, formerly of the Exchange of Montgomery, at the desk, assisted by Mr. Lashley.*

A ball was planned to start the season and to show off the newly renovated Blount Springs Hotel. It was determined this ball would honor three militia companies of note from the Magic City; the Birmingham Guards, the Birmingham Rifles, and the Alabama Zuoaves. A zuoave unit wore garish uniforms based on French units that were extremely elaborate, to say the least. All these units were currently the rage amongst the elite of the Magic City. For the first time since the Civil War, men of the South were allowed to form armed militia units as Reconstruction formally ended. It was really more of a social group than one that readied itself for the defense of home and hearth. (Many of these local groups were called into action during the Spanish-American War and acquitted themselves quite well.)

The décor of the hotel was unsurpassed because Mr. Reed, a Birmingham florist and his assistant, Mr. Smith, were given carte blanche and displayed their rare genius in floral arrangements for the ball. In the parlors were placed tall ladders of white hydrangeas and ferns with the word SUCCESS in silver letters, entwined with green smilax. Chinese lanterns and hanging baskets of blooming flowers festooned the galleries. Flags of the United States, Alabama and the various companies were abundantly placed lending more to the military air of the occasion.

Once the ballroom was reached by the revelers they would see two immense horseshoes filled with roses, dianthus and carnations. Huge wreaths of cut flowers and military designs covered the walls and from the ceiling hung bunting depicting the colors of the various units. Canary red and azure for the Alabama Zouaves, dark red, orange and dark blue for the Birmingham Rifles and the white, gold and blue of the Birmingham guards flowed and waved in the mountain breezes. At one end of the hall was a large green shield with welcome spelled out, and at the other end were BG, BR, and AZ in letters made of flowers.

Of the 400 in attendance, 300 came from Birmingham on a special train, each company of militia singing their special songs and enjoying the camaraderie and the ride of about an hour or so. A short time after leaving Birmingham an accident occurred that put a damper on the festivities when Mr. Ben Carter fell from the train.

Everyone felt sure he was surely killed by this terrible fall and the train was moved onto a side track at Warrior while a party of his close friends went back to look for his body. For the next thirty minutes the sorrow on the faces told the story of the worried crowd as they waited for the return of the group. It seemed like much longer than a half hour but the wait was well worth it as the supposed body came walking up to the train, a little worse for the wear, but alive and ready for the trip and party to continue!

Dixie blared at the station as the train pulled in and the crowd moved quickly to the food created especially for the occasion by the celebrated Denechaud. Between the exquisite decorations, the dancing and the free-flowing wine (some of the choices noted by Mary Duffee included St. Julien, Rhenish Vintage and Widou Clignot) the party roared on into the night.

Many of the men were gallantly dressed in their military uniforms of the highest order and the women in French court dress. The Alabama Zouaves were particularly flashy and brilliant as they danced the waltz, the quadrille, and many other popular numbers to the sounds of the band. To top off the evening everyone was give a satin programme as a souvenir of "the greatest ball of the year".

Duffee proceeds in one of her writings titled *Dear Old Blount* to describe the gowns of many of the ladies. Written in the style of the time, a few of her descriptions follow:

> *Mrs. Gen. Rucker, in a superb toilette of maize faille francaise, the bodice trimmed in point d' Alencon; and a long conet train of rich brocade. Diamonds.*

> *Mrs. S. T. C. Thompson, embroidered shrimp pink, gauze overdress over absinthe green silk. Decollete.*

> *Mrs. T. T. Ashford, elegant toilette of white faille francaise, pearl passenmenteries, front of white, uncut velvet, embossed in fern leaves, decollete and entraine. Pearls.*

> *Mrs. Judge Brooks, one of Alabama's social queens, appeared very handsome in a rich and tasteful evening dress. Diamonds.*

> *Mrs. Ben Green, strikingly elegant dress of rich white silk, front of superb uncut velvet embossed in delicate sprays of wild flowers: square corsage and no sleeves. Diamonds.*

Apparently, the only thing grander than the military dress and floral creations were the gowns the ladies wore. No expense was spared to impress the gentlemen and ladies in the room. The Sloss Brothers had made many improvements and they were grandly displayed at this ball and it was talked about for many years to come.

Management of the Hotel had fallen to the renowned E. F. Denechaud of New Orleans fame. The brothers gave him carte' blanche as to the running of the hotel and dining room and he was excellent at his craft.

He'd honed his skills in the highly competitive restaurant market of New Orleans. He was competing with such institutions as Antoine's and the Four Seasons and was quite successful.

RESTAURANTS.

ANTOINE'S—No. 65 St. Louis street. Board by the day or week. Furnished rooms for boarders. Private saloons up stairs for weddings, baptisms, etc.

FOUR SEASONS' RESTAURANT—No. 111 Chartres street. Furnished rooms. Private saloons. Board and lodging $2 per day. Board by the week or month. J. Bosio proprietor.

DENECHAUD'S—No. 8 Carondelet street near Canal. Every delicacy of the market. Rooms for private and society dinners. Board by the week or month. E. F. Denechaud proprietor.

Denechaud kept good company and strong competition
New Orleans City Directory 1885

The Denechaud House, originally the Denechaud European Hotel and Restaurant, was located at 2107 2nd Avenue North. It adjoined the Florentine Building in downtown Birmingham. The property was owned by Denechaud and operated by his sons Edward and Louis. Opening in 1887, the restaurant was very successful and the building featured one of the most elaborate cornices in town, matched by the ornate window surrounds on the front.

The Birmingham hotel survived only two years, with the sons returning to New Orleans to help operate their father's business there. Since then the building has housed a grocery, sewing machine company, a paint supply store, apartments, and a furniture store.

In the late 1920s, the building housed the Quality Market, one of a row of grocery stores and bakeries stretching across half the block. In the late 1970s, the ground floor was occupied by the Peoples Loan Company. Extensive work in 1985 and 1986 restored the historic facade as well as a painted sign high on the building's east wall, long hidden behind an adjacent structure.

From 1993 to 2002 Designform architects had offices in the Denechaud House. It is currently owned by William Upshaw and Patricia Comer and houses the Comer & Upshaw law firm and a residential loft. Redevelopment of the third floor from office space into a 2,000-square-foot loft was assisted by a City of Birmingham business development loan.

Capt. W. H. Graves
Alabama Department of Archives and History, Montgomery, Alabama

Some of the regulars at the resort were Capt. W. H. Graves and his family. Graves was one of the directors of the Merchants and Planter's Bank of Montgomery, a lawyer of the firm Sayre and Graves, and the author of *Junius Finally Discovered*. He also served as Director of the Montgomery Southern Railway Company. His wife and three children were very popular with most of the guests at the hotel and were there at every opportunity. The girls were known as "the Three Graces" with the eldest, Miss Ellie, considered a great voice. Any time there was a party or gathering, the girls were asked to perform.

Mary Duffee spoke well of Capt. Graves in one of her society columns for the Birmingham Age:

> *Captain Graves and his lovely family have just left on their annual visit to New York. From thence, they go to Boston, where they will place their gifted and fascinating daughter, Miss Ellie, at the famous New England*

Conservatory of Music. After a full course she will complete her studies in Europe, and then, Dear Age, you may look out for a genuine sensation in the shape of a great Southern prima donna. Captain Graves is a perpetual joy and treasure to all who know him; stately inform, handsome of face, the suavity and elegance of his manners win all who come in contact with him. I never knew a more popular man, or one more deserving of the universal esteem he receives from everyone. While eminent in the ranks of his profession, stern and unrelenting in the discharge of his duty, yet in his home he is the tenderest, truest, most lovable of men. Together with his elegant wife, (a daughter of that noble old patriot and true Christian, the late John Whiting, who sacrificed his life for the sake of Alabama and the South & North Railroad) and beautiful children, they have for many seasons been the pivotal center, around which the highest ranks of society at these Springs have revolved; hence they will be sadly missed from scenes they so greatly adorn.

There were several points that had to be visited while in attendance at Blount such as Lover's Leap. This crag gave a commanding view of the town and the landscape around it. There was Cedar Point, River View, Raven's Crag, and Warnock's Mountain. It was said of the latter that you could see all the way to Huntsville's Monte Sano Mountain if you used a spyglass.

Several articles chronicling the social life were written by Miss Duffee during the 1887 season. In August she tells of another ball:

The hotels are crowded and health and good cheer reign supreme. The Mikado Ball was a grand success. I did not attend as my days for such festivities are over; but I saw some of the gallant soldier boys from Birmingham in their pretty uniforms. The fame of the Crescent City was well sustained by Misses Pugh, Hoffman and others. Alabama exhibited some of its rarest, fairest flowers, such as Miss Winn, of Demopolis, Miss Fannie Anderson, the belle of Eutaw, and her sister, Miss Mary, a lady of stately beauty; Miss Breux, a noted belle of New Orleans; Miss Bessie Warren, the attractive belle of my dear old native town, Tuscaloosa; Miss Ledyard of Montgomery; Misses Bannister, Newman, Brooks, Stevens, Graves, Womack, Maury, Armstrong, Blackburn, Shepherd, Cleary, Dennis, King, Wright, Green, Kernon, White, Speer, and Monroe, were, I am informed, exquisitely and appropriately costumed, reflecting the restored glory of the South.

And later it was noted:

> *The Messrs. Sloss have certainly made a signal success of Blount this summer, and deserve all the good things said about them. I know they have been a wonderful help to this entire community by their liberal outlay.*

It was a great thing that the Sloss Brothers had decided to take over the Hotel because things were certainly going swimmingly for the owners and the guests. Patrons numbered in the thousands at this point and it seemed it would only grow from this point.

Mr. and Mrs. Frank Jones
Blount County Museum

Plans were in the works for a new bath house that would be the largest and most expensive in the South. There had to be room for patrons to enjoy the famous Turkish, Russian, Spray, Vapor, Electric and Mud Baths! Baths were only as good as the men that gave them and Blount Springs boasted of two masters in that area. They were John Perkins and Frank Jones. Because of the great reputation of his bath, Jones was also known as Dr. Plugmuckum.

New cottages were going up and were filled almost immediately by no less than Governor Seay and other prominent families in both politics and business. A few examples of those at the resort in September were Dr. Meek of Tuscaloosa, Mr. Stringfellow of Montgomery, Dr. Minor of Greensboro, Col. Warren I. Reese, and others.

It wasn't just the idle rich that came to town. The working class may not have been able to spend a month or two, but they could come for a day trip, a couple of days, or a weekend. The Accommodation ran often enough every day that the family could stay at the hotel or in a cottage and the father could ride back to Birmingham, Decatur, or Cullman to work, the back that afternoon after finishing his workday.

Many fraternal orders continued to come to enjoy a picnic, a dinner, or any number of fun activities. One of those groups was the annual picnic for the Central Alabama L & N employees. A special train of eight cars came from Birmingham in the morning for the several hundred invited workers to enjoy food, dancing and baseball. Baseball had been one of the mainstays of Birmingham and the Industrial Leagues were very big. Each trade group and company had their own team and contests were very spirited.

Also in 1887 the Blount Springs Herald Weekly began publication. Judge Charles W. Ferguson was the editor of the new paper. It was an immediate hit because it only talked about the social scene of the town. It barely mentioned events from Birmingham and nothing of world events or the country at large. Everyone clamored to get a paper to see what someone else was wearing or who at been at each party. It was popular but only lasted less than a year.

One of the most beautiful homes is still there now, and no, it was not ever a hotel. It is Glenwood, the home of Capt. G. D. Fitzhugh. When Col. Jackson came to Blount Springs to finish the South & North Alabama Railroad his friend and fellow engineer came with him. The Colonel bought several hundred acres of land and Fitzhugh bought enough to build his home a few years later. He lived there with his wife and three daughters, Elizabeth, Frances and Grace. They hosted many social events over the years and house parties that everyone wanted to be invited to attend. Being year-round residents they knew everyone and waited anxiously each year for the season to begin so their old friends would once again be around for the festivities.

Glenwood burned in May of 1888 and rebuilt in 1889
Blount County Museum

Mr. Fitzhugh traveled all over the country as a part of his duties as consulting engineer with the Louisville & Nashville Railroad. He was well known for his well-written reports and good-natured demeanor. It was in May of 1888, while he was away on a trip to Priceville, Kentucky that the unthinkable happened. A fire started in a storeroom, perhaps by a mouse and a match. No men were at the house, only the girls and female servants. The fire raged out of control before anyone could do anything to retard it and get it under control.

It was a total loss! Everything in the house was destroyed except for the business papers of Mr. Fitzhugh that his wife was able to hastily grab before she ran out of the house. This was before the season began, so there weren't many men around to help at the time. One of the biggest losses was a brand new piano the family had just received in the last few weeks. They also lost all their clothes and furniture.

Neighbors took Mrs. Fitzhugh and the girls into their home. When word got to the Captain he immediately came home to start rebuilding. Luckily the home was fully insured and it was returned to its original style. Note the house faces what is now called the Clay Road which was the Stage Road to Huntsville in the 1880s. U. S. 31 is located on the old roadbed of the South & North Alabama Railroad. The old road is completely located on private property now and is inaccessible by the public.

Sadly House Bill #398 was introduced into the Capitol chambers to rescind the incorporation of the town of Blount Springs. There just weren't enough people living full-time to keep it. During the season the place would swell to almost 5,000 at times, but off-season was a different story. A legislator named Johnson put the bill on the floor and without much debate it passed. It would be the next year before it actually went into effect.

Gov. Thomas Seay
Alabama Department of Archives and History, Montgomery, Alabama

There was much affection for Blount Springs in government circles. On August 28, 1889 there was a large party for Rueben Seay, son of Gov. Seay. No expense was spared and everyone that was anybody attended. There were always plenty of government officials at the hotel and Seay was one of the most popular.

Mary Duffee was very fond of Seay and talked about him several times in her writings, always in glowing terms. He was from Greene County and grew up on a plantation until his family moved to Greensboro where he attended Southern University. This school later merged with Birmingham College to form Birmingham-Southern College.

The war interrupted his studies. Seay served in the Confederate Army as a private and was captured at Fort Blakely. Afterwards he graduated from Southern and then read law and practiced in Greensboro. Later he was elected to the state senate and served for ten years. In 1886 he was one of four candidates for governor and was considered the dark-horse entrant. Industrialists of Birmingham and many politicians supported him, but the Democratic Convention held 30 ballots before he was named the winner.

In the general election he won by a count of 145,095 to 37,118 for the Republican, Arthur Bingham. He was thought of as a progressive governor being against any kind of prohibition. He supported legislation that was the first child-labor law in the South and provided pensions for Confederate veterans and their widows. The Normal School at Troy and the Normal School for Colored Students (now Alabama State) opened during his term and he did many other things to help education.

Seay didn't run for re-election as governor but instead ran for the Senate in 1890and was defeated. This was the end of his political career and he died young at the age of 49 in 1896.

There was another shocking event that happened in Blount Springs in late spring of the year when John McLean was murdered. McLean was a young man from Warrior that tried to intercede during an altercation between Sam Barker and some other men. He got in between Barker, who was Black, and the other men, who were white. Witnesses stated that without warning, McLean was shot in the abdomen. He died within a few minutes and Sam Barker ran away during the confusion.

About a week after the murder a man was splitting rails at a lumber camp on Red Mountain. He came and talked to Marshall Fitzgerald in Avondale and informed him there was a man at the camp that had committed a murder in Blount Springs. That man's name was Sam Barker. Fitzgerald went to the camp and arrested Barker without a struggle.

When he was searched a number of letters were found on him warning him to stay away from Blount County. One said, *"you would be certain to be catched(sic) if you was to come back."* Other words from the letters said, *"I am not sure you did that thing, but they are mighty excited about it"* and, *"the house has been watched as they is lookin(sic) for you to come back."* The letters were written on L & N Stationary and signed *"your lovin(sic) wife, F. S. Barker."*

Barker was brought to the Jefferson County jail and Blount County officials were notified of his capture. He seemed to match the description broadcast for the wanted man. Mostly he was worried about being lynched when he was returned to the Blount County jurisdiction.

It wasn't planned but there was a Confederate reunion of sorts at the hotel in late July of 1888. Colonel Lemuel Hatch and Capt. Alfred B. Garner were both guests and ran into each other. They were two of the surviving officers of the 29th Alabama. A few other veterans of the regiment were coming to Blount Springs and the officers met them at the depot.

The men were placed in line and marched by martial airs to the hotel where a feast awaited them. Col. Hatch served as their waiter and lavished them with food and drink while Capt. Garner regaled the men with stories of valor and honor. The men of the ranks in attendance were A. G. Jones, James Bentley, A. J. Huffstutler, W. L. Wilbanks, William McMurray, James Blackburn, William Blackburn, S. M. Hays, W. H. Weston, H. M. Whaley, T. R. Betley, G. S. Armstrong, Nathan Armstrong, S. T. Armstrong, Louis McPherson, G. S. White, W. C. Porter, B. T. Porter, Henry Hill and Arthur McPherson.

The men enjoyed this time together and especially enjoyed the service of their former superior officer. There would be many other Confederate reunions over the years at Blount Springs, but this would always be a special one.

Croquet court on the hotel grounds
Tuscaloosa Magazine

17

The Gay Nineties

Through the years one of the most pleasurable pursuits at the hotel was at the bath house. All the different baths were excellent in their own way but the pride of the fleet and the most sought after was the Plug Muckem. Two men were the rulers of the bath, Frank Jones and John Perkins.

John Perkins was good in the baths, but his greater fame was as the livery man. But, make no mistake about it, there was only one "Dr. Plug Muckem" anywhere on the face of the Earth and he was considered a genius at his craft. For only 50¢ patrons found out what heaven was all about at the skilled hands of Frank Jones.

A proper Plug Muckem was composed of several critical steps. First the good doctor administered a regular bath in extremely hot, red sulphur water, followed by a massage with salt and soda. The final step was the pièce *de résistance*. It consisted of a rubdown with his specially prepared herbal mixture and liniment. The secret formula has been lost to the ages. This rubdown was guaranteed to relieve every ache and pain known to man.

The other baths were also popular and were recommended by doctors as treatment for particular ailments. The Turkish bath started by relaxing in a room heated by a continuous flow of hot, dry air. The point of this first step was to start the bather perspiring. Then they move to an even hotter room and after a suitable time wash in cold water. After a full body wash there is a massage and then retirement to a cool room to relax and finish the process.

A Russian bath is much like the Turkish except steam is used in the initial phase in a sauna. While lying in the sauna, a birch twig massage is administered. After the sauna and massage, bathers move quickly to a cold water bath. Mineral water is used to produce the steam and for the cold bath.

Vapor baths involved an invigorating massage with various lotions and concoctions. Afterwards the patron sits in a sauna inhaling the vapors of the lotions along with the heated air. A cold bath is enjoyed, or endured as the case may be, afterwards.

The Spray bath was much like a modern shower whereby water under pressure is sprayed from several spigots at the body. Showers would have been a virtually unknown experience, as running water was not very common. This must have been an invigorating experience because of the novelty of the sensation of pelting water.

An Electric Bath Device of the 1890s
ldysinger.stjohnsem.edu

If a patron requested a mud bath they really enjoyed themselves when an ample supply was applied that had been made with the proper mineral water(s) to achieve the healing or relaxation that was required. Once applied there followed a massage using the slippery mass as a lubricant.

The Electric bath was an early form of a tanning bed. They bathed in light rather than water. The patron would lay on a table and a lid would close over them that was wired with a multitude of lights. These could be regular incandescent or ultraviolet bulbs. Dangers of skin cancer from ultraviolet light were unknown at the time.

Sadness descended over the entire Blount Springs community as they lost one of their leaders when he unexpectedly died. Col James Withers Sloss left this world May 4, 1890 with an estimated worth of $2,000,000. The coming season would not be the same without him. He was one of the driving forces of the improvement of Blount Springs that brought it to the forefront of the social life of the state of Alabama and beyond. Now Mack was left in charge of everything and he would prove worthy of the task over the next decade.

Since Blount Springs had been in operation there was always wine, spirits, and liquor flowing for the guests' consumption. In January of 1890 the liquor license of the hotel was challenged in the courtroom of the Hon. J. W. Ellis. The seat of government had been moved recently from Blountsville to Oneonta and there was friction between the opposite sides of the liquor issue.

The Blount Springs Hotel and Mr. E. S. Betters, a local merchant, had applied for the renewal of their liquor licenses. Merchants Harrell and Fort, along with William Byars, protested the granting of the license before the judge. Two lawyers, Mr. Dickinson and Mr. Hall voiced the dry side, while the Hon. W. T. L. Coper of Cullman spoke for the wet side.

It took two days for the matter to be settled for the dry side. Many of the regulars were devastated by this ruling but the children were still barred from the infamous Devil's Den because the drinking and gambling went on anyway. There was great rejoicing when a liquor license was finally granted for the Blount Springs Hotel in January of 1891. Gambling was still legal due to the special dispensation of the Legislature and more good times were ahead.

There was a showdown in the street in front of Harrell & Fort's General Merchandise. About five o'clock on the 23rd of December, a couple of days before Christmas, three brothers, John, Hiram, and Mack Isbell had been standing around talking for a while. The men had been making threats about another man, W. H. Thomas. They had been all over town talking about what they would do to him when they found him. One phrase heard by several witnesses was they were going to make "meat of him" among other similar comments.

The Isbells were well known in Blount County for causing trouble. A fourth Isbell brother had been killed in Bangor a couple of years before because of their nature. The man who did it was a black man that was serving time as a convict laborer for his crime.

Thomas was quite the opposite. He had come to Blount from Hale County and was well-known as being a peaceable man. Never had he been in any kind of trouble and no one could say any harm against him. Col. Hatch employed him at the stone quarry. There had been two times previously that he had problems with the Isbells and he felt he had to get them before they got him.

From down the street a lone figure moved towards the men. W. H. Thomas came towards them and as he approached he pulled a Smith & Wesson 38 and began firing. After five shots he wheeled his horse and rode down the street and away from the scene.

Four of the five shots hit something. Two were in John and two were lodged in Mack's horse. The wounded man slumped to the ground. Mack's horse ran wildly after the fleeing Thomas. The horse didn't make it far, only about 300 yards, when it suddenly stopped and fell dead. Several men scooped up John Isbell and carried him to Dr. Whaley's office where he died in a very short time.

This certainly wasn't the only showdown in Blount Springs. Alfred King and John Allison were good friends for many years. This relationship lasted until something, or rather someone, came between them. Both had been seeing and courting a particular maiden in the town for a while. This was the first time they both called on her the same night and that's when it happened.

They both went to see who they thought was their girl. It turned out they were seeing the same girl. She dismissed them since they were arguing over her and they left together, continuing their heated discussion. The next day the argument started again as soon as they saw each other, but this time it got very ugly.

Both the men had had enough of the other and the time to talk and argue was over. Knives were drawn and they were not simple pocket knives. Both had long-bladed ones and they were skilled in using them. Bystanders did everything they could to separate the two but it was too late. The cutting was intense and Allison completely disemboweled King. He died within a few hours. Allison was also cut deeply but he survived the fight.

A couple of months later a cashier for the Georgia Pacific Freight Depot in Birmingham left a window open for the cooling May breeze. C. H. Russell left the room to wash his hands and returned to find four men confronting him. They beat the clerk and forced him to open the safe where they found a mere $300. After securing the money he was knocked unconscious. The robbers set fire to the building and made off with their loot. Luckily the fire was discovered and Russell was saved. He was hurt, bruised and embarrassed, but alive. The worst of his injuries was several broken ribs.

One of the thieves had stolen a fire alarm key from a shop operated by a Mr. Wilkinson and turned in a false alarm. The firemen had been sent on wild goose chase to the South Highlands area so that they couldn't answer the real fire at the depot. Their crimes would not be known until they had made good their escape.

The felons boarded an L & N train at that station and got off at Blount Springs. They met two drummers there and beat and robbed them too. A drummer was the name for traveling salesmen at the time, supposedly because they drummed up business. Another crime was added to their credit and they were able to get completely away. No one knows if they were from the area or if they caught another train to make their escape.

Drummers were in Blount Springs because it was a thriving enterprise. There were several general merchandise stores and many other concerns. During the season it was full of people of means and on any given Saturday scores of people were there enjoying picnics and other excursions. Trade unions, Sunday school groups and others chose Blount as a destination because of the many amenities it offered from the beauty of the landscape to ten pins and more.

Trains ran regularly, twice a day, on the South & North Alabama. There was also the Accommodation that ran from Birmingham to Decatur each day. The railroad was always willing to make special runs for groups wishing to use Blount for recreation, as well as any other spots on their line. Money, as always, was at the forefront of the leaders onthe mind of the railroad owners and they did everything they could to promote the places that were accessed by their lines.

The Accommodation made a daily run from Birmingham to Decatur
Cullman Centennial 1873-1973

There was great excitement every day when the Accommodation arrived. Everyone went to the depot to meet the train and see who was coming to Blount. The band was always there and played music as the new arrivals went from the depot up to the hotel in a grand parade. From the hotel everyone then proceeded on to the springs for the daily promenade of men and women in their finest, parasols up and twirling.

Tourism was relatively new for all but the upper class. With the advent of easy access to more places by cheap rail fares, the rising middle class could take advantage of many new adventures. Mary Duffee was hired by the L & N on several occasions to write copy for advertisement of attractions such as Mammoth Cave in Kentucky. These may have appeared in *The Dream of Ellen "N"*, a promotional book for the entire line. There are no credits for writers in that book, but she talked about visiting and writing about Mammoth Cave in other writings. It was probably for this promotional book. She proved very able in this capacity and was asked by many concerns to endorse their products.

Special Correspondent of the South for several Northern newspapers and magazines was one of the titles she had been given. In many ways her fame was greater outside of Alabama than it was in the state. Of course she was well known in Blount Springs and everyone always made a courtesy call on Mollie Duffee when they came to town.

Many times the call could be denied if she didn't want to see the person or just didn't feel the need or desire to visit. She held court from her cabin on the top of Duffee Mountain and rode a horse to town on the days the mail ran to send and collect her voluminous correspondence. Those that did not really know her considered her to be odd, eccentric, and some even thought she was a witch.

She certainly wasn't ordinary in mind or appearance. Mollie Duffee was on an intellectual plane rarely equaled. In reality people did mean a lot to her and she greatly enjoyed any conversation that stimulated her mind and thought processes. The fashions of the times were of little consequence to her. Her preference was an old pair of pants and a comfortable shirt. She was not a slave to the frills, corsets and such of those times.

Poetry and verse filled much of her time, both to read and write. Visitors, when allowed, were often given one of her poems. Sometimes she wrote them as they watched.

Mammoth Cave from *The Dream of Ellen N*
Copy probably written by M. G. Duffee

Other times she would sell her poems to interested parties, usually for one dollar. A family friend told a story about her offering to sell a poem to someone for 50¢. When he tried to pay with a dollar bill and refused the change she exploded! "I work for a living. I don't want your charity!" She stormed away but after a few minutes she returned and apologized for her unladylike actions.

Her style was always in the lyrical and flowery mode of the Victorian Era.

From her poem, *The Hyacinth*:

> *Strange how the perfume of a flower*
> *Could fall across so many years,*
> *And wake from out the perished path*
> *A memory steeped in tears,*
> *And yes, my friend, when o'er your head*
> *I saw the petals gleam*

Once more I felt the thrill of hope
As Exile sees his loved in dream,
While there in bloomed, my favorite flower
The chaste and gentle hyacinth.

In the past decade her Sketches of Jones Valley had been freely given to her friend Charles Hayes in an attempt to help his financially strapped *Weekly Iron Age*. She took twenty subscriptions to his paper as payment for her work and always felt she single-handedly made a great deal of money for him and his paper. After she stopped sending her writings to that paper she continued writing for other ones.

She loved to talk about the area and people of Blount Springs. In *The Blount County News and Dispatch* edition of Thursday, July 23, 1891 she talked about many of them and the article is included in its entirety.

Blount Springs, Ala., By Mary Gordon Duffee

The other day while at the Springs Park, gazing at the lordly trees, the rampart of hills, and the blue heavens that adorned it, there seemed to pass before me the procession of summers of the long ago, when the wealth, beauty and chivalry of the South gathered here, and Alabamians were proud of the fame it had won. I thought of the old pioneers who hunted the deer amid the wild tangle of cane; of the brave men of Blount who filled the ranks of the volunteers and first heard the strains of Dixie beneath the grand old beeches, and marched away-alas! In so many cases so far away that they will return nevermore-and just then a bevy of manly boys and girls came along, whose young lives knew nothing of the war, and I hope will be so loyal to their county and State as were their forefathers. Among them were my young friends back from that noble institution, "Blount College,"-John and Dan Rice-splendid young fellows; Joe Byars, full of energy and talent, and pretty, talented Della Porter in whom we take much pride.

Then I strolled up the old "Tuskaloosa Road," past the pretty home of those worthy people, Mr. and Mrs. Penn McPherson, err by the old freestone spring; next the beautiful residence and part of Mr. Wittich, the great lumber merchant of Pensacola; the cottages of Mr. Mann and Mr. Shannon, most worthy people; and upon the summit of the hill, the homes of Dr. Estill, and that true-hearted man, Isaac Hamilton and his clever family; the well-known and popular resort of Dr. Robinson, with its attractive cottages and well-kept grounds; thence onward 'till a turn in the road brings one to the gate of the lovely home of Col. Brett Randolph, from whose windows can be obtained a view of wonderful scenic beauty and extent.

Then down the hill-side at whose base flows mill creek, and along the margin of the waters to the famous Cold Spring, looking up at the elegant home of Mr. DuBois; next, the lovely residence of our clever merchant, Mr. Charles H. Hooper-whose excellent wife was the daughter of the late Henry Harrell, a man whose virtue, integrity and usefulness were alike an honor and a blessing to this community. On the right of the road, in a romantic glen, is a large never-failing spring of purest water; and a little farther on, the beautiful residence of Mr. William Johnson, of Boligee, Ala. The building, lawn and general surroundings for taste and style are probably unsurpassed in the county. Mrs. Johnson was Miss Katie Byars, the popular belle of this section. Upon the elevation to the right, are the homes of Rev. Travis Byars, Col. Peyton G. King, and that sterling citizen, Mr. Willie E. Byars, whose wife was pretty, gentle Annie Willoughby. Next, the summer cottage of the late Col. Sloss, and the hotel that looks like a castle. Then, past the stores, again the ridge opens on the left, with the summer cottage of Mr. Joseph Brewer, of New Orleans, (Mrs. Brewer is a daughter of Mr. Harris, once the owner of the Springs, a man of blessed memory!) Next is the famous Byars mansion where annually gathers some of the choicest society of the State, and presided over by that noble lady, Mrs. Byars and her charming daughter, Miss Alice, a stately blonde beauty. Their youngest son, Dr. Haden Byars is now at home with them from the Medical College at New Orleans.

A stroll along the old familiar Blountsville road through a valley full of pastoral beauty, brings us to the home of that cleverest of men, Mr. John P. Willoughby, the efficient and popular land agent of the L&N R.R. His home is now occupied by Mrs. Drennen and her much admired daughter, Mrs. Josie Ballenger, and Mr. Dan Drennen. The many friends of the latter will be glad to hear that his health is improving. Immediately opposite, nestling in verdure as green as that of his ancestral Isle is the "sweet home" of Mr. Jno. Crane and his good old mother, whose sterling character, industry and warm, kindly heart are so well and widely known. A few yards brings us to a spring on the left, beyond which resides an excellent man, Mr. Speake; then comes a home of which I love to write, and its inmates, big hearted Walter Harrell, and his amiable, cultured wife, nee Miss Alice Foust, and their lovely children. Here also resides the widow of the late Samuel Foust, whose gentle spirit and Christian worth adorn all womanhood.

Her brother, Judge Gamble, of Jasper, will occupy the "old homestead" this summer. Mr. Charles Fort having purchased the stylish and commodious residence of Mr. Goetter, of Montgomery, opposite the hotel, now dwells there. Mr. Fort has proved by his devotion to church interests, to business and all matters of public interest, a most desirable acquisition to the village, and is untiring in his efforts to promote the welfare of all our people. At his old home is Mr. Worsham, the superintendent of the quarries, and his charming family-and now comes the gem of the valley, the residence of Major George D. FitzHugh, the distinguished Chief Engineer of the L&N R.R. system. The lawn in front suggests Kentucky, the lofty building a Swiss chalet, and the lowering mountain beyond throws cool shadows over all. Flowers that are rarest, bloom on every hand, but none so fair as the daughter of the house, "divinely tall and most divinely fair," Miss Lizzie FitzHugh, who has inherited her mother's wondrous beauty. With them is the modest, amiable Miss Birdie Livingston, a true, womanly spirit, very dear to all who know her, a model for imitation. The interior of the house is elegant in the extreme, and well worth being the abiding place of a man who has done so much for the material progress of Alabama.

Returning past Mr. Hooper's store, we meet our clever townsman, Mr. William G. Byars, who is by his kindly manners and nature, a veritable patriarch amongst us. Next, our worthy Postmaster, Mr. Isom Armstrong, courteous to all; and then comes Mr. James I. Cox, who is as jolly and accommodating as ever, and his good wife so well known in former days as Miss Martha Wood. She works as arduously, and attends to everybody's comfort, before she thinks of her own, the same as ever. The hotel looms up, with its well kept domain, its band of music and usual summer surroundings. Major Hickle keeps a first class tale. The crowd does not come 'till late in the season. Dr. J.C. Lee is at his post as usual.

I don't suppose any place of such note for its Sulphur waters exists where the resident population drink so little of the mineral springs. Our people look upon them as a medicine, and prefer, for general use, the freestone water, of which in wells and springs, there is an abundant supply here. The citizens rarely ever go to the park to take a glass of the sulphur waters. The do not own a dime of the mineral springs, hotel, etc., and have nothing on earth to do with the management, so far as dictating its business affairs. Attending to their own business is sufficient unto them. Our merchants are obliging, and often seriously burden themselves in helping the farmers from one season to another. They pay their taxes, and feel that they are a part of Blount County, and entitled to some consideration, and should not be held responsible for the acts of any individual or corporation.

Well, the day of the barbecue draws nigh, and our citizens look forward with much pleasure to meeting old friends from all sections of our county. There is little excitement about the location of the court house, and only good feeling prevails. The will of the people must be done. I trust there will be no mud throwing at either place, as it is a mighty poor, mean, cowardly sort of business anyway you look at it. The best things in life come only from toil and unselfishness, and only noble sentiments from a pure heart. I rejoice at the prosperity of every locality in old Blount, but I do not like to see a whole community held responsible for the acts of others; neither do I admire flings at other places or their citizens; and I have faith that the men of Blount, whose grandsires built homes in the wilderness, whose fathers and brothers marched, fought and died for the sake of the South, and who are themselves glorious in their efforts to earn their living, build and support churches and schools, are worthy of the day and hour, and capable of thinking for themselves.

The fields give promise of abundant crops; the woodlands are full of wild fruitage; good health prevails, and the glory of a mid-summer sun makes glad the earth. Truly we have much to be thankful for!

Mary Gordon Duffee, July 20th, 1891.

Such was the writing style of Mollie Duffee and she loved it and was a master of that style. That barbecue was held a few days later and, as predicted, it was a joy to those who attended.

The Blount County News and Dispatch of 30 Jul 1891 described the scene:

The morning of the 25th of July dawned upon the hills and lighted the valleys of Blount. The tread of our many feet work her slumbering echoes and merry voices rose in unison to greet the day for many weeks looked forward to with high anticipations. From the first bright hours of morning, a steady stream of humanity moved its eager way to the inviting coolness and restful quiet of the famous Blount Springs. Old men, the "horny-handed sons of toil," accompanied by their wives, mothers and little ones grouped in wide-eyed wonder about them; young men and smiling lassies, all found a hearty welcome at the Springs, whose gates were opened wide to greet them.

On the hill side above the springs long tables were erected which were soon groaning beneath the weight of meats from the large pit faithfully presided over by Messrs. "Pood" Thomas and Ephriam Gossett, and excellent loaves of bread, through the kindness of Major Hickle (of the Blount Springs Hotel) who had one thousand loaves baked for the occasion, the material being furnished by the citizens. Thirty four carcasses were roasted over a pit 3 feet in width, and one hundred yards in length. Numerous lemonade stands furnished cooling draughts and other delicacies. The citizens were indefatigable in their efforts to please all.

The hotel band furnished music, (Charlie Baker furnished music on the violin for Joe Musgrove, Martin South, Ketchum and Willis Allred) and many whiled the hours away in the merry dance.

Prof. Lovett, of Blount College, delivered an excellent address on the "Duty of the Hour," and Prof. Thornton a brief address in behalf of the Alliance.

One of the chief attractions was the "Flying Jinny," and afforded infinite amusement of old and young.

The saloon and all the stores were closed on that day. All in all, it was a day well spent, pleasant and profitable to all-a reunion of friends and a day of social greeting.   Spectator.

Blountsville Items. I took in the barbecue at Blount Springs on Saturday. It was a grand success. There was more dead cows than any crowd could chew. I think there were 2000 people there. Profs. J.A.B. Lovett and Jesse Thornton made speeches, but as I am built like one of Oneonta's boys, the "Flying Jinny" took my eye and the music Brother Bentley's ear, so I missed the speeches, but I hit a quarter of a cow and a ten cent loaf of bread.

These comments prove it was another in a long line of successful Barbeques for the town. This would not be the last and they too would be well received and enjoyed.

18

Crime, Fire, and Politics

Barbeques, fights and beating up drummers weren't the only exciting events in Blount Springs during the early 90s. A gang of safecrackers came to town and caused a big stir when they hit several businesses. The chase and manhunt for the robbers kept the community in an uproar for many days afterward.

Blount Springs Hotel in background with members of the staff in foreground
Blount County Museum

On December 1st and 2nd several newspapers told of the daring crime and its results. Between the hours of 1 and 2 on November 30, 1892 two men, three by some accounts, methodically worked their way through several businesses of Blount Springs, opening their safes, one by one. A third man kept an eye on the night telegraph operator while the other two did the work on the safes.

Chapter 20 – Life After the Fire

The first place they hit was C. S. Hooper's store. The front door was broken and they took $50 from his safe after they blew it open. At W. G. Byars & Son's they bored a hole through the front door and then blew the safe. It yielded $500 in cash and about a $1000 worth of diamonds. These diamonds were the property of Byar's daughter, the late wife of a Mr. Johnson of Boligee. They held great sentimental value to Byars and had been placed in the there for safekeeping. The saloon of O. F. Hickles had everything of value taken from it, but only $15 in cash and the front door of Harrell & Foot was blown open. That noise awakened Harrell who lived near the store.

Harrell hurriedly threw on his pants and, with gun in hand, made his way to the store. He saw a light and went to a window to peek in. One of the men was drilling a hole in the safe door getting it ready for explosives. Harrell moved and made a small noise. The thief turned, saw him, and fired three shots.

By this time Fort, his brother-in-law and business partner, was also there, armed with a double-barreled shotgun. They both fired as the men ran. One of them stumbled and fell like he was wounded, but got up and continued to run. A running gun battle went down the street as the two men hurried out of town with the $2000 and the jewels. There was no time to take the $1500 that was in the last safe of Harrell & Foot. Even though Harrell was able to possibly wound one of the men they still got away, but at least he wasn't robbed.

More men were awakened by the gunfire and they joined in the fray. The chase continued out of town and beyond but the townsmen came back empty handed and quickly formed a posse. One paper reported 100 men in the posse but another said 50. The true number was probably much lower than both reports. The only clues were the burglar tools left at Harrell's store from the aborted safe blowing attempt. The perpetrators were never apprehended.

Hon. Mr. Isaac Goodnight
United States Congress Image

The popularity of the resort and the hotel were not affected by news such as this. People from all over still sought out relief and entertainment there. Newspapers from far away mention inhabitant's visits such as, *The True Democrat* of Bayou Sara, Louisiana which told of Mrs. Nannie Haile planning a trip to Blount. Another report in the *Brenham Weekly Banner* concerned Miss Nettie Jamison returning home to Texas via St. Louis after a lengthy stay at the resort.

Another politician declared his candidacy by sending the postmaster of Bowling Green, Kentucky a letter about his intentions. The Hon. Mr. Isaac Goodnight was congressman for the Third Kentucky District. He was recovering from an untold illness at Blount Springs and expressed his desire to stand for re-election.

Goodnight, a Democrat, served his state from March 4, 1889 - March 3, 1895 and was a member of the powerful Judiciary Committee. His health didn't improve enough and he ended up not running for re-election as he declared in his letter. Besides his health another factor was the harm his absence was causing his law practice. He was elected as a judge in 1897 for the Seventh Kentucky Circuit and served as such until his death in 1901.

Governor Seay was still running the state government of Alabama from Blount Springs every chance he had. From there he announced his appointment of Chancellor Thomas Wilkes Coleman to the bench to replace Judge Somerville. Somerville had resigned from the Supreme Court of Alabama after President Harrison nominated him to serve as a member of the newly created Board of General Appraisers and continued in that post until his death in 1914.

Gov. Seay (center, front row) and some of his Officials on Capitol Steps
Alabama Department of Archives and History, Montgomery, Alabama

Coleman was from Greensboro and previous to this appointment he served as the Chancellor of the Southwestern Chancery Division. After Seay named him to the court in 1890 he served in that capacity through 1900 and then went into private practice in Hale County.

Many tragedies are associated with railroads because of the danger associated with them and rightly so. It was very easy for someone to get hurt and many men have fallen and been killed or maimed or simply caught between two heavy cars at the wrong time. A train moving at its regular speed takes a great deal of space to stop. One man, Thomas Sayre of Nashville, hopped a southbound L & N freighter. He was only 22 when he fell under it shortly before the train was to arrive in Blount Springs. His body was in such a shape that the only way to identify it was through letters he had in one of his pockets.

Chapter 20 – Life After the Fire

There's another story of a runaway that had a connection to the town. Phillip Freidrichs was the son of a New Orleans doctor that ran away from home with two other young men. Dominick Verges and Marshall Currier went on the road with him and had many adventures.

Dominick decided he'd had enough of life on the road and came home, leaving the other two in St. Louis. A short time later Currier wrote home from Trenton, New Jersey that he was doing well but he'd become separated and lost Freidrichs in Syracuse, New York. Another letter drifted in from Currier saying he was in Folkville, Alabama and doing well (Falkville).

The mother of Freidrichs asked him to come back to New Orleans to help them find her son and the boy's father hired the Pinkerton Detective Agency to aid in the search. He was apparently on the way home when he was killed by a train near Blount Springs. Currier's skull was found to have been caved in by the blow and he died instantly. Phillip was never found.

One of the great fraternal organizations of Alabama ended their annual meeting with an excursion to Blount Springs. The ancient Arabic Order of Nobles of the Mystic Shrine, of the Alabama Knights Templars met in Birmingham and capped off their festivities with a trip up the rails for a day of fun. George R. Wheelock was the potentate.

Another year there was a quite different meeting at the Springs. This one was the Alabama Education Association. Amazingly most of the talk was about the same as it is today. Education needed more money, more accountability, and was an important place for children to learn about and improve their character.

The *Weekly Age* of July 4, 1894 had these words of praise for the meeting place:

> *Everybody is enjoying the meeting. Blount is simply delightful now, and the table is fine. Mr. and Mrs. Byers (Byars) and their able and courteous staff of assistants are leaving nothing undone that will contribute to the pleasure of the guests.*
>
> *The association met at 8 o'clock last night and after some resolutions of thanks to the press, railroads and the hotel, Miss Julia Tutwiler read able paper....*

After three days the association adjourned until next year.

In the next year, 1885, Senate Bill 414 passed allowing for the incorporation of Blount Springs College. There are no other records of the college.

A great fire swept through the business section of Blount Springs in March of 1899 that had a devastating effect on the entire village. The blaze was discovered in rooms over the Byars saloon but it was not known how it was started.

The *Weekly Age Herald* described the scene on March 3, 1899

> *The fire was discovered about 12:30 o'clock in the rooms over Byer's(sic) saloon, thought it is not known how it caught. The flames quickly spread from one store and building to another until all of the active business houses in the town except that of McPherson & Son were burned down. The hotel also escaped, though the fire was just across the street from it. The flames continued to spread for about two hours, when the fire went out for want of anything else to burn.*
>
> *One of the features of the day was the stubborn fight which the employes(sic) of the Louisville and Nashville railroad made to save the depot building. There were five freight trains passing through Blount at the time, and their crew all got off and assisted in fighting the fire. With the assistance of a good-sized hose and water from the railroad tank, they finally succeeded in saving the building.*
>
> *The losses in detail were as follows: Two business houses in which the saloon was located, owned by the Blount Spring Company, valued at $2000 and covered by insurance. One store and one dwelling, owned by D. C. Rice, valued at $800; no insurance. One store and dwelling house for C. E. Fort, valued at $1500; no insurance. One barn burned, valued at $100. Byars & Byars' stock of goods was lost, valued at about $3000; insurance, $1500. W. F. Harrell lost about $3000 worth of goods; well covered by insurance. G. W. Green had a $1500 stock, most of which was saved; no insurance.*

This devastation would affect Blount for quite a while as it wasn't very easy to recover from such losses, but they did move on and build back even bigger.

July was a dark time in Blount Springs after the murder of Justice of the Peace, J. K. Hamilton. One afternoon there was some trouble between Hamilton and a black man named Henderson Tunstall. That night Hamilton took two men with him to Tunstall's home to execute a warrant for his arrest.

Tunstall was not willing to go peacefully. After a short scuffle both sides started firing pistols, each side claiming they only fired in self-defense after the other started it. No one knows for sure which side did indeed fire first, but Tunstall had several flesh wounds and Hamilton lay dead.

Chapter 20 – Life After the Fire

Running into the woods the fugitive wandered around the hills and valleys for two or three days. Finally making his way across the Mulberry he was discovered by two farmers. He claimed he was trying to get to Deputy Sheriff McMurry's home to turn himself in. Fearing there would be trouble Deputy Sheriff McMurry took him through the woods to Cullman and put him in the jail.

News reached Blount Springs of his capture and that he was incarcerated in Cullman. Friends of the dead man started talking about a lynching and some even attempted to board the northbound train to go to Cullman. Forty men from Blount went to Cullman but they weren't sure he was there.

Cullman County Sheriff Algood telephoned the governor and asked for help to protect his prisoner. The Cullman jail was guarded by forty citizens including State Senator Brown, Probate Judge Fuller and Representative Cofer until the militia arrived.

When the Governor learned of these threats he called out the Birmingham Rifles and the Jefferson Volunteers. Gov. Joseph E. Johnson ordered both units to Cullman to guard the prisoner and prevent a lynching. After these units arrived it was decided Tunstall would be safer in Birmingham. He was taken in the middle of the night to the larger city and remained there until time for his trial.

More threats were made towards the man and it was told he would not live if he returned to Blount County. When the time for his trial came he was taken to the courthouse at Bangor under heavy guard. Sheriff Sanders and Deputy Sheriffs McMurry and Tidwell formed his guard and were heavily armed. Traveling with them were William Vaughn, the United States District Attorney, Julius Davidson, Assistant US Attorney. Henderson Tunstall's attorney also accompanied this group. It took only a few days to decide his fate once the trial started, guilty as charged.

Capitol Park in 1910
Public Domain

Gramb's Military Band was one of the regulars at Blount Springs on the weekends. They also performed often in Birmingham and other cities. In 1895 they played for a crowd of over 2,000 at Capitol Park. The leaders of the city had long wished for the state capital to be moved to the Magic City and had created the park as an incentive. It never happened and was eventually renamed Linn Park to honor one of the city's great citizens, Charles Linn.

During the summer of 1899 one of the most important occasions ever to be hosted at the Springs was in honor of one of its own. On June 26th a delegation of important people came from Birmingham to meet the train that was bringing the newly installed Grand Exalted Ruler of the Benevolent & Protective Order of the Elks.

Elk President and Entourage in Blount Springs
Public Domain

At their annual meeting in St. Louis, Basil Manly Allen was selected for this singular honor. Much toasting and regaling was in store for the Birmingham attorney as his friends and brothers brought him in to a hero's welcome of pomp and circumstance at every turn.

Mrs. Elizabeth Fitzhugh Talley
The Birmingham News

During this period many important families from across the South continued to visit their summer homes and cottages in Blount Springs and the surrounding areas to be part of the social scene that was so well developed in the area. Many of the people that had been a part of Blount Springs for many years and enjoyed the resort town were gone. Now the younger generation was taking over.

Now their children were taking over. The Fitzhugh daughters had all married but often returned with their new families to visit and enjoy the surroundings they had known much of their lives. Elizabeth continued her riding and many years later she was still considered to be one of the finest riders at Blount Springs. Her ancestral home is still standing and regarded by many to be their dream home, even though most

People have only seen the back. It remains a strikingly beautiful home.

One of these families was the Randolphs. Carter Randolph had been the first to build a cottage at Blount Springs and he and his family enjoyed it for many years. After his death the family continued to visit and his son Brett took over the home. Brett Randolph and his family were well known for the house parties they held at this home.

The Randolph Home, later the Clay Home
The Birmingham News

Another member of the family from Greensboro was Richard Beverly Randolph. He was the son of Dr. Robert Carter Randolph and part of the family that frequented Old Blount since he was a very young man. He married Florence March 5, 1857 in Mobile. She was the daughter of George and Louisa Goff.

They met while her father owned the Goff House and courted in Blount Springs. Perhaps Pivot Rock was one of their places to court and it is a possibility that he asked her to marry him there.

Richard Randolph
Ancestry.com

Pivot Rock was well-known as the chief courting walk of Blount Springs. Many romances blossomed there and great families can trace their beginning back to Pivot Rock. It is still in existence today and continues to be a marvel as to how it stands on such a small diameter.

Florence Goff Randolf
Ancestry.com

Richard died suddenly without warning September 11, 1866 at the age of 36. He was buried in the family cemetery in the city of Greensboro. Augustus Benners was a good friend of Randolph's. They went fishing together quite often and Benners was his lawyer in several cases. He spoke of him in his journal:

> *Another of our valued and estimable citizens is gone to his long home. Mr. Richard Randolph died last night at 12 o'clock. It has cast a gloom over our Community--of him it may be truly said that no one could ever speak harshly or slightingly. I never heard anyone say aught against him. Poor Dick--his earthly troubles are over Peace to his ashes-*

Pivot Rock, circa 1904
The W.S. Hoole Special Collections Library, The University of Alabama

Florence was only 32 at his death. They had five children with the youngest, Smith Randolph, born June 27, just three months before his father died. She would live until 1906 when she died at the age of 63. They lived at the Brakes near Greensboro, visiting Blount Springs as often as possible.

William Edgar and Travis Byars
Ancestry.com

William Byars had been the business partner of his father in their mercantile operation and in managing the Blount Springs Hotel for a time. He continued running their businesses after his father' death in 1902.

Travis was the oldest son and a minister of the Methodist Episcopal Church. He served in other cities but continued to come home to Blount Springs. Another son, Henry Hayden Byars became a physician in Perryville, Alabama.

All during this time Mary Duffee continued to earn a living by endorsing products through her testimonials. This had been a time honored tradition for products at the time. One product she wrote about was Pe-Ru-Na, a cure all created by Dr. Samuel Brubaker Hartman of Ohio. Mary also endorsed and sold subscriptions to The Youth's Companion, a magazine dedicated to young people with items that would be of interest to them.

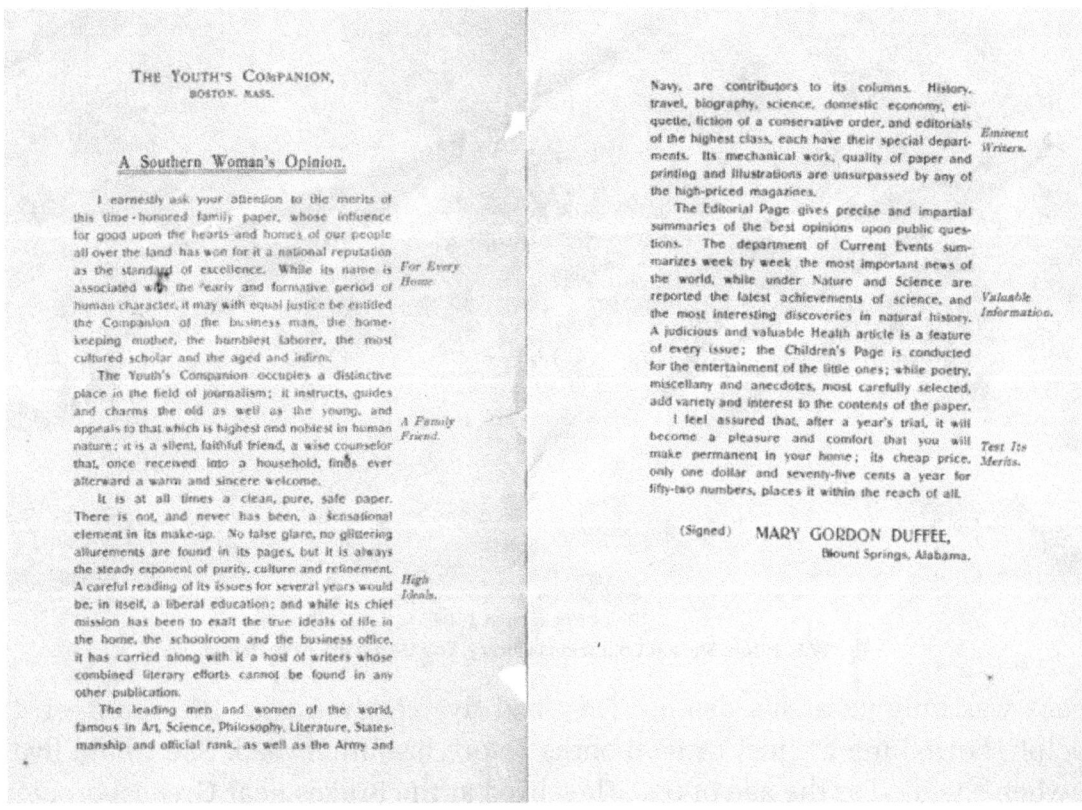

The Youth's Companion

19
Dawn of a New Century

The new century dawned over Alabama with a population of 1,828,697. 1,001,152 of those citizens were White and 827,307 were African-American. 216,714 lived in cities and 1,611,983 lived in the country. Birmingham's population went from around 38,000 to 132,000 from 1900 to 1910. By 1920 it had become the 19th largest city in the United States.

Postcard Showing City Hall and Downtown Birmingham, Circa 1900
W. S. Hoole Collection, University of Alabama, Tuscaloosa, Alabama

The Alabama Polytechnic Institute was one year past the tenure of John Heisman as their coach and the University of Alabama's team was called the Crimson White, after their colors. W. C. Handy was an instructor at Alabama A & M and the leader of their band. Birmingham had a population of 38,415, but in just ten short years it shot to 132,685, proving the nickname, the Magic City, was appropriate.

Chapter 20 – Life After the Fire

More excitement occurred in Blount Springs when on a March Friday night the bookkeeper for the Blount Improvement Company walked into his bedroom located over the store. He moved from the door to his bed and put his pistol under the pillow as he did every night. As he walked back towards his dresser he was shot in the thigh. When he turned toward the sound of the gunshot he saw a man three or four feet away with a smoking gun. Running at him he began wrestling and trying to subdue the gunman. The assailant was finally able to get out of Mason's grasp and he ran down the steps into the darkness. It was never known who it was or what he was after.

Hoo-Hoo Button
phoenixmasonry.org

In November, an L & N express train was approaching Blount Springs when the engineer saw a man standing beside the tracks looking at the train. Just before it got to him, he stepped in front of the engine. He didn't die immediately but was unconscious. On the way to Birmingham for medical help he died.

He wasn't able to talk and had no form of identification on him except a Hoo-Hoo button in his lapel. The International Concatenated Order of Hoo-Hoo, Incorporated is a fraternal and service organization whose members are involved in the forests products industry. There was a number on the button and the coroner was able to contact the secretary of the Hoo-Hoo Order and determine the name and address of the man. He was W. W. Perkins of Doniphan, Missouri and the way he got to this point is a sad story.

Mr. Perkins was an attorney for the lumber company and had gone to St. Louis on company business back in May. While he was there he went on a wild spending spree and used his client's money for his pleasure. After he sobered up he realized what he'd done and went into hiding. The company and his family searched but could not find him. He looked like a tramp when he was killed. Apparently he'd been wandering since his days of indiscretion. To the engineer it looked like he planned to kill himself and all agreed with this assumption.

Soon after A. J. French, a lawyer from the Doniphan Lumber Company of Missouri came to town to identify the body. Instead of taking Perkins' body home to his family, French left money to pay for burial in a Birmingham cemetery. Perkins was an important in his home city, but he had fallen from grace because of his actions.

There wasn't a Hoo-Hoo Lodge in Alabama, but one of the several large fraternal organizations of Alabama was the Knights of Pythias. The Enoch Lodge of Pratt City held an annual picnic and many times it was at Blount Springs. One such day of revelry was a June Saturday in 1900. Between seven and eight hundred people attended.

from The Knights of Pythias Complete Manual and Text-Book

Six train coaches were filled to capacity and arrived in town about 10:00. They enjoyed games, dancing, bathing and a trip through the Great Southern Cave. A roundtrip ticket for the ride from Birmingham was 75¢, 40¢ for children. The Lodge cleared over $250 and used the money to help pay for their building. It was a fun time for everyone and a great success.

In 1899 the rates for the Blount Springs Hotel were $10.50 a week, going up to the Season Rate of $12.50 during July, August and September. Rates stayed the same for the new year of 1900 and the crowds of patrons would grow each year. Amenities included the free use of water for drinking and bathing, a first class orchestra, livery, billiards and bowling lanes. Many walking and riding trails were also available, but most important was the daily promenade to the spring yard. Many also enjoyed the veranda of the splendid hotel.

Guests were still coming for lengthy stays from all over the South. George Carmichael and family came from Ocala, Florida, the Rev. J. L, Wyatt and his family came from Hopkinsville, Kentucky, Miss Bennie Plosser of Atlanta, Georgia and the Marsh family from Pensacola to name just a few. Gov. Jelks and other members of the government continued to patronize Old Blount. The growing industrialist class of Birmingham was well represented and society was still a reason for attendance.

One group that made their way to the resort for a convention in 1902 was the teachers of Blount County. For three days in April the grounds and hotel were filled with educators listening to speakers, attending seminars on how to be better teachers, and socializing with others that enjoyed the same vocation. This was an annual meeting all teachers attended but it was extra special when

Program for Teacher Meeting of 1902
Blount County Museum

the people could also enjoy the amenities of the famous Blount Springs.

Working class people from Birmingham and all along the railway now had the means to enjoy the many pleasures offered by Blount. Mostly through daytrips, but none the less, they could avail themselves of the various attractions. Not only Birmingham provided patrons, but other towns along the line. The hotel also catered to the German immigrants of Cullman. A German dance was offered each Saturday night to encourage more patronage from the growing town.

1908 Barons Baseball Program w/Drennen Ad
Public Domain

The Blount Springs Company held the deeds since 1887 when the holdings were bought from Col. Jackson. J. W. Sloss was dead and the other partners were ready to get out of the hotel business. The property around the hotel and several thousand more acres were taken over by Mel Drennen, mayor of Birmingham.

The Drennen family had many interests in Birmingham and had had a summer home about four miles from Blount Springs for many years. Originally the family had settled in Arkadelphia and later moved to Birmingham and many of the family had become very successful businessmen. A hardware store at 2nd Avenue and 20th Street was well established and there was also a Wagon and Carriage company in the family. Years later this would evolve into one of the most successful automobile companies of Birmingham, Drennen Chevrolet.

Mel Drennen in 1904
Public Domain

He had long enjoyed and admired Blount Springs as a summer home. Finally, when he felt the time was right, it became his. As Mayor of Birmingham since 1899, he had a dream of making Blount Springs a recreational suburb of the Magic City. In 1903 he took over ownership and started making changes that would improve the area even more. One of his first improvements was to dam up Cold Creek. He had long wanted there to be a place for swimming and boating. This made those pursuits possible.

The new swimming hole was the first thing to be seen from the train window just before entering town when coming from Birmingham. Trainmen always blew the whistle to draw everyone's attention to the fact they were passing the landmark and slowed down for a really good look. This was the first hint of the many wonders to come during a stay at the resort. Children were especially thrilled by the sight of the ole swimming hole.

Postcard Showing a View of the Dam and Boating
Courtesy of Mike Tumlin

Rev. Walter Blythe Drennen came from Tennessee as an infant with his parents and settled in Arkadelphia. Rev. Drennen was a planter as well as a leading Republican active in politics, both state and national. He and his wife Matilda had eleven children. Walter Melville Drennen was born in Arkadelphia in 1851.

Mel Drennen attended the common schools at Arkadelphia. The family started a mercantile business there and eventually started a branch store in Birmingham. That one developed quickly and profitably and caused them to close the original one and move their entire operation to the larger city. The brothers settled in Birmingham and continued to enlarge their business empire.

Besides being mayor of Birmingham, Drennen was a member of the firm of Drennen & Company; director of the Birmingham Mutual Fire Insurance Company; president of the Martin Cracker Company; manager of the Palos Coal & Coke Company; and president of the League of Alabama Municipalities. He was vice-president of the National Good Roads Association and was a member of the Benevolent and Protective Order of Elks.

In addition to his business honors, quite a few accomplishments were credited to the administration of Drennen as mayor. During his tenure a new City Hall was completed in 1901 at the cost of a quarter of a million dollars, along with several public schools, many street improvements were done and other improvements of note. The city completed water filtration plants at both their water plants, sidewalks were established and many streets were paved. His legacy in Birmingham and Blount Springs lives on to this day and beyond.

James Knox Duffee was Captain of Company K, The Blount Guards, 19th Alabama Regiment. They fought at Shiloh, Chickamauga, Missionary Ridge, New Hope Church, Marietta, Franklin and Bentonville. After the war he was never the same and probably suffered from what is now known as Post Trauma Syndrome. He never married and stayed at the cabin atop Duffee's Mountain the rest of his life. Charles Henry Hamilton, son of Rev. John H. Hamilton, wrote about his trip to Duffee Mountain for the funeral of the youngest Duffee son.

> *It was about the year 1903 when Captain Duffee died. My father, the Rev. John H. Hamilton performed the burial for him. He was buried under a big poplar tree beside his father and mother. These graves was(sic) a stone's throw from the old house they lived in. The house was built of wood. The front porch faced Blount Springs and had an 8 foot porch with railing around it. I went into the house with Miss Mary at this time and one room was piled about half way up the walls with newspapers and magazines, all kind of reading material and letters. She saved everything. The next room was full of twigs piled up with only a narrow place to walk through. Miss Mary was so afraid of fire, after her parents died, and would not allow a fire in the house. She would take a few twigs of wood outside the house and had a brick circle with rocks piled around this circle in which she would place the twigs and make a fire to make her coffee and to boil water. She did most of her cooking outside. The home*

> *was a six room house built on a "L" shape. Three rooms run back of each other. She lived in the east room and the house faced south of Blount Springs. The last room was the kitchen and next to it was a dining room. The other room was her brother's. After the funeral of Captain Duffee, that day, she told my father to come into the house and she gathered up all her brothers clothes and all his belongings and said, "Here John, take all these things for your boys. I don't want anything that belonged to my brother left here. Do as you please with any of them. I don't want them in the house.*

At this point Mary didn't come down the mountain because of her ailments. Her mother had already died in 1896.

Rev. Hamilton's wife had been bitten by a rattlesnake. Doctors in Blount Springs thought her arm would have to be amputated to save her life. Mrs. Hamilton would have none of this and was carried to a doctor in Birmingham that was able to save her life and her arm.

Mary wrote to Rev. Hamilton to express her sympathy and grief about this calamity to his wife.

> *"...cruelly born down upon you and the dear noble woman who deserves a better fate! How often has my heart gone out to you in the recent sad, darkened days. Truly, the ways of Providence are fast finding out. You have always seemed such an humble, patient-spirited Christian, so entirely submissive to the Father's will, - your wife such a true and noble help mate, both of you striving through paths of honest industry-to rear your children God-fearing and upright. I can but wonder in arrangement why this blow fell on your household!*

In this letter she expressed the reason she stayed on the mountain and didn't come down any more. She had an infirmity in her left side that would not go away. There is no other mention of this malady in other correspondence. With her brother's passing, she was left alone on the mountain. People still came to see her, when she granted them an audience. M

ary and Issac Points came each day to bring food. They also took care of getting her correspondence to and from the post office. The Points lived near her on Duffee's Mountain and were tireless in taking care of her. Their children received an excellent education in northern schools and went on to become successful professionals in later years. One of the daughters became a teacher and taught in colored schools in Blount County.

A Mr. West of Mountain Brook recalled the summer of 1904 when his father and

grandfather leased the Blount Springs Hotel around 1904. His grandfather had been in the hospitality business for over 30 years. He had a loyal staff that moved with him from location to location. These summer and fall seasons were very popular with the gentry of the South and he had been quite successful in the business. His grandfather and father were Mabson and West. Mabson was a popular hotelier in Montgomery and wanted to try his hand working with the summer resort crowd. The Blount Springs Hotel seemed to be a sure thing for them to be successful.

Spring Yard Circa 1904
The W.S. Hoole Special Collections Library, The University of Alabama

Food was one of the best reasons for success in the hotel business and Mr. West had people that were extremely talented in its preparation and service. Albert Diggs was the head waiter and he was assisted by his well-known and loved cooks, Big Mack and Little Mack. Pegleg Rufus was also well-known as one of the best meat cooks in the state. Food was an art form in their hands.

Social activity was most important at the hotel, as important as drinking the waters for health. There was always a full time orchestra ready when the trains arrived to greet the guests. At lunch and dinner they entertained and then played for a dance every night in the ballroom, with Saturdays still reserved for a German dance. Patrons at the resort

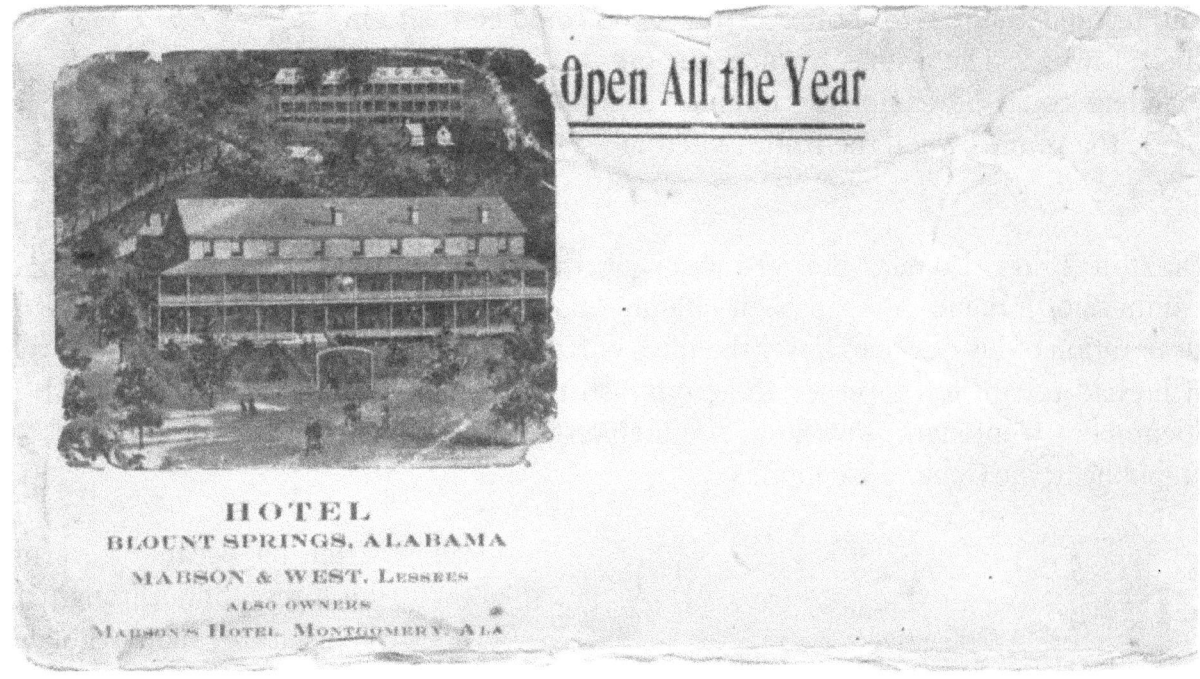

Envelope from the Hotel Stationary
Blount County Museum

would sit around the springs on benches, in the gazebo, or around the pavilion that housed the skating rink and bowling alley with their long-handled dippers, as they moved about to the various springs for the one that was the cure for their ailment.

The afternoons were usually reserved for baths and, best of all, Dr. Frank Plug Muckum was still available for the most desirable treatment at the resort. After one of these famous baths everyone always felt refreshed and ready for the many other entertainments that could be enjoyed at the resort.

Towards dusk each evening the promenade of ladies in their finery would begin at the hotel and proceed to the spring yard as the men watched the beauty parade by. There were some mothers that brought their daughters to the Springs to find the most desirable beaux and abet their courting, hopefully leading to a happy marriage. Besides the spring yard and the many meandering walking trails, one of the most popular things for couples to do was take a walk to Pivot Rock. There were many first kisses at that spot and more than one marriage proposal uttered around this timeless landmark.

About twice a year the "Booster Trains" came through town to everyone's enjoyment. Businessmen from the various towns along the line would use these to advertise the wonderful products and services available to the public by bringing samples, drinks both soft and hard, special varieties of food, and printed material to show everyone what could be found in their towns. The whole town came out to see what new wonders could be sampled. Blount Springs Sulphur Water made the rounds when the train visited other towns along the L & N.

Gov. Braxton Bragg Comer
Alabama Department of Archives and History, Montgomery, Alabama

Braxton Bragg Comer, the president of the state railroad commission, made a speech at Blount Springs making a declaration of his desire to lower the rates of freight in Alabama. He stated that day that if he had to run for governor to accomplish this goal he would. He went on to beat incumbent Lieutenant Governor Cunningham in the Democratic Primary and then the Republic in the General Election.

Child Laborers at Avondale Mills, Birmingham
Alabama Department of Archives and History, Montgomery, Alabama

After he became governor he forced bills through the Legislature that regulated freight rates, bringing them in line with Georgia and the other states neighboring Alabama. He also emphasized education during his term. Several college buildings were named in his honor due to his push for better schools. It must be remembered this was only for the benefit of white students. Black schools were not able to get additional funds. In fact, they were mostly denied any money and some of them closed.

Comer was made chairman of Avondale Mills after he was Governor and helped bring more jobs to Central Alabama through this large company's expansion. Due to his influence not only was the Birmingham facility enlarged, but an additional factory was built in Sylacauga.

Ironically, after he fought for more money for education, he opposed child labor laws and aided in the creation of the widespread use of children in the mills at sub-standard pay and conditions.

He was a proponent of convict labor and helped to promote this new form of slavery in the post-slavery South. Much of the public was behind this idea because it made money for the state and it made more profit for the industries that took advantage of it. A good deal of the profits made in the Mineral District was due to the labor of these convicts.

Politicians running for office and speaking at Blount were nothing new. But in 1908 the famous William Jennings Bryan made a whistle stop tour through the South. Between Cullman and Birmingham, Blount Springs was the only stop.

Bryan Campaign Button
museum.msu.edu

Bryan was famous as one of the leading political figures in the country. He had risen to national prominence as a Congressman from Nebraska and this was the third time he was running for President of the United States as the Democratic nominee. He was considered one of the best orators of the day.

As a devout Christian and a supporter of the Popular Democracy Movement, he was one of the leaders of the Free Silver Cause and had a great deal of influence over many other conservative groups. Later he was one of the most vocal proponents of Prohibition. Hfamously was a part of the prosecution of the Scopes Trial of 1925, often referred to as the "Scopes Monkey Trial" where he served as a fervent protector of the *Bible*.

John Scopes had dared to teach the Theory of Evolution in a small Tennessee school. The state had created a law against teaching Darwin's Theory, even though it was in the state approved text book. H. L. Mencken of the *Baltimore Sun* helped finance the defense and sensationalize the case by calling it the "Monkey Trial". This was the first trial in the United States to be broadcast live on the new medium of radio.

A big change came to the hotel and Blount Springs in 1909 when Alvin Sinclair assumed the management. He wanted to uphold the high standard of service and hospitality, but he decided it was time for a big change. Instead of trying to appeal to the "Old Guard" he went for the younger people.

Chapter 20 – Life After the Fire

The emphasis was now on bringing in the children of the older generation that were now adults. "Come join us" was the new theme of the Blount Springs Hotel and activities were geared toward them. The society columns reflected this new atmosphere and the young were encouraged to come and visit.

In 1909 one of the new social clubs of Birmingham came to visit Blount Springs. The Growlers was formed in 1908 by a group of young men, some in high school and some recent graduates. Founded on the principals of friendship, they later evolved into doing many charitable activities. They eventually changed their name to the Redstone Club in 1927. They have done many

The Growlers in 1909
Encyclopedia of Alabama

good works throughout their long history but are also well known for their annual Christmas Dance that still occurs.

Once again Blount Springs was the epicenter of another kind of great excitement when a gang of train robbers entered the mail car of a train while it was waiting at the Blount Springs Depot. The masked men stepped into the car and with a "flourish of revolvers" held up the clerks. First reports were that they got away with $40,000. The dastardly thieves boarded the train at Blount and went immediately to the mail car. J. M. Chamberlain was in charge and C. A. Hoover was his assistant. Both clerks were well aware the L & N and some other companies' payrolls were in that mail car.

Broyles, just north of Birmingham
L & N RR Map

After it was made clear to the clerks what would happen if they didn't cooperate, they were told to lie down. The bandits were not reticent to intimidate the clerks by hitting them. One of the clerks cleverly sprawled over the Birmingham pouch. It was the one that held the payroll for a couple of Birmingham mills and amounted to quite a bit of cash. Payrolls were almost always in cash at that time. The men quickly ransacked the mail car looking for money. They found several small amounts in different pouches but not the big score they had expected to find.

Chamberlain recalled the thieves showed their inexperience when they threw that money down and kept searching for the big score. One of the finds was several thousand dollars worth of railroad stock coupons they scattered on the floor in their frenzied search. Disgusted, they took five dollars out of the pocket of Chamberlain.

Before they made their escape the men tied both clerks to a wooden table. When the train neared the small station of Broyles they signaled the engineer to stop and jumped off. Running into the nearby woods they made their escape. In a few minutes the two clerks were discovered bound in the car. They went on into the station and telegraphed the news of the robbery to Birmingham. A posse was formed to chase the bandits but they were never found.

Almost 20 detectives and Secret Service agents were assigned to the case and worked the next few days to find clues. At Broyles they found two separate scraps of torn overalls that were similar to what the bandits had worn. No other clues were ever found, but it was determined that they had only gotten a very small amount of money and not $40,000 as was first reported.

Summer Outings on the Louisville & Nashville Railroad

BLOUNT SPRINGS, ALA.

Blount Springs is situated on the main line of the Louisville & Nashville System of Railroads, in Blount County, Alabama, in the heart of the foothills of the famous Cumberland Mountain Range, thirty miles north of Birmingham and 175 miles south of Nashville, Tenn. The climate is delightful, the temperature being medium the year around.

Under the management of the Blount Springs Hotel Company, we are prepared to furnish the patrons with a diversity of amusements, and a dining-room second to no American-plan hotel in the South. The comforts of a country home, combined with the conveniences of a city, cannot fail to be appreciated by an intelligent public.

A high-class orchestra is engaged, giving a concert in the mornings from 11 to 12 o'clock, and from 8 o'clock in the evenings until nearly midnight.

As a health resort Blount Springs is historical. Long before Alabama was admitted into the Union as a Territory this famous group of sulphur springs was a landmark and meeting place for the Cherokee and Creek Indians.

Able physicians are always resident on the grounds, so that invalids have the advantage of the best attention. The hot and cold sulphur baths, which can be taken in the hotel, are said to possess curative qualities equal to the celebrated Hot Springs of Arkansas. Dyspepsia and miasmatic affections, especially, are quickly removed by the use of these waters. Address proprietor Blount Springs Hotel Company, Blount Springs, Ala., for rates, etc.

Visit beautiful Blount Springs, Ala. On the L & N
L & N Travel Literature

The L & N encouraged travel and sought to bring people to the many attractions that lay along their tracks. Advertising was posted in stations and also newspapers across the South, into Ohio and other Northern states touting the wonders to behold all along the line. Many of these attractions were popular during the same season as the hotel and were varied in their appeal.

Chapter 20 – Life After the Fire

It was becoming easier to travel to all these exotic destinations and for people all over the United States and the growing middle class of Alabama. You could visit from Niagara Falls to Mammoth Cave, from Blount Springs to the Florida Beaches, all on an L & N rails.

When the original tracks were built there was a need for expediency and the road bed was not constructed with the correct grade throughout the length of the line. By 1913 the Louisville and Nashville had taken total control over the South and North Alabama Railroad. They began re-routing and reconstructing parts of the roadbed that were not at the recommended grade.

It was decided the tracks should run from Warrior to Hayden and then back to the regular line. This caused the tracks to be moved away from Blount Springs. The new route came in east of the springs and further up the mountainside. This move foreshadowed the demise of Blount Springs as a popular trip, because it made it harder for people to get directly to the hotel by train.

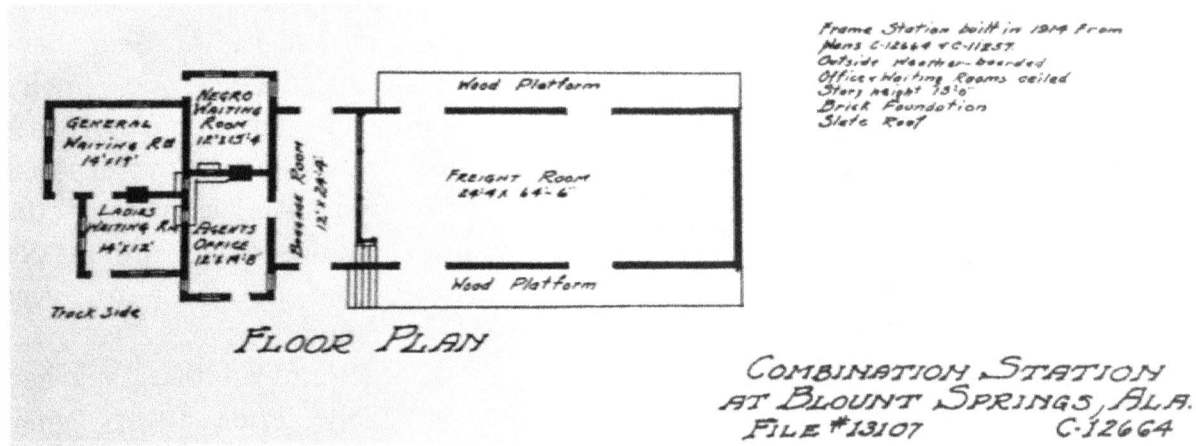

Floor Plan for the new Blount Springs Depot
L & N Archives discovered by David DeBandi

Reid's Gap was abandoned and a new depot for Blount Springs was built near the new tunnel. This change was completed in 1914 and the old rails were torn up. That roadbed was donated to the state to serve as a highway in 1923 and it is now where US 31 runs. This was the beginning of the end of the importance that Blount Springs held with the society of the South.

Blount Springs was saddened when the people learned of the death of Col. J. F. B. Jackson. At the age of 82 he proceeded from his home on 7th Avenue between 18th and 19th Street, to a neighborhood store. He went to buy a few things his wife Sallie wanted. Jackson had a hearing problem, couldn't see very well, and was quite feeble by this time in his life. He simply stepped in front of a streetcar. Ironically, the streetcars were made possible by the Birmingham Gas & Illuminating Company, a business he founded.

Col. Jackson
The Birmingham News

It appeared there were no serious injuries from the accident and Jackson would only be sore from the impact and have a few bruises. He did go unconscious for a few minutes so he was taken to a local infirmary. He died the next afternoon shortly after 2:00 on Sunday, January 14, 1912. He was buried in Elmwood Cemetery alongside his daughter Elizabeth. Many leaders of Birmingham served as pallbearers for this important pioneer of Birmingham including several judges, George B. Ward, and General Rucker.

Later Sallie would join him in 1916. When she died she left a portion of her estate to Hillman Hospital. The Jacksons had never forgotten the loss of their daughter and the importance of hospitals. A ward for the children of Louisville & Nashville Railroad workers was dedicated as a memorial to Elizabeth.

Mary Duffee had not been seen in town for several years, but she was well remembered and many still climbed the mountain to go visit her when they were up for a stay. She held court in her deteriorating six room cabin. Many believed when her brother died he wasn't buried. They thought she had left him in his bedroom. This was part of the mystique of the "Witch of the Mountain".

Charles Hamilton thought the world of Miss Mary and he described her the way he remembered her from his childhood.

> *Miss Mary was six feet tall, slender and always dressed in a Mother-Hubbard dress or in men's clothes. She always carried a long rifle with her and she rode horseback, always side saddle. Her hair was sandy, combed to the back of her head and tied with a ribbon in a knot. She weighed about 130 pounds and wore high top laced shoes. I never saw her with a hat on. She would put a shawl over her head in bad weather and a croaker-sack around her shoulder and tied it under her neck fastened with a safety pin.*

1915 brought the event that really ended the prominence of the resort and changed its future. Early in June the news went out all over Alabama that fire was raging through Blount Springs. That was all that was known, because the telegraph wires were down which made it difficult to get news of the blaze and its aftermath.

Chapter 20 – Life After the Fire

By the next day the terrible truth was known. A fire started in the kitchen of the Blount Springs Hotel and soon spread and went out of control. This hotel, including the Mountain House, was a total loss. A few of the surrounding cottages and several stores were also lost to the conflagration. No lives were lost so the biggest tragedy of all was the lack of insurance. Losses were estimated to be in the neighborhood of $45,000.

The prediction in the newspaper accounts was true. None of the hotel buildings were ever rebuilt. There would be life after the fire in Blount Springs, but it would never regain the grandeur that had been the essence of the town since the 1870s. Several attempts at re-capturing the wonder of the resort would come about, but all ended below the high mark the Blount Springs Hotel set as the center of social life for so many, and for so long.

BLOUNT SPRINGS HAS $45000 FIRE.

BIG HOTEL AND SEVERAL COTTAGES DESTROYED.

On Thursday afternoon, June 3rd the big hotel at Blount Springs and several cottages were destroyed. The fire is reported to have started in the kitchen of the main hotel, completely destroying that building The Mountain House, located on the mountain about two or three hundred feet from the main hotel, quickly caught and in a short time several of the cottages were enveloped in the flames. Other cottages and store houses were badly damaged.

Practically all the buildings damaged and destroyed were the property of the Blount Springs Hotel Co., owned by W. M. Drennen, of Birmingham. Mr. Drennen estimates the loss at $45000. with only $13000. insurance.

It it is probable that the burned section will not be rebuilt.

The *Southern Democrat*

20
Life After the Fire

The town didn't die immediately but it did change drastically. Several cottages were still in good shape and some of the smaller hotels were still in business, but it just wasn't the same without the social hub of the Blount Springs Hotel and all its finery.

Another problem confronting the businesses there was the spreading ownership of automobiles. Dependency on the train was over and people were gaining the freedom to go where they wanted, when they wanted. It was a new world of mobility and other places of interest were appearing all over the countryside taken advantage of by many former Blount Springs patrons.

Henry Lee Badham, Sr.
BPL Digital Coll.

Henry Lee Badham and his family had been regulars at the hotel for many years and then around the turn of the century bought a home on Alabama Street. They built a home on a lot previously owned by Dr. Constantine and next door to the Randolphs, just south of the Mountain House. It was prime property in Blount Springs and the Badhams were the right people to occupy such a choice spot.

They were well known for their wonderful house parties. Everyone lucky enough to attend any of their events was certainly assured of a great time and much hospitality. Their house was large enough to accommodate a good crowd and they even had a large sleeping porch to allow many to stay over for more fun the next day.

The Badhams were part of the elite of Birmingham as he was the Director of the Bessemer Improvement Company and had an interest in several mines. She was a member of the Alabama Equal Suffrage Association, mother of ten children and one of the best hostesses in Birmingham and Blount Springs.

Their oldest son, Henry, Jr. graduated from Yale in 1912just like his father had before him. After graduation he returned to Birmingham and worked with his father. He also joined the National Guard and served during the Mexican Border Campaign when the Army tried to catch Pancho Villa. When

Mrs. Lottie Badham
The Woman Citizen

World War I started he signed up with the newly formed Aviation Section of the United States Signal Corps.

After his service he worked with a group of men that helped found the Birmingham Aer o Club and eventually landed the 106th Observation Squadron for the city. Badham rose to the rank of Major and became the commander of this group. He also constructed an airstrip in Blount Springs. It was not unusual to see his plane in the air over the mountains of Blount County. He is a member of the Alabama Aviation Hall of Fame.

Henry Badham, Jr. Alabama Aviation Hall of Fame

In the middle of August, 1920, Charles Hamilton had grown up and was now a minister himself. He was married and had two young children. They made the hard climb up to see Miss Mary Duffee so his wife and daughter could meet the women he so much respected and admired.

When I got near Miss Mary's house and near to her window, I called out to her, "Miss Mary," for a few minutes I heard no reply. And again I said, "Miss Mary, can I come in to see you?" She said, "I don't want to see anybody, go away!" I said, "Miss Mary, I am Charlie Hamilton, Rev. John Hamilton's son that you used to give me nickels when I was a little boy. I want to see you again, please." And she said, "If you are Charlie Hamilton, open that door and come in. I want to see you too." I opened the door and told her I had my wife and daughter with me, and she said, "Please come in." It was a sight I will never forget. It almost broke my heart to see her. She was frail, white as snow. Her bed had fallen in through the floor partly and she was lying cross-wise on a bed. Even though it was summer time, she had old quilts on her. She held out her feeble hand and I held it with tears in my eyes. And she also began to shed tears. With her voice weak, she said to me, "I am glad you came. I don't have many more days left." We stayed about 30 minutes and I asked her if I could take her down the mountain to be cared for until her death and she said, "No. I want to die here and you know where to bury me." I saw it was making her weak to talk and when we got ready to leave, I said, "Miss Mary, are you a Christian? Do you believe in God and the resurrection of Jesus Christ?" She answered me and said with tears in her eyes, "Charlie, I have been a Christian all my life. I do believe in God. I have never done anyone any harm. I love God and hope to be with him soon." She asked me to have a prayer with her and I did. She was lying cross ways on this bed and my wife and I helped to put her straight in bed. And I fixed the floor the best I could with what I could find. She was clean. Her hair combed back as she always wore it. She said, "Thank you, Charlie for coming and God bless you and your family."

Mary and Isaac Point would go every day and clean her up, change her bed and night clothes, bring her food and feed her. I sure hated to leave her like that, but it was all I could do. I could not get back the next day. I had told her when I left I would be back again to see her. Two days later a runner from the mountain came down looking for me and said that Miss Mary was dead and had requested for me to bury her. I was a local minister at the time. I knew what I had to do and, with God's help, I did just what I knew Miss Mary would want me to do.

On Duffee's Mountain
David DeBandi

Mary died August 21, 1920. Mary and Isaac Point had stuck with her and took care of her the best they could. Nieces and nephews begged her to let them provide a home for her, but she didn't want to leave her beloved mountain. She was buried alongside her father, mother, and brother near the cabin she lived in for close to 40 years. Charlie kept his promise to Miss Mary and remembered her fondly until the day he died.

The most famous citizen of Blount Springs, Mary Gordon Duffee had died atop Duffee Mountain. Mollie had been an institution since the early 1850s when her father first brought the precoucious girl from Tuscaloosa, along with his family, to run a hotel. Her writings left a lasting memory of Blount Springs and how life was during the best years of its existence.

She had also written accounts describing her annual journey from Tuscaloosa to Blount that are a lasting endowment to historians. She pushed Thomas Owens of the Alabama State Archives to get those articles published as a book, writing extensively to him about this project in 1908. She even worked with editing them into a work she would be proud to leave for posterity. In some of the letters she remarked how she would be leaving some people out because they didn't deserve to be remembered.

Unfortunately it would not be published in her lifetime, but did finally become a reality in the 1970s. Sketches of Alabma is one of the most important sources for historians and those with interest in the early history of Central Alabama. It still stands as one of the greatest sources of information about the settlers of Jefferson County.

Even in death, Mollie Duffee proved to be true to part of her reputation. Some called her the "Witch of the Mountain" because of the peculiarities she exhibited. As she lay in state in her home of many years a sheet was draped over her body.

Mary "Mollie" Duffee in 1902
Blount County Museum

As family and friends sat and stood around for her wake, as was the custom of the time, the sheet moved. It was almost imperceptible at first and some looked to see if what they thought happened really had. In just a moment their fears were confirmed when the sheet moved again. The room was quickly cleared as they thought the "witch" might have overcome death. To the crowd's relief, one of her many cats poked its head from beneath the shroud to the amazement of the gathered mourners.

The graves are sunken now and the nature Mary Duffee loved so much has reclaimed the mountain. The Winesap orchard has lived through maturity and disappeared into the woodland floor. Duffee's cabin has fallen in, rotted and totally disappeared from view. It would take an archeologist to determine exactly where everything was, except for the still standing fireplace.

There are many descendants of the Duffee family scattered around the United States and they have continued to make a mark on the lives of other people. The spirit of Mary Gordon Duffee lives on through her poetry, her family and her landmark book.

William Rice built a hotel on the main road in 1923 and called it The Rice Hotel. It wasn't a big hotel, only sixteen rooms, but it was very popular and stayed full most of the time. There were two floors and a porch ran across two sides of both floors. No grand dining room for dances was there, bands didn't play for dinner, and the grounds were not extensively landscaped, but it was cozy and Mrs. Rice kept up the tradition of delicious and abundant food. A loyal clientele kept the place busy and it was a highly popular summer vacation stop along the old railroad bed. The place where the tracks had run was now the main road from Warrior and would later become U. S. Highway 31.

The Rice Inn
Blount County Museum

He had a large family and this seemed a great way to provide for them. There were five daughters and Blount Springs was a great place to raise them. The Rice House was over the hill from the Baptist Church for black people and across the road from the Badham Family retreat. The Church was located where the Blount Springs Baptist Church is presently located and near their home, so the daughters would rush from their own church services to listen to the beautiful singing of the black church as it flowed down the hillside into their valley. They would sit on the porch and listen as long as they could.

Unidentified woman in front of the Rice Inn
Wallace Community College Genealogy Department Hanceville, Alabama

Unfortunately tuberculosis took Mr. Rice's life in 1932. His wife tried to take over running the hotel for a couple of years by herself. Some of her older girls lived in Birmingham and finally talked her into selling the hotel and moving all the family there. In 1934, at the height of the Great Depression, she sold the building to a man from Cullman. Birmingham became her home as she moved in with one of her daughters. The new owner had the building torn down and used the lumber to construct another home in Cullman.

Later in the 1920s the town saw big plans for the future unfold. In an effort to make his land valuable again, Drennen and Robert Jemison put together a grandiose scheme to make Blount Springs a resort town once again. Plans were drawn up for new streets and homes to be built. There were plans for swimming, boating and even an 18 hole golf course and country club and luxurious homes.

Robert Jemison, Jr.
realtor.org

This would have a distinct twist making it much different than the standard suburb with four homes lined up on blocks that were of the standard size. The idea was to use the countryside much as it was before development. Homes would be on oversized lots with the majority of trees and greenery left as nature created it. These would be grand homes also, suited for the gentry that had frequented Blount Springs and would be built to suit the cream of Birmingham society.

Everything was advancing quite smoothly and the plan was falling into place. Money was available and Drennen's 8,000 acres would provide plenty of space for the venture. Sadly, in the year 1921, Mel Drennen finally died from the tuberculosis that had plagued him for years. With his death the plan also died, at least as it concerned Blount Springs.

Instead of going through with those plans in Blount County, it was decided to create the new suburb nearer to Birmingham. That suburb was Mountain Brook, just as it was to be named after the sister community, just down the road from Blount Springs. Jemison took those same ideas and created the community on the southern edge of the newly moved Birmingham Country Club.

Country Home Lovers Praise Mountain Brook Estates

From *Jemison Magazine*

Originally the club was founded in 1898 in North Birmingham, but moved to Lakeview in 1900. The old course in North Birmingham remained as a municipal course for many years. It was located where Carver High School now stands. While at Lakeview it hosted Teddy Roosevelt on the same trip he visited Blount Springs. They also hosted several Women's Southern Golf Association tournaments. Highland Golf Course is a reminder of the old club during its time at that location. Jemison was instrumental in getting the Club moved to its present location as part of his new fashionable development.

A second nine holes course was added and new homes were constructed in the pastoral setting as promised, the difference being it was not near Blount Springs. Bankers, industrialists, and other well-to-do families hurried to buy land and build homes in the very well advertised area. Jemison created a magazine specifically to promote the new development and serve the people that lived there. It was aptly titled *Jemison & Company Magazine: Devoted to the News of Mountain Brook Estates, Inc.*.

Many people still came to Old Blount and enjoyed the mountain air and camaraderie during vacations. The old hotel wasn't there to be the center of the social world but many enjoyed house parties and other social events. There was one three story hotel still in operation and the Badhams, Willoughbys, Lights, Coles, Burdettes, Burgesses, Gladdens, Hobers, and others came from Birmingham, while the McCoys and Lees came from Cullman, along with other families from scattered towns around Alabama and the South.

Many of the yearly visitors were the children of some of the regulars of years past. Cabins and homes were still owned by individuals or in the family for all to enjoy. Members of several families, including that of Dr. Robinson continued to visit as did the descendants of the Randolphs and many others. Other families and groups still used the area for reunions and picnics also.

Judge and Mrs. Brown enjoying their cabin at Blount Springs
Blount County Museum

One of the stalwarts that came every year from Montgomery was Judge Joel B. Brown and his wife. As soon as the Supreme Court adjourned for the Spring Session they made their way to enjoy the good life in their mountain cabin. They built it on the old road near the Badhams where the judge enjoyed his hobby of building clocks.

Avondale Mills created a camp for the families of its employees to use and enjoy. They were able to enjoy swimming, hiking, fishing and open air concerts by bands and singing groups. One of the groups that often sang there were the Jordans. They were a family group from Birmingham with 10 children. One of those Jordans, Irene, became a soprano of reknown with the Metropolitan Opera.

Comer Family Reunion at Blount Springs, circa 1930
Wallace State Community College Genealogy Department, Hanceville, Alabama

Three doctors invested in 2,500 acres with a dream to create the Mountain Brook Dairy. Dr. E. M. Prince, Dr. D. S. Moore, and Dr. Joe Moore hired over 50 people to operate and maintain one of the most modern dairies the state of Alabama had seen up to that point. Besides the best equipment, provisions were made to keep the employees happy and healthy at the farm.

The company built tennis courts and provided places to play volleyball, basketball and other sports on the grounds. One of the greatest things the doctors did for their workers was the creation of a swimming area on one of the coldest waterways in the South. Dr. Prince took sawdust from his sawmills and made a beach. On that beach he commissioned one of the prettiest beach houses ever seen, made entirely of walnut with an inlaid design in the floor. Remains of the swimming area are still used today by local families and their children.

Blount Springs has been home to many fine folks since its glory days as the "Saratoga of the South" and "Alabama's Fountain of Youth". There are only a few of the buildings left from those days, but many others have been built. Several years ago one of the descendants of Mel Drennen started the Blue Hole Village above Cold Creek. There are many beautiful homes there and many young folks have moved into the area.

The springs still run and the smell of rotten eggs pervade the air of the old spring yard where a hundred years ago the elite of Alabama and the South made the promenade from the hotel to see and be seen. Many families started in Old Blount as young men met young ladies and married after meeting there. Pivot Rock is still there and could tell many, many stories of young love and probably many first kisses.

The only signs of the Blount Springs Hotel are the rocks of the foundation and a hole where the basement might have been. Many people have trespassed on this private property and used metal detectors to look for buried items that could be valuable. There are some stone stairsteps and pillars on the spot where the Mountain House once proudly stood. Trees have grown throughout the property but many signs of the landscaping are still recognizable, such as walkways and paths.

Through the woodland property surrounding the hotel site can be found numerous footings and a chimney or two marking the site of many cottages where eventful summer memories and decades of laughter and enjoyment for those priviledged enough to have stayed there were made. The woods are also full of danger as most cottages had cisterns that are now hidden and present an easy opportunity for danger to anyone that walks through unaware of them.

Remains of the Mountain House in a photo by the author

Much of this property is in good hands now and will be preserved as it is. The sites of many cottages including the Randolphs, the Badhams, and Judge Brown are owned by a family commited to preservation. They also own the site of the Rice Hotel, the Avondale Camp and much of the old road to Birmingham. Many other cottage sites are on their land and will be protected from future danger of encroachment. The top of Robinson Mountain is still full of families living in homes built during the resort era and will be preserved.

The Baptist Church on US 31 is doing well and serving the area. The Top Hat Barbeque is a thriving concern and has become well-known throughout the state as an excellent restaurant. It has been in the Pettit family since the 1960s and will be for many years to come as the next generation takes over. A popular motorcycle establishment occupies the former site of the South & North Alabama Railroad.

Its legacy is barely known to the young of today, but that is true of many other great sites that are important in Alabama history as well. Our duty to the young is to relate the stories of days gone by so they know where their people have been, while they forge the future of where our progeny will go.

Photographs of Blount Springs

Blount Springs Hotel
from the Blount County Museum

RAILROAD STATION—BLOUNT SPRINGS, ALABAMA

Post Card of Blount Springs
Blount County Museum

Waterfalls Swimming Area in the 1950s
Blount County Museum

Photographs of Blount Springs

CONCERT IN SPRING YARD, 1884, BY GRAMB'S BAND OF BIRMINGHAM

Blount County Museum

DUFFIE'S MOUNTAIN—BLOUNT SPRINGS, ALABAMA

Postcards of Blount Springs
Blount County Museum

Pivot Rock
Circa 1904 photograph by Eugene Smith
The W. S. Hoole Collection, University of Alabama

Pivot Rock
Circa 1904 photograph by Eugene Smith
The W. S. Hoole Collection, University of Alabama

On the Hotel Grounds
Wallace Community College Genealogy Department, Hanceville, Alabama

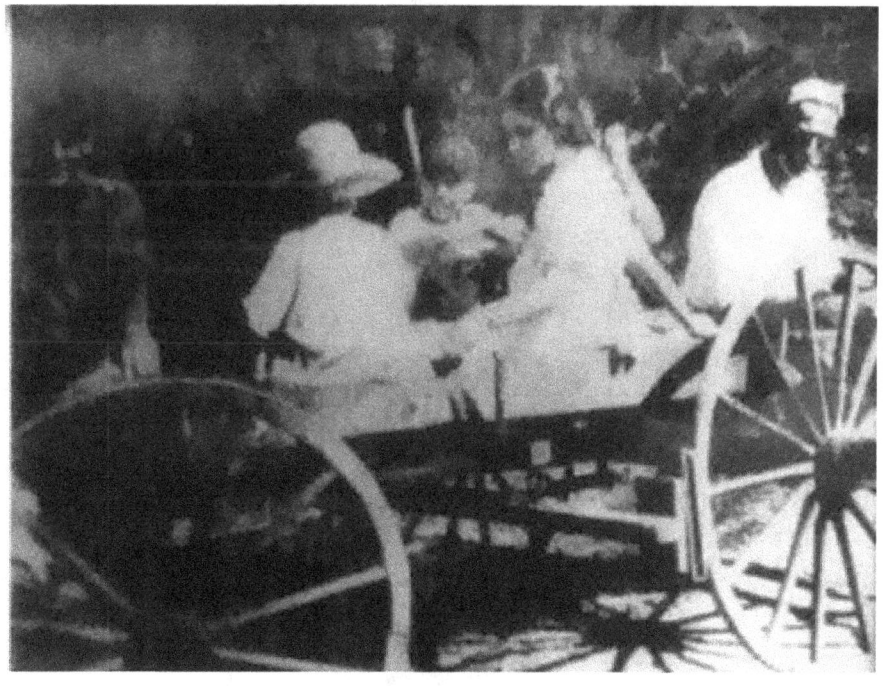

Wagon Ride
Wallace Community College Genealogy Department, Hanceville, Alabama

Rice Hotel
Mrs. Evelyn Howell Sapp

Road by the Spring Yard

Mrs. Evelyn Howell Sapp

Blount Springs Methodist Church
Legend has it the church was built by a one-armed man. It burned to the ground in the late 1970s.
Some of the beautiful stained glass windows are now in the Smokerise Methodist Church.
Blount County Museum

Resources

Reference Material

Books

Armes, Ethel, *The Story of Coal and Iron in Alabama*, Birmingham, Alabama, Published under auspices of the Chamber of Commerce, 1910.

Benners, Augustus, *Disunion, War, Defeat and Recovery in Alabama*, Macon, Ga., Mercer University Press, 2007

Blount County Heritage Book Committee, *The Heritage of Blount County*,

Christopher, Charlotte and Watson, Tom, A History of Blount Springs, Self-Published, 1998

DuBose, John Witherspoon, Jefferson County and Birmingham, Alabama, Historical and Biographical 1887, Birmingham, Caldwell Printing Works, 1887

Henderson, Aileen Kilgore, *Eugene Allen Smith's Alabama*, Montgomery, Alabama, NewSouth Books, 2011

Herr, Kincaid A., *The Louisville & Nashville Railroad, 1850-1963*, Lexington, The University Press of Kentucky, 2000

Interstate Directory Company, *City Directory of Birmingham and Gazetteer of Surrounding Section for 1884-5, Volume II*, Atlanta, H. H. Dickson, Book and Job Printer, 1884

Louisville and Nashville Railroad Passenger Department, *The Dream of "Ellen N"*, Cincinnati, John F. C. Mullen, 1886

Myer, William G., *Federal Decisions, Cases Argued and Determined in the Supreme, circuit and district Courts of the United States*, St. Louis, Mo., The Gilbert book company, 1887.

Owen, Thomas McAdory. *A Bibliography of Alabama*. Washinton: Government Printing Office, 1898.

Pioneer Club, *Early Days in Birmingham*, Birmingham: 1908

Ramage, James A., *Rebel Raider, The Life of General John Hunt Morgan*, Lexington, Kentucky, The University Press of Kentucky, 1986.

Robbers, Madge Thornall, *The Personal Correspondence of Sam Houston*, Enton, Texas, University of North Texas Press, 1996.

Seale, William, *Sam Houston;s Wife*, A biography of Margaret Lea Houston, Norman, Oklahoma, University of Oklahoma Press, 1992.

South and North Alabama Railroad Company, *The Charter of the South & North Alabama Railroad Company and Acts Amendatory Thereof*, Montgomery, Alabama, Advertiser Book and Job Printing, 1876

Sulzby, James F., Historic Alabama Hotels and Resorts, Tuscaloosa, The University of Alabama Press, 1960

Thomas E. Huey, *Ruhama, The Story of a Church*, Birmingham, Birmingham Printing Company, 1946

Waldo, J. Curtis, *Visitor's Guide to New Orleans*, New Orleans, Southern Publishing & Advertising House, 1875

Walton, George Edward, *the Mineral Springs of the United States and Canada*, New York, New York, D. Appleton & company, 1873.

Wiggins, Sarah Woolfolk, *the Journals of Josiah Gorgas*, 1857-1878, Tuscaloosa, Alabama, The University of Alabama Press, 1995.

Williams, Stephen K., *Cases Argued and Decided in the Supreme Court of the United States Book 14*, Rochester, New York, the Lawyers Co-operative Publishing Company, 1884.

Wooster, Louise C., *The Autobiography of a Magdalen*, Birmingham: Birmingham Publishing Company, 1911.

Information and/or Photographs

Alabama Department of Archives and History - Montgomery, Alabama

Birmingham Public Library Digital Collection - Birmingham, Alabama

Birmingham Public Library Southern History Archives - Birmingham, Alabama

Cumming, Anne, Blount Springs, Alabama, The Making of the New South, history class Report

DeBandi, David for his photographs and information

Huntsville Historical Quarterly – Huntsville, Alabama

Lewis, Jim for his fantastic family picture of the spring yard

Odom, Jonathan, for his videos and information

Porter, Essie Leonora, Reminicing about Blount Springs, Blount County Museum

Reeves, Dr. Rebecca for Bangor Cave Club photograph

Reid, Irene for photographs and oral history

Sapp, Mrs. Evelyn Howell for her photographs and oral history

Tumlin, Mike for photographs, information, and most importantly, moral support

United States Census 1810 - 1950

The W. S. Hoole Special Collections Library, University of Alabama

Wallace State Community College Genealogy Department - Hanceville, Alabama

University of Alabama Geography Department for maps of Alabama

Websites

University of Alabama Geography Department Map Collection
http://alabamamaps.ua.edu/

Letter written by Matthew Duffee in Blount Springs, Alabama To his son, George G. Duffee in Mobile, Alabama, December 28, 1875
http://trees.ancestry.com.au/tree/55681929/person/13857095416/storyx/d0cb372d-41c6-4fe8-9925-bdec3f46d9bc?src=search

Letters of Minnie Anderson, Blount Springs to Mother, Baltinglass
http://ied.dippam.ac.uk/records/29489

University of Alabama Libraries
http://acumen.lib.ua.edu/

Encyclopedia of Alabama
http://www.encyclopediaofalabama.org/face/Home.jsp

Ancestry
http://ancestory.com

Jefferson County Historical Association
http://www.jeffcohistory.com/

Information on George Goff
http://wc.rootsweb.ancestry.com/cgi-bin/igm.cgi?op=GET&db=fittingsbf2&id=I117

Mary Gordon Duffee Information
http://archiver.rootsweb.ancestry.com/th/read/ALABAMA/2007-10/1192580678

Autaugaville History
http://www.autaugaheritage.com/Statesville.htm

Autauga County Census for 1830
http://www.usgwarchives.org/al/autauga/census/1830

Mary Louise Goffe
http://wc.rootsweb.ancestry.com/cgi-bin/igm.cgi?op=GET&db=fittingsbf2&id=I816

Mary Louisa Goffe Burton Burial
http://www.findagrave.com/cgi-bin/fg.cgi?page=gr&GRid=29656624

Marriage of George and Louisa Goff
http://www.genealogyforum.rootsweb.com/files/AL/DallasCoMarriages.htm

Sketches of Towns
http://algensoc.org/alabama-indexing/TCndx.pdf

History of 39th Georgia
http://files.usgwarchives.net/ga/whitfield/history/other/gms353historyo.txt

History of Dalton Guards
http://dalton150th.com/1861_Apr_-_June.html

Report to the Governor of Alabama on the Alabama Central Railroad, Montgomery, 1859 - Milner
http://www.bhamrails.info/Milner_report_Gov.htm

Mary Gordon Duffee Information
http://bama.ua.edu/~sholl001/try/MGD.htm

Newspapers and Publications by City

Newspaper	City	Retrieved From:
The Meridonial	Abbeville, LA	Library of Congress
Athens Weekly Banner	Athens, GA	Georgia Historic Newspapers
Banner-Watchman	Athens, GA	Georgia Historic Newspapers
Southern Banner	Athens, GA	Georgia Historic Newspapers
Atlanta Constitution	Atlanta, GA	Georgia Historic Newspapers
Atlanta Daily herald	Atlanta, GA	Georgia Historic Newspapers
Atlanta Georgian	Atlanta, GA	Georgia Historic Newspapers
Atlanta Georgian Tribune	Atlanta, GA	Georgia Historic Newspapers
Sunny South	Atlanta, GA	Georgia Historic Newspapers
The Sunny South	Atlanta, GA	Georgia Historic Newspapers
Weekly Constitution	Atlanta, GA	Georgia Historic Newspapers
Weekly Iron Age	Birmingham, AL	Library of Congress
Birmingham Age Herald	Birmingham, AL	Birmingham Public Lib. Dig. Coll.

Birmingham Iron Age	Birmingham, AL	Birmingham Public Lib. Dig. Coll.
Birmingham News	Birmingham, AL	Birmingham Public Lib. Dig. Coll.
Birmingham Weekly Herald	Birmingham, AL	Birmingham Public Lib. Dig. Coll.
Bismarck Tribune	Bismarch, ND	Library of Congress
Blount Springs Herald	Blount Springs, AL	Blount County Museum
The Blount County News and Dispatch	Blountsville, AL	Library of Congress
Burlington Weekly Free Press	Burlington, VT	Library of Congress
Clarksville Weekly Chronicle	Clarsville, TN	Library of Congress
The Columbia Herald	Columbia, TN	Library of Congress
Columbus Daily Enquirer	Columbus, GA	Georgia Historic Newspapers
Columbia Democrat and Bloomsburg General Advertiser	Columbus, GA	Georgia Historic Newspapers
Sun and Columbus Sunday Enquirer	Columbus, GA	Georgia Historic Newspapers
Weekly Columbus Enquirer	Columbus, GA	Georgia Historic Newspapers
The Cullman Tribune	Cullman, AL	Cullman County Archives
The Donaldson Chief	Donaldson, LA	Library of Congress
Cambria Freeman	Edensburg, PA	Library of Congress
The Jones Valley Times	Elyton, AL	AL Dept. Archives & History
The Findlay Jeffersonian	Findlay, OH	Library of Congress
Fort Worth Gazette	Fort Worth. TX	Library of Congress
Gadsden Times	Gadsden, AL	Library of Congress
The Hickman Courier	Hickman, KY	Library of Congress
The Hawaiian Gazette	Homolulu, HI	Library of Congress
The Huntsville Weekly Democrat	Huntsville, AL	newspaperabstracts.com
The Southern Advocate	Huntsville, AL	Library of Congress
The Iola Register	Iola, KS	Library of Congress
The State Journal	Jefferson City, MO	Library of Congress
Mower County Transcript	Lansing, MN	Library of Congress
The Ohio Democrat	Logan, OH	Library of Congress
Le Meschacébé	Lucy, LA	Library of Congress
The Evening Bulletin	Marysville, KY	Library of Congress
Medford Mail Tribune	Medford, OR	Library of Congress
Memphis Daily Appeal	Memphis, TN	Library of Congress
The Milan Exchange	Milan, TN	Library of Congress
Nashville Union and American	Nashville, TN	Library of Congress
Nebraska Advertiser	Nemaha City, NE	Library of Congress
New Orleans Commercial bulletin	New Orleans, LA	Library of Congress
The Morning Star and Catholic Messenger	New Orleans, LA	Library of Congress
New York Tribune	New York, NY	Library of Congress
The Evening World	New York, NY	Library of Congress

The New York Times	New York, NY	Library of Congress
Daily Press	Newport News, VA	Library of Congress
Omaha Daily Bee	Omaha, NB	Library of Congress
Southern Democrat	Oneonta, AL	Library of Congress
The Paterson Press	Patterson, NJ	Library of Congress
The Pensacola Journal	Pensacola, FL	Library of Congress
The Pensacola Journal	Pensacola, FL	Library of Congress
Perrysburg Journal	Perrysburg, OH	Library of Congress
Public Ledger	Philadelphia, PA	Library of Congress
Arizona Republican	Phoenix, AR	Library of Congress
Keowee Courier	Pickens Coutny, SC	Library of Congress
Pittsburg Dispatch	Pittsburg, PA	Library of Congress
Pratt City Herald	Pratt City, AL	Library of Congress
The Pulaski Citizen	Pulaski, TN	Library of Congress
The Daily Dispatch	Richmond, BA	Library of Congress
The Time Dispatch	Richmond, VA	Library of Congress
Sacramento Daily	Sacramento, CA	Library of Congress
Deseret Evening News	Salt Lake City, UT	Library of Congress
The Salt Lake Tribune	Salt Lake City, UT	Library of Congress
The San Francisco Call	San Francisco, CA	Library of Congress
The Scranton Tribune	Scranton, PA	Library of Congress
The Selma Times-Journal	Selma, AL	selmatimesjournal.com
The Semi-Weekly Shreveport News	Shreveport, LA	Library of Congress
The Somerset Herald	Somerset, PA	Library of Congress
The St. Louis Republic	St. Louis, MO	Library of Congress
Daily Globe	St. Paul, MN	Library of Congress
St. Paul Daily Globe	St. Paul, MN	Library of Congress
Staunton Spectator	Staunton, VA	Library of Congress
Tulsa Daily World	Tulsa, OK	Library of Congress
The Tuscaloosa News	Tuscaloosa, AL	Library of Congress
Evening Star	Washington, DC	Library of Congress
The Times	Washington, DC	Library of Congress
The Washington Herald	Washington, DC	Library of Congress
The Wheeling Daily Intelligencer	Wheeling, WV	Library of Congress
Willmar Tribune	Willmar, MN	Library of Congress

Please direct any comments and suggestions to gregburden@gmail.com
or talk with Amy Rhudy at the Museum.

Blount County Memorial Museum and Historical Society

204 2nd Street North
Oneonta, Alabama

Mailing address:
P. O. Box 45
Oneonta, AL 35121

Amy Rhudy, Curator
205-625-6905

http://www.blountmuseum.com/

arhudy@co.blount.al.us

This book is only one version of the Blount Springs story.
Much more happened during the time covered by this book
and much more has happened since the time of this book.

The sincere hope is that others will write and contribute more
to this ongoing story and more information will be discovered in attics, at yard sales
and in the memories of the many people that have lived in Blount Springs, visited
Blount Springs, or have any kind of connection to this fabulous place and story.

Alabama history is very diverse and so many stories are waiting to be told and read.

If you have any item or story connected to Blount County in any way,
the Blount County Museum is an excellent place for you to donate materials
and your time so everyone can share in our wonderful history!

www.ingramcontent.com/pod-product-compliance
Lightning Source LLC
Chambersburg PA
CBHW080539170426
43195CB00016B/2614